What a delight to be able to honor Dr. Ted Yamamori's life of mission and his intentional encouragement of those he influenced! This Yamamori Festschrift underscores the contributions to the global mission community and the creative foresight that enabled him to serve his generation well. Ted's life and ministry is a reminder that God places each of us on this earth to write a distinctly personal script. This Festschrift is yet another reminder of our need to call out a new generation who, like Ted, will live their lives with intentionality and courage to give voice to new ideas and creative ways of approaching the mission of God.

Charles Cook, PhD
Professor of Global Studies and Mission,
Executive Director, Jaffray Centre for Global Initiatives,
Ambrose University, Canada

Dr. Ted Yamamori has lived one of the most remarkable lives and ministries of any Asian-American Christian. In a world where the top music group or the head of the World Bank can be Asian, it's easy to forget how much our global society has truly changed. Ted had the stature, leadership, and respect as an Asian-American influencer long before these changes. He was a trailblazer in academia as a researcher and scholar, and in nonprofit executive leadership as president of Food for the Hungry International. He has also impacted my life, not only as Lausanne International Director, but as a friend who grew up in Nagoya, Japan, where I lived for thirteen years and served as president of Christ Bible Seminary. He has been a voice of prophetic wisdom, insight, and encouragement to me.

Dr. Michael Y. Oh
Executive Director/CEO, Lausanne Movement

I remember hearing the name Tetsunao Yamamori when I was in college, mainly through his writing. From his thesis on church growth in Japan in the 1970s and his works on relief and development, to his encouragement of and engagement with those using business in mission, Ted has poured his life and work into causes that would push forward the gospel of the kingdom globally. Later in his life, I was on a board with him and appreciated his wisdom and encouragement both to those around him and to younger leaders.

Greg Parsons, PhD
Global Strategist, Frontier Ventures

Among many leaders who talk about integral mission, Dr. Ted Yamamori is one of the few I have interfaced with who also lives it out. I first met Dr. Ted when he pioneered the Tentmakers International Exchange (TIE) that aims to advance and develop tentmaking missions. He provided stewardship to TIE while leading Food for the Hungry International. This book is a testament to his considerable influence and impact as a modern-day father of integral mission not only to me, but to many other holistic mission leaders and practitioners.

Bishop Efraim M. Tendero
Global Ambassador, World Evangelical Alliance

Since my first conversation with Dr. Ted Yamamori at an Urbana Missions Convention in the 1970s, I have drawn richly from him through print, presentations, and in-person dialogues. In his illustrious ministry career, Dr. Ted has been God's global envoy to advocate for God's concern for the poor, holistic/integral mission, and business as mission. He also helped the Lausanne Movement to embrace diaspora missions as a major focus and served as a senior advisor to the Global Diaspora Network. To make this kingdom impact, Dr. Ted has been a tireless missional road warrior across the planet and overwhelmingly deserves the honor of this Festschrift.

Rev. Dr. T. V. Thomas
Chairman, Global Diaspora Network

Missionary Statesman, Strategist, and Servant

GLOBAL LIBRARY

Missionary Statesman, Strategist, and Servant

A Festschrift for Tetsunao (Ted) Yamamori

Editor
Sadiri Joy Tira

Associate Editor
Laurie Nichols

© 2023 Sadiri Joy Tira and Laurie Nichols

Published 2023 by Langham Global Library
An imprint of Langham Publishing
www.langhampublishing.org

Langham Publishing and its imprints are a ministry of Langham Partnership

Langham Partnership
PO Box 296, Carlisle, Cumbria, CA3 9WZ, UK
www.langham.org

ISBNs:
978-1-83973-776-3 Print
978-1-83973-820-3 ePub
978-1-83973-822-7 PDF

Sadiri Joy Tira and Laurie Nichols hereby assert their moral right to be identified as the Author of the General Editor's part in the Work in accordance with sections 77 and 78 of the Copyright, Designs and Patents Act 1988.

All rights reserved. No part of this publication may be reproduced, stored in a retrieval system or transmitted, in any form or by any means, electronic, mechanical, photocopying, recording or otherwise, without the prior written permission of the publisher or the Copyright Licensing Agency.

Requests to reuse content from Langham Publishing are processed through PLSclear. Please visit www.plsclear.com to complete your request.

Scriptures taken from the Holy Bible, New International Version®, NIV®. Copyright © 1973, 1978, 1984, 2011 by Biblica, Inc.™ Used by permission of Zondervan.

British Library Cataloguing-in-Publication Data
A catalogue record for this book is available from the British Library

ISBN: 978-1-83973-776-3

Cover & Book Design: projectluz.com

Langham Partnership actively supports theological dialogue and an author's right to publish but does not necessarily endorse the views and opinions set forth here or in works referenced within this publication, nor can we guarantee technical and grammatical correctness. Langham Partnership does not accept any responsibility or liability to persons or property as a consequence of the reading, use or interpretation of its published content.

"Behind every great man is a great woman."
(*The Fort Arthur News*, Texas, 1945)

"[A great woman] brings him good, not harm, all the days of her life. . . . Honor her for all that her hands have done, and let her works bring her praise at the city gate." (King Lemuel; Proverbs 31:12, 31)

This book is dedicated to
Mrs. Judy Saunders Yamamori,
a godly and great woman.

Contents

Foreword xi
    By Douglas Birdsall

Preface xiii

Introduction 1
    By Laurie Nichols

1   Ted Yamamori: Friend, Brother, and Co-Servant in the Kingdom 3
    By LeRoy Lawson

2   Collaboration: Leading within the Lausanne Movement 15
    By Joseph Handley

3   International Student Ministry: From Blind Spot to Vision......... 31
    By Leiton Chinn

4   Church Growth in the Japanese Context of Complex Disasters 43
    By Masanori Kurasawa

5   Kingdomization through Integral Mission of House Church
   Networks 53
    By David S. Lim

6   Church Planting in All Seasons: A Personal Reflection 71
    By Sadiri Tonyvic Tira Jr.

7   Business as Mission: Roots, Scope, and Future 81
    By Mats Tunehag

8   Brewing All the Good You Can: Discovering the Prophetic
   Calling of Kingdom Business 95
    By Cody Lorance

9   Mobilizing Thousands to Move in among the Urban Poor:
   A Brief History of MoveIn................................... 111
    By Nigel Paul

10 Pentecostal Holistic Mission: Looking Back and Looking Forward... 125
    By Wonsuk Ma

11 The Impact of the Pandemic on Theological Education:
   A Hybrid Assessment.. 145
    By Steven Ybarrola and Juliet Lee Uytanlet

12	Reframing Leadership to the Digital Native: Making Discipleship an Immersive Experience 157
	By Philip Yan
13	Diaspora Mission and Bible Translation 171
	By S. Hun Kim
14	People, Places, and Partnership in Transnational Missions 181
	By Stanley John
15	Home: Reflections on Next-Generation Diaspora 191
	By Lorajoy Tira-Dimangondayao
16	Training Leaders for Diaspora Missions in South Korea: The Yamamori Strategy Models 203
	By Tereso C. Casiño
17	Peace in the Land of the Morning Calm 225
	By Barnabas Moon

Afterword 237
    By Sadiri Joy Tira

Bibliography of Tetsunao Yamamori's Books 239

Editors and Contributors 243

Tributes 247

Partners 251

Foreword

One of the highest values of the Lausanne Movement is the development of emerging younger leaders whose lives are committed to the grand enterprise of world evangelization. Ted Yamamori is globally respected as a brilliant scholar, prolific author, successful CEO, and mission statesman. As great as his lifelong contributions are in each of these spheres of leadership influence, I believe Ted's greatest legacy will be through the scores of younger men and women from around the world who treasure him as an exemplar of Christian leadership, and as a mentor of immense wisdom and generosity of spirit.

Like the gifted men and women who have made invaluable contributions to this Festschrift to honor Ted's distinguished global leadership, my life has also been greatly enriched through his life. For forty years, Ted has been a mentor, a friend, and a colleague.

Our paths first intersected in 1982 when he paid a visit to my office in Tokyo. I was just getting started as a young American missionary in Japan. He was already established as a Japanese-born leader of a dynamic global organization based in the States. I was honored that he would come to see me, and I was greatly surprised when it became evident that this energetic visionary and multi-gifted CEO had come to ask for advice and input on a project he was launching in Osaka, Japan.

He taught me a lesson that has stayed with me all my life: A senior executive increases his or her capacity for effective leadership when he or she combines proven leadership competence with leadership humility. This enables a lifelong learner to continuously gain wisdom from others, regardless of the learner's status as a seasoned leader or as a young person just beginning his or her journey. Interestingly, the humility of the senior leader serves to boost the competence and confidence of the younger leader.

Twenty-two years later, when I was appointed to serve as the new executive chairman of the Lausanne Movement, I turned to Ted to ask if he would be willing to join me by serving as the new international director for Lausanne. I was thrilled when he accepted the invitation to serve with me for two years, from 2004 to 2006. Our challenge was to revitalize Lausanne and to bring a new generation of younger leaders into the movement. He brought wisdom, energy, credibility, and a global network of trusting relationships. In the course of just twenty-four months, we worked together to build a team of twelve international deputy directors; rebuilt the four pillar working groups of the Lausanne Movement: Theology, Strategy, Communications, and Intercession; and convened a Younger Leaders Gathering in Port Dickon, Malaysia, that brought together 550 younger men and women from nearly a hundred countries.

That provided the energy and momentum for convening the Third Lausanne Congress on World Evangelization in Cape Town, South Africa, in 2010. This would not have been possible without the friendship and partnership that Ted extended to me back in Tokyo in 1982 when I was just getting started.

It is a quadruple honor for me to write the foreword for this book. The first and most immediate honor is simply to speak words of gratitude to Ted for a lifetime of service to Christ, and for forty years of friendship. Thank you, Ted! "Thanks a million" doesn't even come close to conveying the debt of gratitude I owe to you as a friend, mentor, and Lausanne colleague. Thanks be to God!

Second, it is an honor to write at the request of my dear friend, Sadiri Joy Tira, the editor of this book, and the former Lausanne global catalyst for Diaspora. Writing for Joy is like writing for Ted. These two statesmen are cut from the same divine cloth in terms of their passion, energy, brilliance, and productivity. Thank you for the friendship and for the honor, Joy! Who could have imagined that such a life-giving friendship and globally impactful partnership would have begun in a cemetery in Macau where we went to visit the grave of Robert Morrison, a missionary pioneer to China.

Third, it is an honor to shine the light on the many friends and protégés of Ted who have written the chapters of this book. It has been my honor to work alongside many of them as a fellow missionary and within the context of the Lausanne Movement.

Fourth, it is an honor to write as the "honorary" chair of the Lausanne Movement. This is where my life was most powerfully impacted by Ted. We were colleagues who provided senior leadership for a global movement. We served in "the spirit of Lausanne." This is the spirit of humility and friendship, study and prayer, partnership, and hope.

Thank God for the life of Ted Yamamori, and for his lifetime of service to Christ, the church, and the world. His life personifies the spirit of Lausanne. I trust that your reading of this book will enrich your mind and will fill your spirit with hope.

Douglas Birdsall
Honorary Chairman of the Lausanne Movement

Preface

This book, a Festschrift, is a collection of published writings (i.e. essays and tributes) to honor a scholar. Indeed, the person being honored by his colleagues, friends, and students is Dr. Tetsunao Yamamori, for his contributions to global Christian missions and world evangelization.

At the beginning of the third millennium and in the context of the twenty-first century, the landscape of global mission (Matt 28:18–20; Acts 1:8) is markedly different from that of the first century. To be noted are the sociocultural dynamics, political-economic forces, globalization, climate change, international migration driven by wars, regional conflict, poverty, and educational advances, as well as the trade of commodities and technological and scientific research. In the midst of this landscape are two paradoxical images of human suffering and the dynamic growth of the global church of Jesus Christ.

The gospel writer describes wars and rumors of wars, nations rising against nations and kingdoms against kingdoms, and famines and earthquakes in various places (Matt 24). This description has echoed through the ages and remains familiar in the twenty-first-century landscape. The words of Jesus Christ recorded in Matthew 16:18–19 also have reverberated through the centuries and continue into our own: "I will build my church, and the gates of Hades will not overcome it."

As we meet the challenges and opportunities of global mission in the twenty-first century, we have invited a diverse group of scholars and reflective practitioners to contribute their expertise and experiences. And although they come from various geographic and cultural backgrounds, they have one thing in common: all have been impacted by the life and ministries of Dr. Ted Yamamori.

In June 2018, during the historic consultation on "Hybridity, Diaspora, and *Missio Dei*" sponsored by the Lausanne Movement and the Global Diaspora Network (GDN) and hosted by the Biblical Seminary of the Philippines, GDN honored Dr. Yamamori by presenting him with a plaque of appreciation for being instrumental in the birth and formation of the network. However, even at that time, I felt strongly that the octogenarian global leader and humble servant of Jesus Christ should be honored with something even more enduring that reflected his investment and participation in global missions. The following month, I was invited to participate at the Triennial Conference of the Asian Missiological Society in Bali, Indonesia. There, Dr. Greg Parsons gifted me a copy of his PhD dissertation that had been published as a book: *Ralph D. Winter: Early Life and Core Missiology.*[1]

It was then that I knew I wanted to shepherd into being a similar type of book that honored the man I knew had impacted so many involved in global missions in the twentieth and twenty-first centuries. I believed that a Festschrift of this sort could both honor my friend, professor, and mentor, and also inform, instruct, and inspire global missions enthusiasts, supporters, and students focused on kingdom work today and into the future. For further reading and research about the work of Dr. Yamamori, see the bibliography at the end of this book.

I must express heartfelt thanks to the publisher, Langham Global Library, and the contributing writers, endorsers, and the leadership of the International Graduate School, Quezon City, Philippines, for allowing this idea to come to fruition. May it serve as a source of inspiration and as a roadmap to mission endeavors for years to come.

Soli Deo gloria.

Sadiri Joy Tira, DMin, DMiss
Editor
Edmonton, Canada

---

1. Greg Parsons, *Ralph D. Winter: Early Life and Core Missiology* (Pasadena, CA: William Carey International University Press, 2012).

Introduction

By Laurie Nichols

> There is no retirement for a Great Commission Christian. The Lord has given us marching orders. Until he calls off that command, the order remains in effect. The truth of the matter is that when Jesus calls you into ministry, you must respond. I have reached 70 years of age, but I am healthy, and my mind is still somewhat intact. I want to serve the Lord wherever I am needed for as long as the Lord provides me with good health. I suspect that until I draw my last breath, my conscious thought will be ministry, ministry, ministry. – Dr. Tetsunao Yamamori

I remember first hearing Ted Yamamori's name when I was attending the Wheaton College Graduate School in 2005. I had just been asked to become the Editorial Coordinator for a new online publication called *Lausanne World Pulse*, which was part of a global movement of evangelicals called the Lausanne Movement. In the years that followed, I met Ted only once in passing, but I have felt the reverberations of his missional influence all around me. In all honesty, I wish I could have spent some time with him. And yet in some ways, through my work and friendship with Sadiri Joy Tira, I feel as though I have. The more I've learned about Ted, the more I see those qualities and passions in Joy (though he may shy away from that similarity!).

After the Global Diaspora Network formed post-Cape Town 2010, I began to more intentionally learn about this concept of "diaspora" that seemed to be taking center stage as a new – yet not new at all – opportunity for God's kingdom to expand into all corners of the earth.

After all, as people travel, the gospel goes with them. The movement of people was God's plan all along. "Go!" Scripture implores us, "and make disciples of all nations" (Matt 28:19a). Joseph. Esther. Daniel. The narrative of God's people taking God's hope to the nations is nothing short of miraculous. In so many ways, God is calling us all to do the same – to move when he asks, to go when he calls.

And yet, as you will find in this Festschrift, Dr. Yamamori's scope and impact extend beyond diaspora missiology and mission. His impact, as reflected in the following chapters, covers a wide swath of God's global mission. He has been both an academic and a practitioner. He has cared about thought and about action. He has been a friend, a mentor, and a leader. This book at times may appear disparate as it swings from being deeply scholarly and bookish to wildly Spirit-led and movement-oriented. This is intentional as it reflects the heart of a man who cannot be put into one box. (The reader may also note that each contributor refers to Dr. Yamamori differently, sometimes more formally, sometimes more personally; we have kept the author's voice in this regard to reflect his or her relationship to Dr. Yamamori.)

Each topic addressed in this book is relevant for a new generation of God's mobilizers and leaders: friendship, collaboration, international student ministry, church growth, integral mission, Business as Mission, entrepreneurship, caring for those in poverty, Pentecostalism, theological education, discipleship and the digital world, Bible translation, history and diaspora, hospitality, leadership, and working in difficult contexts. One would be hard-pressed to find a leader more impactful in so many areas than Ted Yamamori.

You may be asking yourself, "Why should I read this book if I don't know Dr. Yamamori personally?" Our response would be to look at the state of global missions today and the work of God's people throughout the world. There is hardly a sector untouched in some way by Dr. Yamamori's influence. As the former leader of several major organizations committed to global missions (e.g. Lausanne Movement and Food for the Hungry International), and as an academic who formed many minds and hearts in the academy, the global missions movement owes much to Dr. Yamamori.

We all stand on the shoulders of those who have gone before us. The more we understand those men and women, the more effective we will be in continuing God's mission. Few have impacted global missions and diaspora missiology and ministry in the twentieth and twenty-first centuries more than Dr. Ted Yamamori. As Joseph Handley writes in chapter 2, "the breadth of Dr. Tetsunao Yamamori's influence for the modern mission movement is astounding. Few leaders have this expanse in their lifetimes, especially with the quality of work that Ted has shown over the years."

Our hope is that as you learn about Ted Yamamori through the words of over a dozen of his closest friends and colleagues, you will both become a better student of global missions and be stirred to better understand your own role in advancing God's mission however God has called you.

1

Ted Yamamori: Friend, Brother, and Co-Servant in the Kingdom

By LeRoy Lawson

You young people don't know anything about one of the best blessings of a Christian life. It's not your fault. You are too young. It's the joy of growing old with your Christian friends.

I was introducing an old friend as the chapel speaker at Hope International University when I made the above comment. I'm considerably older now than I was that day, but this is one lesson I had already learned. This chapter is about such a friendship – a very old, deeply cherished one.

It began in 1957 when Japanese student Tetsunao Yamamori arrived at Northwest Christian College (NCC) in Eugene, Oregon. To this day, he reminds me that I was the first person on campus to greet him.

As we shook hands in proper American style, neither of us could have imagined that sixty-five years later we'd still be best friends doing life together. I am half a year younger than him, but as the more experienced student (I was, after all, a sophomore and he a mere freshman), I took it upon myself to show this newcomer the perils and possibilities of academic life in the States.

Even though I was a year ahead of him, I could only marvel at his proficiency in his second language. Fortunately, his English was not perfect; every now and then I was able to catch him in a mistake, which helped me retain a modicum of self-respect. One favorite comes from his English Composition class. His assignment was to write an essay about "apple polishing" – which he did, carefully detailing how you start the process with an apple and a soft cloth. On another unforgettable occasion he complained that the used car dealer had sold him "a melon."

The truth is, though, I had few opportunities to tease him. In time, his ability to understand and communicate in my native tongue seemed to outstrip my own. But his English studies didn't begin when he landed on American soil. In Nagoya, his hometown, he had attended a public school for nine years before entering tenth grade at Nanzan High School, a Roman Catholic institution, where he worked on mastering his second-language skills.

I wanted to get to know as much about him as I could. Part of the fun was rolling the syllables of the family's names over my stuttering tongue. Ted's parents were Yasumitsu and Yaeki Hattori Yamamori. His father had two sons from a previous marriage, twins Kiyomitsu and Mototsugu, about fifteen years older than Ted. His mother gave her husband five more boys: Koji, Setsumasa, Tetsunao, Shoji, and Yasuyuki. In Japanese, Ted explained, Tetsunao means "Iron Will Honest." Yamamori is "Mountain Forest." I was impressed. My name means that my father admired his cousin enough to name me after him. After several attempts to repeat Ted's Japanese name, his linguistically tongue-tied fellow American students happily settled on "Ted."

The Yamamoris maintained a prosperous upper-class home. Yasumitsu, a successful entrepreneur, operated several businesses, concentrating on textiles (clothing). Ted surprised me one Christmas with a high-quality shirt (like the Pendleton brand we boasted of in Oregon). At his request, his parents had sent it to me. I bragged about that shirt for years because of the label: it read "Large." Being somewhat diminutive of stature, I'd never had a "large" shirt before, and I certainly couldn't afford such an expensive one. I wore it for so many years that the collar eventually gave out. It was designed for large men – and it fit me!

Ted and I are almost the same age, but we are from different worlds. Our people had been enemies. They scorned us Americans and we sneered at those Japanese; in World War II, our nations ordered our armies to destroy each other. It was an unequal struggle. Ted's homeland was devastated. Mine was virtually untouched. The closest the war came to me was watching the US Navy reconnaissance blimps fly over Tillamook, my hometown. Just outside of town two huge blimp hangars each housed six of them. Decades after the war ended, a downed Japanese plane could still be found beneath the undergrowth near the beach just a few miles north. That was all I knew of the hostilities in Oregon.

For Ted's family, the war was more personal. A US bomb fell on the family compound, damaging buildings but missing the people. Fearing for his boys' safety, Ted's father had arranged for four of them to be housed outside the city in a Buddhist temple. The fifth son, an infant, remained with his parents. For several months, that temple was the only home these Yamamori brothers knew. There they became acquainted with hunger. Food was in short supply throughout Japan, a fact Ted never mentioned in the earlier years of our friendship but about which he spoke more freely many years later when he headed up Food for the Hungry International.

It was after the war that Vernon Kullowatz entered Ted's life. Ted was still a Buddhist at the time, like the rest of his family. Vernon was actually Major Kullowatz of the United States Air Force, Senior Chaplain at the Nagoya Air Force Chapel in the American Village, home of many US soldiers occupying Japan following the armistice. A Japanese acquaintance who worked at the chapel introduced Chaplain Kullowatz to Ted, describing him as a bright teenager eager to learn English. He was so eager, in fact, that he offered to babysit the chaplain's young English-speaking children.

The chaplain invited Ted home to meet his family, and Ted reciprocated – on occasion bringing the Kullowatzes to get acquainted with the Yamamoris. As Ted and the chaplain's friendship deepened, so did Ted's curiosity about the chaplain's Christian faith. In time, Vernon led his young protégé to Christ and Ted was baptized before leaving for America. For many years, he was the only Christian in his family, but he subsequently had the joy of leading (directly and indirectly) several others to Christ.

Even though the Yamamori finances sustained a severe blow during the war, Mr. Yamamori was still able to buy passage for Ted on a ship from Yokohama to Seattle, a three-week crossing including a three-day stopover in Honolulu. Chaplain Kullowatz had taken advantage of connections with his alma mater in Eugene to arrange for the first phase of Ted's American education. Northwest Christian College (NCC) awarded Ted a rare scholarship that took care of his tuition and fees. The school also hired him to clean the library each evening – a job that covered his modest living expenses.

So, we were fellow custodians, Ted and me. He worked for NCC, and I cleaned restrooms in offices around town for University Cleaners. We were grateful for the jobs. If student loans had been invented, we still had not heard of them. At least nobody offered us one – for which governmental neglect I later gave thanks, since we also didn't have the burden of repaying student loan debts. This was our life then: we studied, and we worked.

Worked. That's one of my dominant memories of my new friend. The man could work! When he wasn't in class or studying or imbibing a bit of American collegiate culture, he worked. He sometimes seemed to work and study around the clock, treating sleep as a luxury that he couldn't afford. But then, exhausted, he could also sleep around the clock to catch up. As someone who couldn't hit the books past 11 p.m. and had to have eight hours of sleep, I was in awe. Envious, even.

We did make something of a name for ourselves, however, exploiting Ted's prowess in judo. He brought his black belt with him from Japan. In our circles, that made him something of a celebrity. Most of us didn't know a thing about the martial arts. That was only one of my obvious shortcomings, I'm afraid. My teenaged children later concluded after looking through my high school and college yearbooks, "Dad, you really were a nerd, weren't you?"

Yes, I was. But Ted wasn't. Still, though unevenly matched, we could put on a good show: Ted, the athlete; Roy, his nerdy fall guy. Together, we impressed audiences (at least we thought we did) with our demonstrations. He knew what he was doing. I provided comic relief.

As you can see, I was already in awe of Ted's intelligence, his ability to adroitly adapt to and negotiate the peculiarities of his newly adopted culture. What I saw in those college years he continued to exhibit as he went on to graduate studies on a scholarship at Brite Divinity School of Texas Christian University (TCU) and then again at Duke University, where he lived in the president's home. He moved with an ease and immediate "at-home-ness" I knew better than to try to emulate.

While at TCU, East Dallas Christian Church employed Ted to work with the church's young people. I thought it was remarkable that the church had the vision to hire an international student for this assignment. He served so effectively that the church promoted him to assistant pastor. It was also in Dallas that Ted met and wooed the love of his life, Judy Saunders. (That is, I thought she was Judy. Only in checking details for this book did I learn she is really Julia Lee, named for an older aunt. She kept that secret for years.) She was also working in the youth activities program at the church. As Ted's much more experienced American "brother," I wondered from afar about this relationship. She was, after all, ten years younger, and it was already apparent that Ted had daunting career challenges ahead of him. Did she know what she was getting herself into?

She did not. Who would have guessed that this Texas charmer with her beguiling accent and somewhat sheltered homelife would someday be partnering with one of evangelical Christianity's most influential international leaders? I suspect she was only thinking that she was in love. I know he was.

When they married in Texas, Ted was twenty-nine and Judy was nineteen years and one month. For his nuptials, I had to cheer from half a continent away. I had no doubt about whether this union would last. Judy herself confessed that her family was a little worried. Judy was young and Ted was a foreigner – a foreigner who spoke of whisking his bride off to his homeland once he had completed his studies.

That wasn't an empty threat. Beginning with our days at NCC, Ted and I had dreamed seriously of teaming up in ministry – in Japan. The dream faded in time, on my part because my uncertain health couldn't get a green light from mission boards' physical examiners; they didn't like my asthma and attending complications. And on Ted's because, influenced by the Church Growth Movement's focus on fields receptive to the gospel, Ted reluctantly concluded there were other ways to maximize his contribution to the kingdom. Japan faded as the field of choice, but effective evangelism remained his lifelong passion.

Back to Judy's family for a moment. The young bride-to-be's mother was nervous, admittedly, but as Judy puts it, "her mother's instinct kicked in and she took Ted in immediately." And Ted's parents? They had already faced up to the probability that he would meet someone in America since his studies had kept him there so long.

My wife Joy and I got our first good look at Judy when, on their honeymoon trip from Dallas to Durham (even their honeymoon was dictated by his studies!), they stopped by Johnson City, Tennessee, where I was teaching at Milligan College. I must have scared them as I took the five Lawsons and the two Yamamoris sightseeing in our tiny Chevy Corvair. Today's safety experts would be horrified!

Here's what we quickly concluded about Judy: Once again, Ted had proved his astuteness. I suspect he was attracted by her beauty and lured by her quiet but sparkling personality, but for certain he was captivated by her combination of gifts. She promised to be then what she proved to be over their lifetime together: an invaluable teammate, strong in all the places Ted needed her strength, patiently rising to the many challenges his burgeoning career threw her way, the practical "can do" person who translated his ideals and visions into achievable action. And what she was in her youth we still see after more than fifty years of marriage. These two are teammates!

My concerns back then about the stresses this cross-cultural marriage might have to endure proved unfounded. Oh, there were a few early incidents. On that honeymoon trip from Dallas to Durham they drove through a small town in Arkansas. When they stopped for gas, the attendant left the gas cap off. Ted quietly told Judy the act was deliberate, racially motivated. Then there was that butcher in Texas who questioned Judy, with obvious disapproval, about why she had chosen to marry a Japanese. That incident rang true to me because, while we were students in Oregon, I took Ted with me for Thanksgiving dinner in Southern California. My father had remarried after my parents' divorce. His wife's brother was also invited to dinner. I learned after dinner that he had to be persuaded not to storm out of the house because he wasn't going to eat with anyone from Japan. This happened in the late 1950s. The end of the war between us was only a little over a dozen years past. Tensions were still real. I shared some of Judy's mother's concern. Ted, for the most part, has been oblivious to such slights.

Even that early in Ted's career, he was an internationalist. He didn't hate Americans for bombing Japan. He didn't hate anyone, not even Japan's longtime rival, Korea. He seriously believed the heart of the Christian faith was found in Jesus's sacrifice for all the people of the world, and that it was to be expressed in love for God and love for one's neighbor. It was that simple.

These beliefs motivated Ted while he was still an undergraduate to think and act like a world Christian. His mentor at NCC was Dr. Donald McGavran, who was establishing his Church Growth Institute, giving birth to the Church Growth Movement. McGavran's passion for leading people groups to Christ and Ted's love of his native country resonated. Their time together in Oregon cemented a mutual affection, Ted adopting Dr. McGavran as a father figure. He and his wife, Mary, became part of the Yamamori family and they embraced Ted and Judy as part of theirs. McGavran's pioneering church-growth thinking has been reflected in much of Ted's writing over the years.

Chronology of Ted's Lifetime of Service

The following chronology of Ted's life demonstrates the scope of his ever-expanding ministry.

1957–1962

Ted was a student at Northwest Christian College in Eugene, Oregon, where he identified more fully with the Christian churches that Chaplain Vernon Kullowatz had introduced him to, where Dr. McGavran became his most influential mentor, and where Ted and I soon became "best friends for life." Chaplain Kullowatz's parents, who lived in Southwest Portland, gladly adopted Ted as their Japanese son – a tie that brought Ted and me even closer, since thanks to Ted they also took this young preacher under their wing and into their home, providing free weekend lodging for my first year as a church planter in nearby Tigard.

1962–1966

Ted was a Bachelor (now Master) of Divinity student at Brite Divinity School of Texas Christian University and served in ministry with East Dallas Christian Church. His courtship of Judy Saunders happened during this time, and they married in 1967.

During the summer of 1965, East Dallas Christian Church asked Ted to speak to the congregation about his life to that point. They wanted to know more about his spiritual (and geographical) journey so far. He presented his "Unfinished Autobiography" that evening. For the rest of his ministry, he remained faithful to the principles he laid out on that occasion. Here are just two:

- "My father always said to all seven of his sons, 'Boys, be ambitious. Choose one field and become an expert in it. That way you can contribute to the world.' My life motto became, 'Be ambitious to contribute to the world.'"
- "My mother's biggest contribution to my life was her sustaining love. Therefore, my path through life has been and always will be, 'Be ambitious, work hard, and remember to show God's love to all people.'"

As we follow Ted's life and his ministry through the ensuing years, it is apparent how strongly these parental lessons influenced him. It has never been enough for him to feed hungry bodies while ignoring the rest of the person. Feed them, care for them, and show them God's love. These are the roots of Ted's symbiotic ministry.

1966–1969

Ted did his doctoral studies in the Sociology of Religion at Duke University in Durham, North Carolina. He and Judy spent six months during this period in Kyoto, Japan, at Doshisha University, where Ted did research for his PhD dissertation.

1969–1972

Ted served as assistant professor in the Religion Department of McMurray University in Texas.

1972–1976

Ted served as chair and associate professor of sociology and dean of students at Milligan College in Tennessee. This position grew out of a good-natured tug of war between two friends who had long wanted to work together. Ted, a member of the faculty committee searching for a new academic dean at McMurray, proposed my name. Joy and I were invited to Abilene for an interview. The conversation went well, but I felt it would be untimely for me to resign my position as vice president of Milligan College. Instead, I extended my president's invitation to Ted to join our administrative team in Tennessee. He accepted, and the Yamamoris moved to Johnson City. Proof of Ted's gracious spirit came a year later, when I left the college to return to pastoral ministry, this time in Indiana. He forgave me for deserting him.

1976–1978

Then it was Ted's turn to move on. He accepted the offer to become academic dean and professor of sociology at our alma mater, Northwest Christian College in Eugene, at a time when NCC's administration was troubled. The outcome was that both the president and the dean stepped down from their positions. How does one explain God's providence in such matters? What seemed, at the time, like a step backward in Yamamori's upward career trajectory was in fact more like a blip or mid-course correction.

1978–1979

Ted joined Win Arn's "Institute for American Church Growth" in Pasadena, California. Arn was applying the insights and principles Dr. McGavran gained personally in India, and through his research on other foreign mission fields, to the church in America. Ted's own spiritual and academic odyssey, as well as his personal relationship with McGavran, attracted Arn's attention.

1979–1981

Ted served as director and professor of intercultural studies in the developing International Studies Program at Biola University in La Mirada, California.

1981–2001

When founder Larry Ward invited Ted to join him at Food for the Hungry International (FHI) in Scottsdale, Arizona, his goal was to prepare Ted as his successor. The transition was completed in 1984 when Ward retired and Yamamori was named president, the position he held until 2001. During these twenty years FHI's staff expanded from fifty employees to 1,500 worldwide, regularly adding field offices and collaborations with partner organizations. As CEO, Ted of necessity developed yet another aptitude to his growing skill set: he was the primary fundraiser. The mission's annual budget and donor base grew steadily during those years, a growth that continued after he retired.

20 July 1990

During most of his years of international travel, Ted relied on his Japanese passport, but on 20 July 1990 he was sworn in as a citizen of the United States. He was proud to be an American, but he never lost his love for his native land. On 1 January 2022, eyes glued to his TV, he celebrated the Japanese New Year in absentia.

2004–2006

After completing his stewardship with Food for the Hungry International, Ted stepped into various leadership roles with the Lausanne Movement. He held the post of international director from 2004 to 2006 and continues as a senior advisor.

This brief chronological sketch is as impressive for what it leaves out as for what it includes. Ted has never limited his attention to the demands of his salaried positions. Other contributions were made as senior fellow of the Center for Religion and Civic Culture of the University of Southern California; chair of the international board of advisors for two joint-venture international universities (Pyongyang University of Science and Technology in North Korea and Yanbian University of Science and Technology in China); president/CEO of WorldServe Ministries (concentrating on China and Cuba); adjunct professor of holistic mission at Asbury Theological Seminary; and consultant with Christian Missionary Fellowship International. These are just the ones I know about. There are others.

And then of course there are all those books – twenty-eight of them. I encourage you to check out his bibliography at the end of this book, which also includes books translated into other languages.

I know a little about these activities because over the years Ted invited me along on journeys to some of his projects in places such as Peru, Bolivia, Ethiopia, Eritrea, Afghanistan, Japan, Korea, China, South Africa, and Congo. These weren't just junkets, although there was no shortage of enjoyment. They were everyday work for him, but mind-expanding opportunities for me. Ted talked a lot about symbiotic missions, in which evangelism goes hand in hand with social action. They were holding hands in every country where Food for the Hungry International served. In these trips, he introduced me to his bigger world. As college students, we had dreamed of becoming missionaries in Japan. God called him to a far larger mission field. He called me to a supportive role. These travels together convinced me that God made the right call for both of us.

Several of his travels involved consultations in which he brought together experts to explore various issues in world evangelization. I tagged along as a devotional leader to the one in Manila, and while there, the group visited Smoky Mountain, the municipal garbage dump where up to twenty-five thousand ragpickers scratched out their meager living under conditions so appalling that afterward I had to discard my clothes and shoes. There was no ridding them of the filth and stench.

But the lives of these poorest of the poor were being transformed. Thanks to the vision of one man, a Roman Catholic priest, they were finding jobs, housing, and hope. He told us his story: He had consulted Mother Teresa to see where he could best serve God, and she recommended Manila. He took her advice, but when he arrived in the Philippines, he had no idea what to do. The needs were overwhelming, so he prayed, and God's answer became clear: He was a priest and so he would start a church. Since then, that church has been changing the lives of the people in the garbage dump.

That consultation resulted from and gave proof of Ted's longstanding philosophy of ministry and his conviction that symbiosis is exactly what the gospel calls for. Symbiosis is the holding together and the mutual dependence on the proclamation of the good news and its praxis, love in action. This conviction guided his personal life, his leadership of Food for the Hungry International, and his participation in many other ministries.

I close by calling attention to two characteristics of Ted's life and ministry. The first is *collaboration*. Ted has enjoyed teaming up with many coauthors over the years; I take pride in being his first, and beyond a doubt, the greenest of them. While we were together at Milligan College, Standard Publishing Company asked us to produce several books on the burgeoning field of church growth. We were grateful that Standard would gamble on a couple of neophytes.

Introducing Church Growth and *Church Growth: Everybody's Business* were the results, our only joint ventures in publishing.

For Ted, of course, they were just the first of many collaborations. He has been a networker par excellence. Most of his books are coauthored or are edited compilations of essays by experts in a variety of fields. They include such notables as Donald Miller, René Padilla, David Dageford, Sadiri Joy Tira, and Kim-Kwong Chan among others. To me, most of his collaborators were just names. I came to know of them primarily through my friendship with Ted, who seemed to know everybody.

The second characteristic to note is his *partnership with Judy*. Let me share a story. Ted had invited me on one of his trips to South America. We flew separately across the continent and met at the airport in Miami, Florida, to go on together from there. I arrived in time to join him, but my suitcase didn't. I was a newcomer to international travel in those days and I checked with the luggage counter for Eastern Airlines (this is a very old story), but that exhausted my expertise. Ted, however, knew exactly what to do. He called Judy, told her my problem, and left it in her hands to solve. Judy was his administrative assistant with Food for the Hungry International. It seemed a natural move to call her – but Judy wasn't with us. She was in Scottsdale. It took her only a few minutes to sort the problem out. She sent us on our way as scheduled. My luggage caught up with us on the next flight, as she said it would. Ted made many good decisions in his life, but next to his submission to Christ as Lord, marrying Judy was the best.

And that partnership wasn't limited to working hours, of course. Ted and Judy know how to parent, and grandparent. What joy it has given this old friend to see the admiration the families of daughter Kelli and son Steven have for their parents and grandparents. We have all known prominent leaders who seem to have sacrificed their wives and children for the sake of their careers. That was not so with the Yamamoris.

Ted is concluding a remarkable ministry. If anyone can expect to hear, "Well done, good and faithful servant," Tetsunao Yamamori is the one.

2

Collaboration: Leading within the Lausanne Movement

By Joseph Handley

The breadth of Dr. Tetsunao "Ted" Yamamori's influence for the modern mission movement is astounding. Few leaders have this expanse in their lifetimes, especially with the quality of work that Ted has shown over the years. This chapter focuses on leadership, particularly within the Lausanne Movement, of which Ted served as international director as well as senior associate for holistic mission.

In my own research, with keen attention to the Lausanne Movement, I discovered six distinct themes pertinent to this approach to leadership.[1] We begin with highlighting the importance of this polycentric theoretical model by looking at collaborative leadership and partnership.

Collaboration and Partnership

In looking at the history of the Lausanne Movement, Dr. Doug Birdsall, former executive chairman of the Lausanne Movement, made an interesting observation: "Consensus on a common goal is perhaps the most obvious ingredient for both intra- and inter-organizational collaboration. Individuals

---

1. Joseph W. Handley, "Polycentric Mission Leadership" (PhD diss., Fuller Theological Seminary, School of Intercultural Studies, 2020), ProQuest: 27745033. Much of this article was adapted from the dissertation chapters.

and organizations are unlikely to work in partnership if their goals are not in alignment and mutually beneficial."[2]

In his book *Well Connected*, Phill Butler points out that what attracts people and keeps them committed to a partnership are (1) great vision and (2) seeing results.[3] According to Butler, once you have a compelling reason to work together and a desire for strong results, you must build trust. "All durable, effective partnerships are built on trust and whole relationships."[4]

Butler also, however, emphasizes this point:

> Spiritual breakthroughs are not a game of guns and money. No human effort, expenditure of resources, or brilliant strategy will alone produce lasting spiritual change. Our partnerships must be informed and empowered by God's Holy Spirit in order to be effective. The challenges of relationships, cultural and theological differences, technical and strategic issues, and sustainability can only be dealt with in a process rooted in prayer.[5]

Mark Oxbrow adds that "multi-cultural partnerships need multi-cultural objectives: we need to understand what is valued as 'success' or 'achievement' in each culture."[6] Kärin Primuth reflects this, noting that multicultural networks are a demonstration of biblical unity:

> Networks offer a context to build trust across cultures and to genuinely listen and learn from our partners in the Majority World. They provide a platform for dialogue with our brothers and sisters in the Global South to mutually define what the North American Church can contribute to today's mission movement.[7]

Global business leaders are suggesting this type of collaboration as well. Angel Cabrera and Gregory Unruh suggest that "global leaders craft solutions by

---

2. S. Douglas Birdsall, "Conflict and Collaboration: A Narrative History and Analysis of the Interface between the Lausanne Committee for World Evangelization and the World Evangelical Fellowship, the International Fellowship of Evangelical Mission Theologians, and the AD 2000 Movement" (PhD diss., Oxford Centre for Mission Studies, 2012).

3. Phill Butler, *Well Connected: Releasing Power, Restoring Hope through Kingdom Partnerships* ([UK]: Authentic & World Vision, 2006), 41.

4. Butler, *Well Connected*, 51.

5. Butler, 101.

6. Mark Oxbrow, "Better Together: Partnership and Collaboration in Mission," Paper, Forms of Missionary Engagement, Edinburgh 2010 study, in *Witnessing to Christ Today, Volume II*, eds. Daryl Balia and Kirsteen Kim (Oxford: Regnum, 2010), 116–47.

7. Kärin Primuth, "Mission Networks: Connecting the Global Church," *Evangelical Missions Quarterly* 51, no. 2: 215.

bringing together people and resources across national, cultural, even organizational boundaries."[8]

The ability to navigate across a variety of cultures, stakeholders, and global scenarios is a vital trait for empowered leadership in a globalized era. These leadership skills are captured in the six themes discovered in the research I did for my dissertation. They are seen in figure 2.1 and highlighted by the interviews with Lausanne Movement leaders in the next section.

POLYCENTRIC MISSION LEADERSHIP THEMES

Theme	Component of the Theme
Charismatic	Charismatic	Value-based	Spiritual
Collaborative	Collaboration	Network	Participate	Shared	Collective
Communal	Community	Contractual or Cooperative	Own Ecosystem	Mutual Vision	Team
Relational	Empowerment	Encouragement	Relational
Entrepreneurial	Entrepreneurial	Freedom to Structure
Diverse	Diversity	Cross-cultural

Figure 2.1

Interviews with Lausanne Movement Leaders

In interviewing thirty-three key leaders who were leading significant movements for the kingdom of God within the Lausanne Movement, I was able to discern issues, trends, and challenges they face, how they have grown and been formed as leaders, and how leadership has changed in the past twenty years. Each leader was chosen for either effectiveness in leading a current network, or the promise the leader showed in getting his or her networks established.

In analyzing the data, it became apparent that there are leadership aspects that are timeless as well as factors that can change over time. Long-standing leadership traits that several noted included being biblically formed, being committed to strong character formation, and demonstrating Christlike servant leadership. Faithfulness and humility are traits that find themselves deeply interwoven into this thread of spirituality. Other, more tangible threads related to the need for vision, passion, and relational competence.

---

8. Angel Cabrera and Gregory Unruh, *Being Global: How to Think, Act, and Lead in a Transformed World* (Boston: Harvard Business Review Press, 2012), 12.

All the leaders pointed to a spiritual dimension in their life story of how God clearly intervened and called them to ministry. Over and above this aspect of calling was a deep sense of the need for the Lord's presence to enable them to serve the way in which they served.

The common issues driving the need for changes in leadership included globalization, economic disparity, migration, and technological advancement. They also advocated moving away from a broad vision toward a more clearly defined set of outcomes, complete with measurable qualities, as being important in the current era.

The changing leadership environment is significantly impacted by diversity and cross-cultural engagement. The need for more strategic and directional leadership was apparent as well. Brad Smith highlighted the importance of *gift-based leadership* rather than *trait-based leadership*. He felt that moving away from the more trait-oriented approaches is critical to faithful, missional leadership today and into the future. He characterized the leadership changes needed like this: "[Leadership is] much more dispersed and distributed (not management by objective). [We need a] vision and values approach – not [simply] by goals and objectives."[9]

The relational theme was strong in all the interviews, especially highlighting an increased need for cross-cultural engagement and collaboration. Smith suggested that "giving away power" is critical to success in this age. Talking about ownership, he stated, "The ownership – confidence of indigenous leaders to lead their own way and let Westerners get out of the way [will be key for leaders of the future]."[10]

Augmenting this was the importance of possessing cross-cultural leadership skills. Samuel Chiang noted, "We have neglected the honor/shame perspective so deeply that we don't know how to regain it. Our theological basis is so shallow that we need to redevelop it."[11]

A final common thread was a need for further creativity and innovation. Whether it was a conversation about technology, the diversity of the world, communication patterns, or something else, there was a sense that creativity will be crucial for leaders in the future. As Tuvya Zaretsky said, "[We are]

---

9. Brad Smith, Cape Town 2010 Table Talk designer. December 2014 interview via Skype.

10. Brad Smith.

11. Samuel Chiang, catalyst for Orality; CEO of the Seed Company. June 2014 interview in Manhattan Beach, California.

constantly looking for innovative ways to engage around spiritual issues and lots of interesting methodologies in our network."[12]

With this summary, we now turn our attention to the core themes present in this polycentric theoretical model for leadership.

Common Themes for Collaborative Leadership
Charismatic

The theme of charisma stood out as primary in the interviews. While this is true for many studies on leadership theory, I was under the impression that this would be less prevalent for spiritual leaders.[13] However, I learned that this theme had more to do with character than personality. The theme uncovered in the research refers more to the depth of character and an ethos based on values and spirituality. As the GLOBE Study of CEO Leadership Behavior and Effectiveness revealed, these values are seen to be more important in this aspect of leadership than the popular idea of a winsome, charismatic presence.[14]

Nana Yaw Offei Awuku stated that "Christlike character as the call of Christian leadership will be our greatest distinguishing mark for both the church and mission today. The world is going through its own crisis of leadership and probably only the outstanding Christ-centered character that stands the test of time will be the most distinguishing."[15] Ramez Atallah also highlighted this important aspect of charisma: "The number one priority in the church today is integrity at all levels, financial, sexual, moral and many other ways. The deterioration of commitment to integrity or the lack of our understanding of integrity is threatening the very fabric of the church."[16]

Character is certainly key to charismatic leadership. Beyond this, though, for mission leaders in particular, spirituality is paramount. Byron Spradlin emphasizes that "private, personal, intimate, worship walk with the Lord is number one. Powerful public ministry comes from passionate private worship

---

12. Tuvya Zaretsky, catalyst for Jewish Evangelism. December 2014 interview via Skype.

13. To understand this leadership theory, see Boaz Shamir, Robert House, and Michael Arthur, "The Motivational Effects of Charismatic Leadership: A Self-Concept Based Theory," *Organizational Science* 4, no. 4 (1993): 577–94.

14. Robert J. House, Peter W. Dorfman, Mansour Javidian, Paul J. Hanges, and Mary F. Sully de Luque, *Strategic Leadership across Cultures: The GLOBE Study of CEO Leadership Behavior and Effectiveness in 24 Countries* (Thousand Oaks: Sage, 2014), 268.

15. Nana Yaw Offei Awuku, global associate director for Generations. October 2018 interview via Skype.

16. Ramez Atallah, former vice chair of the board. May 2018 emailed questionnaire.

walk with the Lord."[17] Mac Pier put it this way: "To me the most important thing in leadership is getting revelation from God. The depth of our influence is in proportion to our intimacy with God. If you are in tune with God, people will trust you even if your ideas are audacious."[18]

Finally, when looking at charisma as a theme, vision became vital. Phill Butler characterizes this aspect:

> Cast vision! You have to believe in your vision and hold out a goal and give them a chance to participate. The more a movement is like Lausanne and WEA, the more it has to define its purpose. The biggest challenge is defining its clarity and vision and focus, and then alignment of all its tentacles. . . . They must say, "This is the beach we're going to take!"[19]

Collaborative

There is power in participating in a network or collective to achieve a common goal. Of the thirty-three people interviewed from the Lausanne Movement, twenty-four emphasized the importance of working together as key to their recruitment within the movement or network they led, to their success within the network they served or the movement overall, or to advising others desiring to serve within the Lausanne ecosystem.

Nana Yaw Offei Awuku captured this theme well: "Nobody anywhere should set the agenda for the global church today. It must be a collaborative effort. All of us must do it together. No one can do it alone."[20] Similarly, Anne-Christine Bataillard noted, "[To be effective] we need to stop looking at our differences, respect each other and work together. We will then have much more impact."[21]

Yet the work of collaboration is easier said than done. Butler commented, "Everybody talks about collaboration, but nobody does it. It's an idealized and realized value – there's a huge difference."[22] Michael Oh put it this way: "Perhaps the greatest opportunity is ground level, and broader level, collaboration.

---

17. Byron Spradlin, catalyst for the Arts. December 2014 interview via Skype.

18. Mac Pier, catalyst for Cities. July 2019 interview via phone.

19. Phill Butler, catalyst for Partnership. December 2014 interview via Skype.

20. October 2018 interview via Skype.

21. Anne-Christine Bataillard, former catalyst for Children and Evangelism. May 2019 interview via Skype.

22. December 2014 interview via Skype.

The vision for Lausanne IV, in fact, is to mobilize the global church toward catalytic collaboration to address the greatest opportunities and gaps of the Great Commission."[23]

Two leaders noted how important this theme is for success in the Lausanne Movement when sharing how leadership today is different from how it was ten to fifteen years ago. Lindsay Olesberg stated, "[To serve as a leader today] there's an expectation of higher levels of collaboration and partnership within your own organization and teams."[24] Bodil Skjøtt expressed it this way: "We can do more together than if we stay by ourselves. . . . [Now] people are more willing to network. Lausanne has introduced me to a strong emphasis on partnership and networking."[25]

For a leader to be effective within the Lausanne Movement today, that person must be collaborative in his or her approach, willing to work in a team-centered paradigm where no one rises above the others and all work together toward the goals of their network within the movement.

Communal

Twenty-two leaders among those interviewed commented on the importance of community and teamwork. Collaborators form a community, establishing a bond where vision is shared, and they function as a team. In this grouping, ownership is taken to a deeper level of commitment.

Speaking about effective kingdom leadership, Chiang recognized "the ability to bring together people who might create culture together. Trust in the key leader allows others to be comfortable with each other and talk and create. [We need] a new understanding of *koinonia* – a philosophy of *koinonia* at the Godhead level means so much."[26] Leighton Ford reflected, "It's not a program but life-on-life mentoring. Leaders come together and listen to the Lord and one another. [It's important to] trust peers and fellow leaders. [It's important] to value others and make sure everybody has a voice."[27]

Olesberg spoke of the power of friendship in relation to this theme as she shared her advice for future Lausanne Movement leaders. She believed that

---

23. Michael Oh, CEO of the Lausanne Movement. December 2015 interview in King of Prussia, Pennsylvania.
24. Lindsay Olesberg, catalyst for Scripture Engagement and Scripture Engagement Director for InterVarsity. July 2018 interview via Skype.
25. Bodil Skjøtt, catalyst for Jewish Evangelism. June 2018 interview via Skype.
26. June 2014 interview in Manhattan Beach, California.
27. Leighton Ford, former executive chair. December 2018 interview via Skype.

"in Lausanne, good friendships are the coin of the realm. . . . Deep relational investment [is a priority]. People want to know, 'Are you going to be a part of real community here or not?'"[28] Awuku illustrated this further: "Partnership for global mission will have strength that closely parallels global friendships. I think that in the next years ahead of us, as important as results may be, the strength of authentic relationships of trust, openness, friendship, [and] common shared purpose between Global North and South leaders will be critical."[29]

Leaders who work with others in community bring change to their various networks and issue groups; they foster an environment that has momentum to go farther together. As the teams work together, comradery builds, vision coalesces, and action begins to take shape.

Diverse

Diversity highlights the importance of having a variety of perspectives and vantage points that include things such as gender, regional perspective, age, and cross-cultural acumen. Twenty-two of the thirty-three leaders weighed in on diversity. They shared their ideas related to the shifting of momentum from the West to the Global South and to dynamics related to culture.

Doug Birdsall captured these changes and leadership trends: "Leadership of the Majority World is recognized by global leaders as bringing freshness and creativity. Leadership has gone from multinational Western initiatives to working in many nations."[30] Esme Bowers agreed, noting "the changes in faces [in leadership] from 1997 to today: before it was all white and now it's a big group of black, Asian, and mixed faces. [There is also] a huge swing toward women moving into positions of making decisions. Everywhere we go, we need to make place for women."[31]

Several saw diversity as imperative for global leadership and for the Lausanne Movement, including Las Newman: "[We must] embrace multiethnic, multicultural church and community in a globalized world. The rise of global

---

28. July 2018 interview via Skype.

29. October 2018 interview via Skype.

30. Doug Birdsall, former executive chair and honorary co-chair. February 2015 interview in El Segundo, California.

31. Esme Bowers, board of directors. October 2018 interview via Skype.

Pentecostalism and the growth of Christianity in the Global South [is one of the biggest changes I am seeing]."[32] Joseph Vijayam stressed the following:

> A rise of leadership in missions from the Global South. The rise of women in Christian leadership. The rise of younger leaders all over the world who are taking a more significant role. One of the big surprises is that the church in the Majority World both is younger and has a higher representation of women than in North America and Europe. We will continue to face this issue of the diaspora and migrant peoples. [We must] always keep it a priority to engage people from all over the world. I can't stress the importance of [this enough]. . . . If we don't continue to stress the need to involve people from different parts of the world, we can quickly become irrelevant in places where the church is growing at its most rapid pace.[33]

Sadiri Joy Tira (the editor of this book) stated:

> The world has become borderless. There are cultural borders but because of technology, no longer [a] global village but global apartments. The world has shrunk more today than fifteen years ago. [For Lausanne], the regional leadership is very diverse. International Deputy Directors are strategically balanced. If you look at the list of Senior Associates, there is a strategic balance of leaders from south, east, west, and north – no longer perceived as another Western, imperialistic leadership. In the past it was another Western-driven, colonial model.[34]

Patrick Fung also spoke to the theme of diversity:

> Mission changed from linear to multidirectional, from West to the rest, and now to the diaspora, from the diaspora, and of them. It is much less linear. We see the emergence of the Global South mission movements. . . . Lausanne will need to have a bit more input from the Majority World and reset their mindset – Western and Majority World leaders. The Majority World needs to come out of the mindset of [having] no power and nothing to

---

32. Las Newman, global associate director for Regions. December 2019 emailed response with follow-up call via Skype.
33. Joseph Vijayam, senior associate for Technology; CEO of Olive Technology. August 2018 interview via Zoom.
34. Sadiri Joy Tira, Global Diaspora Network. December 2014 interview via Skype.

contribute (inferiority complex). Not in an arrogant manner [but] demonstrating humble godly leadership for the kingdom. Both come together to learn and appreciate one another. Appreciate the gaps. Let's listen to each other.[35]

It is within this diversity of leadership that is multigenerational, multinational, multiethnic, and multicultural, as well as from different socioeconomic or political backgrounds, that strong bonds can develop which help overcome obstacles, create unified momentum, and catalyze ideas toward a better future.

Entrepreneurial

The fifth theme is entrepreneurial and includes independence from overarching structures in terms of decision-making and setting agendas. This is displayed when groups are free to practice their expertise in their areas of specialty, creatively defining their own realities and managing, collecting, and building their own resources. Whether in a conversation about technology, the diversity of the world, communication patterns, or something else, creativity is crucial for leaders.

While the comments of only seventeen of the thirty-three leaders related to the entrepreneurial theme, it was well represented in the literature reviews related to the study. Ram Gidoomal captured the essence of this theme in his assessment:

> [Mission has changed] from everywhere to everywhere. Decentralization of power from Europe and the US to closer to the ground. Shift the power bases to the regions of the mission. [The] secular world is now doing this too. [We should ask] who are the people on the ground, and are they being empowered? Delegation that empowered [others]. As Lao Tzu said, they will all say, "We did it." [This is] the art of letting others have their way. My principle is doing myself out of a job. This operates in a healthy environment.[36]

Emphasizing it to a greater degree was Pier, who described what effective leadership looks like today:

---

35. Patrick Fung, board member. August 2018 interview in Singapore at the OMF Center.
36. Ram Gidoomal, former chair of the board. February 2015 interview via Skype.

[We need] starters, incubators, planters. . . . What makes them effective: [is] risk-takers, [holding an] Ephesians 3 view of the world. God can do more. [It means being] alliance-builders. For me and my role, [it's] trying to have a Barnabas-style leadership. Trying to find the Pauls and empower them. Barnabas is a networker and resource provider. Investing in other leaders and other efforts. A dime invested in us is a dollar for others. We try to be multipliers.[37]

Butler amplified this theme, adding, "Risk-taking is more important today. We need to be risk-comfortable. And we need to adopt the innovation curve. There has to be a dreamer and then the model-maker."[38] And in his counsel for the Lausanne Movement, Tira exhorted, "Lausanne needs to be careful not to become an organization run by a CEO. It is a network and a movement."[39]

Polycentric leadership requires freedom of expression and operation. Lausanne leaders recognize something pivotal about polycentric governance: to lead well today, there must be the space to guide and shape within one's own group and sphere of influence. Entrepreneurial engines must be activated for mission networks to thrive.

Relational

Relational encompasses empowerment and encouragement, as well as personal skills. It is important to note the connection between encouragement and relational aspects of leadership. Here is where the idea of emotional intelligence comes into play.

The relational theme elicited the fewest responses in the interviews, with only thirteen of the thirty-three interviewees commenting. This could be due to the similarities this trait shares with the communal theme. Chris Wright noted this quality when answering a question about effective Christian leadership and what shaped his leadership: "John Stott [had] a very strong capacity for friendship. He had a great intentionality about developing friends. He didn't just get to know people: he knew their names, children, families, and prayed

---

37. July 2019 interview via phone.
38. December 2014 interview via Skype.
39. December 2014 interview via Skype.

for people. He was very relational. That is an element of effective Christian leadership: warmth and fellowship."[40]

Perhaps no one captured this relational theme more adeptly than Attalah. He spoke of the relationships that had impacted him and the importance for how we should treat one another:

> During that time [living in Canada], I began my friendship with Leighton Ford, who was the youngest trustee of the seminary, and that relationship changed my life. . . . Within that context I have tried to keep my leadership a people-centered leadership. I lead basically in a pastoral way rather than an administrative way, and I think that is desperately needed in our very mechanized, organized, and systematized world.
>
> Fruitful kingdom influence is mentoring others in the long term so that you can build into their lives principles of life and leadership that will help them be transforming agents in the next generation. Since I have lived a very long time (I am seventy-two now) I can look back to my investment in young men and women, some of whom I didn't think would add up to much, and now see them being influencers within the church and within society. That is the most rewarding experience I have ever had in my life, and I am continuing to invest in younger people today in the hopes that this multiplication of mentorship will bring some fruit in the future as it has in the past.[41]

Toward a Collaborative Model of Leadership

Ted helped to set the stage for this type of collaborative model to emerge. His approach to most of his writing projects was collaborative in nature, choosing to align with others as either coauthor or recruiting others in a collaborative venture to pull together a strong resource. In choosing others to write with, he drew from a vast array of leaders exhibiting the diversity imperative for a polycentric form of leadership. The authors and subjects of this Festschrift reflect people Ted influenced and relationships that have endured over time.

---

40. Chris Wright, former catalyst for Theology Working Group. January 2016 interview via Skype.

41. May 2018 emailed questionnaire.

Ted's own research revealed this type of model as well. Matthew Krabill highlighted this collaborative form of leadership, noting Ted's research on global Pentecostalism with Donald Miller through the Center for Religion and Culture at the University of Southern California. Key to these movements were what Krabill describes as networks of cooperation.[42] Similarly, Richard Flory and Brad Christerson highlighted this essence in their research on Network Christianity as well, with particular attention to Ted's research.[43]

Ted further illustrated these principles in sharing wisdom for ethnic church planting in America. Several of his insights corresponded with this collaborative model of leadership. These included abandoning an assimilationist approach; acknowledging the heterogeneous nature of persons; recruiting local/indigenous leaders; and using strong ethnic, communal, and relational ties.[44] No doubt, these ideas stemmed from a lifetime of leadership and study. "Paul" Kiichi Ariga noted his influence from when he was commended by Ted to receive the McGavran Church Growth award in 1979. He stated that his ideas of "'Symbiotic Ministry' integrating the gospel and social actions may have prepared the way to Lausanne 1974."[45]

Steve Hoke strengthened this affirmation by referring to Ted as an empowering leader:[46]

> When I first met Ted in 1980, he was building an organization from the grassroots, and he selected a handful of very capable emerging, younger leaders to help construct that foundation. In inviting them into a life of global service, Ted was humble, available, and present as an alongside coworker and servant leader.[47]

While he led the way with symbiotic ministry, he did so through empowering others. Thus, Ted was ahead of his time and exemplifies this spirit of collaborative leadership within the Lausanne Movement.

---

42. Matthew Krabill, "Menno Was a Migrant with No Headquarters: The Polycentric Ecclesial Existence of African Immigrant Mennonite Congregations in LA" (PhD diss., Fuller Theological Seminary, 2019), 224.

43. Richard Flory and Brad Christerson, *The Rise of Network Christianity: How Independent Leaders Are Changing the Religious Landscape* (New York: Oxford University Press, 2017), 207.

44. Tetsunao Yamamori, *The Church Growth Handbook*, ed. Win Arn (Pasadena: Church Growth Press, 1979), 184.

45. Paul Ariga, November 2021 emailed correspondence.

46. Steve Hoke, November 2021 interview via Zoom.

47. January 2022 emailed correspondence.

The most powerful affirmation of these qualities came in a conversation with Doug Birdsall. He said that he and Ted had a good working relationship and that Ted's encouragement after the Younger Leaders Gathering in 2006 was pivotal in his life. Ted suggested that the event was the best he had ever attended, which surprised Doug since Ted had been to lots of conferences. The feedback Ted gave to Doug, a younger leader, was especially motivating. In addition, Doug shared how Ted was pivotal to gaining confidence among international leaders. They trusted him as a seasoned veteran leader who had good relationships across the globe. Doug said that Ted could relate to everyone and did a wonderful job on a monthly call soliciting everyone's perspective.[48]

Doug's assessment was echoed by Tira, who coauthored several books with Ted and co-labored with him for the Lausanne Movement. Joy shared how Ted took him under his wing and gave him a platform so that Joy shone and Ted was rarely seen. He was a true friend who came alongside and encouraged Joy as a younger leader. Joy expressed it this way: "He is there as a silent advocate, and his presence is like a pillar and reassuring. When I was down, discouraged, and disappointed, he lifted me up and prayed for me." In their coauthoring partnership, Ted said, "Joy, this is yours! Your name should be first!" Joy continued, "Dr. Yamamori is an inspirational, pastoral, motivational leader. A courageous and big thinker; very generous, and gracious. . . . He is my hero, my friend, my adviser, my teacher."[49]

These qualities are those that have made Ted a truly global, polycentric leader. It was Christlike, servanthood-focused leadership like this that infused the Lausanne Movement in a way that shaped many of us within it. Lausanne carries this collaborative spirit because of servants like Ted.

Today, the Lausanne Movement may be unparalleled in its influence in the development of the world Christian movement. Given the call for radical collaboration by non-Western leaders, may we see more collaboration fostered in the coming years and leaders who rise up and exhibit these six themes in serving our Lord.[50]

References

Birdsall, S. Douglas. "Conflict and Collaboration: A Narrative History and Analysis of the Interface between the Lausanne Committee for World Evangelization and

---

48. January 2022 interview via mobile call.
49. January 2022 emailed correspondence.
50. T. V. Thomas, Global Mobilization Consultation, Brazil, December 2019.

the World Evangelical Fellowship, the International Fellowship of Evangelical Mission Theologians, and the AD 2000 Movement." PhD diss., Oxford Centre for Mission Studies, 2012.

Butler, Phill. *Well Connected: Releasing Power, Restoring Hope through Kingdom Partnerships.* [UK]: Authentic & World Vision, 2006.

Cabrera, Angel, and Gregory Unruh. *Being Global: How to Think, Act, and Lead in a Transformed World.* Boston: Harvard Business Review Press, 2012.

Flory, Richard, and Brad Christerson. *The Rise of Network Christianity: How Independent Leaders Are Changing the Religious Landscape.* New York: Oxford University Press, 2017.

Handley, Joseph W. "Polycentric Mission Leadership." PhD diss., Fuller Theological Seminary, School of Intercultural Studies, 2020. ProQuest: 27745033.

House, Robert J., Peter W. Dorfman, Mansour Javidian, Paul J. Hanges, and Mary F. Sully de Luque. *Strategic Leadership across Cultures: The GLOBE Study of CEO Leadership Behavior and Effectiveness in 24 Countries.* Thousand Oaks: Sage, 2014.

Krabill, Matthew. "Menno Was a Migrant with No Headquarters: The Polycentric Ecclesial Existence of African Immigrant Mennonite Congregations in LA." PhD diss., Fuller Theological Seminary, 2019.

Oxbrow, Mark. "Better Together: Partnership and Collaboration in Mission." Paper, Forms of Missionary Engagement, Edinburgh 2010 study. In *Witnessing to Christ Today, Volume II*, edited by Daryl Balia and Kirsteen Kim, 116–47. Oxford: Regnum, 2010.

Primuth, Kärin. "Mission Networks: Connecting the Global Church." *Evangelical Missions Quarterly* 51, no. 2: 214–18.

Shamir, Boaz, Robert House, and Michael Arthur. "The Motivational Effects of Charismatic Leadership: A Self-Concept Based Theory." *Organizational Science* 4, no. 4 (1993): 577–94.

Yamamori, Tetsunao. *The Church Growth Handbook.* Edited by Win Arn. Pasadena : Church Growth Press, 1979.

3

International Student Ministry: From Blind Spot to Vision[1]

By Leiton Chinn

In April 2009, more than twenty-five former students and scholars from about fifteen countries and all continents, spanning three decades of academic life in Boston, reunited at the Park Street Congregational Church's FOCUS Forum. These accomplished Christian women and men, from a vast array of professions, gathered in the sanctuary to testify to God's grace as they served him in their homelands or other countries as nation-builders and transformation agents. Returning to Park Street Church, which was my church from 1967 to 1968, I felt as if the sanctuary was "holy ground," and the international graduates who were giving reports had also met God and his people here.

These former students from several colleges and universities in the Boston area are Christ's ambassadors and witnesses around the world today. In plain sight, they embodied and exhibited a core value of international student ministry (ISM) – that is, sharing the love and life of Christ with foreign students in holistic and authentic ways while they are among us, and contributing to their development as the world's future leaders.

Seeing God's exhibit of international disciples in the sanctuary testified to the value of, and need for, international student ministry and its strategic worldwide impact.

As I sat in the sanctuary beholding God's work among international scholars, researchers, and graduate and undergraduate students over the years,

---

1. This chapter is an updated and abridged version of an unpublished paper given at the Lausanne Diasporas Strategy Consultation held in Manila in May 2009.

I thought back to the time in 1975 when a former international student gave a powerful message in the same sanctuary for the World Missions Conference of Park Street Church. That message, "The Great Blind Spot in Missions Today," was about ministry among international students, and how the church often failed to see the tremendous opportunity and potential for world missions to and through foreign scholars. That message certainly applied to the church in 1975, and while there has been encouraging progress in moving from blindness to sight and vision, there remains the need for the Holy Spirit to remove and replace various shades of blindness with clarity and vision.

Personal Journey from Blindness to Vision

It was a privilege for me to attend California Baptist College on a "Foreign Student Scholarship," even though I was an American-born citizen from Hawaii (prior to statehood Hawaii was considered the "foreign mission field" by the Foreign Mission Board of the Southern Baptist Convention). Because of the scholarship, I attended a Thanksgiving conference for international students and felt at home with students from all over the world. I did not, however, catch the vision for ISM through that exposure and experience. On campus, I would walk by the room of students from Asia, and not really "see" them. I smelled their cooking spices and heard their foreign accents, but still I did not recognize them as part of my world.

I saw superficially, but I was blind to accept them. If they were not obviously hurting or needing help, they could be in their world, and I was busy in my world with my American friends. There were no negative feelings toward them, and if we happened to engage briefly, it was fine . . . like our American greeting in passing – friendly, but superficial.

For four years, I saw internationals on campus, but I did not engage with them on any personal level (to my loss). I did not have xenophobia (the dread of foreigners), but I also did not practice hospitality (to show love to foreigners). The blinders of ethnocentrism (and the privacy of the American culture) are prevalent, even in Christian campuses and churches as well as in the broader community. I was blindly insensitive toward my international student neighbors, and many diaspora mission practitioners and researchers may see the same dynamic in their own contexts of diaspora ministry.

Soon, I went from campus life to military duty and began serving in Korea. I experienced Christian hospitality by an older Korean who befriended me even though American military personnel were not always well thought of. This man introduced me to the Korean community and church and discipled me. He risked reaching out cross-culturally to connect with me and enriched my life and experience of being a stranger in a strange land. I left Korea with a deep love for the Korean people and the country, so much so that I returned there four years later as a self-supporting "tentmaker" missionary.

At that time, I thought that I could best serve God as a layman rather than as a professional missionary, and serve him in another country rather than in the US. But God had another plan for me. He soon led me back to the US with a strong conviction to minister in my home country.

He also led me to seminary. In my second year at Columbia Graduate School for Bible and Missions (now Columbia International University), I had a strong desire to return overseas, and was confused and bewildered since I believed God had led me to remain in my country. It was in that perplexing situation that I met a person working in ISM. I had never heard of ministry among international students and was interested to learn more. The following day, I received a newsletter from the World Evangelical Fellowship (now World Evangelical Alliance) describing different missionary endeavors, including ISM. There was just one sentence about ISM, but it really resonated with me, and I wondered if God was calling my attention to international student ministry.

I realized that God was solving my dilemma of staying home but also being involved in global missions, by ministering to the world he brings to our campuses. It was the solution to what had seemed to be an irreconcilable problem. The blinders came off my eyes, and I saw the vision of international student ministry as global missions at home and on our campuses.

The seminary soon allowed me to initiate a ministry to international students at the nearby University of South Carolina.

A few months later I substituted as a volunteer leader of a church-based ISM in Atlanta, Georgia, and through that summer experience I received my call to full-time missionary service in ISM. I sensed that many churches in North America, and the world, were blind to the rich and ready opportunity to participate in global missions by relating with and serving international students in their communities.

Just as Jesus saw and felt compassion for the multitudes as harassed and helpless, like sheep without a shepherd, and told the disciples to ask the Lord of the harvest to send workers into the harvest field (Matt 9:35–38), I saw that the church was practically blind to international students. This realization broke my heart and the burden to share the vision of ISM with the church became my passion and call to full-time missionary service. I took a leave from my seminary to travel for a year to share the ISM vision at mission conferences in the US and Canada. This was in 1977.

For over four decades I have been privileged to be a mobilizer, advocate, and vision-caster for ISM in North America, and increasingly at the global level in the last twenty years. As an ISM ambassadorial chef, I serve the ISM vision *entrée* utilizing the following two basic ingredients, mixed and stirred in a missional wok, and presented in person or publication:

Insights for the Biblical Basis for ISM

Sharing the vision for ISM includes sharing some of the biblical basis for ministry among "strangers" and other relevant scriptures pertaining to the broader field of diaspora peoples. The Old Testament contains multiple commands for God's people to love the alien and foreigner in the land, as summarized in Leviticus 19:33–34: "When a foreigner resides among you in your land, do not mistreat them. The foreigner residing among you must be treated as your native-born. Love them as yourself, for you were foreigners in Egypt. I am the LORD your God." The New Testament has numerous injunctions to practice hospitality and to welcome strangers. An early brief overview of diaspora theology is contained in "Diaspora in the Bible" of the Lausanne Occasional Paper #55, stemming from the Lausanne 2004 Global Forum for World Evangelization in Thailand. Subsequently, numerous diaspora missiology texts and publications have emanated from the directive and encouraging leadership of Dr. Enoch Wan, Dr. Joy Tira, Dr. Tetsunao (Ted) Yamamori, Dr. Samuel George, and the Institute for Diaspora Studies of Western Seminary, the Global Diaspora Network, and the Global Diaspora Institute at Wheaton College.

One of the biblical perspectives I usually share with the ISM vision is how often people will meet God while they are away from their homeland. We see this in Acts 2 with people from all around the Mediterranean world hearing the gospel in their own language while they are in Jerusalem. Additionally, the church was born as a multilingual, multiethnic body. The number of "Jerusalems" housing or hosting many thousands of foreign-language speakers continues to grow in places such as Toronto, Sydney, New York City, Paris, London, Sao Paulo, and Amsterdam.

Acts 8 records the account of the traveling Ethiopian treasurer who was returning from Jerusalem but needed to know more about the Messiah who is prophesied in Isaiah. The apostle Philip was diverted from a great evangelistic ministry in Samaria to meet the African on the desert road to explain the good news of Jesus. The government official believed, was baptized, and went home rejoicing – and may have started the church in Ethiopia. I wonder how many international students and scholars also return home rejoicing because someone noticed their need for biblical explanation and understanding and shared the good news of Jesus with them.

Acts 9 tells the story of Saul (a seminary student from Tarsus studying under Gamaliel in Jerusalem) who was persecuting the followers of Jesus. Saul encountered Jesus on the road to Damascus and became Paul, the great missionary church planter among the Gentiles. Thousands of international students encounter Jesus while studying abroad, and become Christ's ambassadors in their host country, back home, or in another country.

Acts 10 recounts two cross-cultural conversions: the Italian military commander and his family stationed in Caesarea who were prepared by God to receive the gospel, and Peter's transition from socioreligious bias-blindness toward Gentiles, to accepting God's repeated revelation and reality that Gentiles are not impure or unclean. Once Peter received God's declaration that foreigners are acceptable to him, Peter was not hesitant to enter the presence of the Italians and share the good news of Christ. Sharing the ISM vision gives sight to the church to accept foreign students and to connect with them, and many foreign students have been prepared by God to receive the gospel presented by the host Christian community.

One of my Bibles has the paragraph title "First Convert in Europe" in Acts 16, which introduces the conversion of Lydia in Philippi, Macedonia. Lydia met Paul and received Christ on European soil, but she was from across the sea in Thyatira, in the Asian province which Paul had been forbidden by the Holy Spirit to enter. Perhaps Lydia went back to Thyatira for business or to visit and was a witness in the place and to the people that Paul and his missionary team were prevented by God from visiting in Acts 16:6. So it is with many converted international scholars, faculty, and students who receive Jesus abroad and return to a place and people that missionaries have been prevented from going to.

Many international students arrive in a new country and culture as vibrant Christians and need to be received by a hospitable church and Christian friends who may encourage them and enable them to grow and serve. This was the situation for Apollos, a native of Alexandria, Egypt, who had arrived in Ephesus and was speaking boldly of Christ in the synagogue. In Acts 18, Apollos was befriended by Priscilla and Aquila, who invited him to their home. There, they explained the way of God more adequately to Apollos, who later went to Achaia and had a powerful apologetics ministry. Priscilla and Aquila were like "host families" and friends today, who invite Christian international students to their homes as a place for fellowship and growth.

One area for proactive hospitality could be inviting international students at seminaries, Bible colleges, and Christian schools for fellowship and meals in a Christian home. And let us not forget or ignore the reality that many Christian international students arrive as God's missionaries to our countries, communities, churches, and campuses already prepared, ready, and willing to serve and minister. Let us be quick to recognize their gifts for ministry and receive them and partner with them as equal co-laborers in God's field of our own place.

Gaining Vision of the Strategic Nature of ISM

What was a "great blind spot in missions" in 1975 has been gradually diminishing as the church continues to gain vision about the strategic value of ISM, and a better understanding of international students and scholars who are:

- Already on our campuses, in our communities, and in our churches. We do not need to wait to go somewhere, over there, get a visa, or purchase a plane ticket. Despite the temporary reduction of international student numbers during the COVID-19 pandemic from 2020 to 2022, the growth of students studying abroad has been projected to grow by 5 percent each year through 2030.[2]
- Sufficiently conversant in our language to study in our schools (or maybe in a language institute to enhance the learning of our language) and appreciate the opportunity to practice our language with us.
- Generally curious to learn about our culture, history, and country (or city/town), and may wish to have friends who can be cultural mentors.
- Often more open, curious, and responsive to learning about Jesus Christ while living abroad.
- Freer to consider the gospel if they are away from a restrictive society, culture, and religion that is hostile toward Christianity.
- Often from unreached people groups where the church does not yet exist or is in an infant stage.
- Appreciative of hospitality and welcome relationships of mutual intercultural interaction, as well as the intergenerational social

---

2. Sudeep Load and Anip Sharma, "Global Student Mobility Trends – 2021 and Beyond," LEK, 29 June 2021, https://www.lek.com/insights/ar/global-student-mobility-trends-2021-and-beyond.

context of host families where younger children, parents, and grandparents are valued along with peer-age adults.
- Potential world leaders politically and in their professions, nation-builders, and transformation agents.
- Christian returnees who are significantly establishing the universal church. For example, many of the top evangelical leaders of the church in Malaysia and Singapore today were students in Australia in the 1960s and 1970s. John Sung came to Christ in the US in the mid 1920s, returned to China as an apostle, and revival spread like wildfire. His first missionary endeavor was to Manila in 1935, and revival spread through much of the Far East. At about the same period that Sung was building a ministry in China in the late 1920s, Bakht Singh of India, a Sikh, was being attracted to Christ over a span of months while studying in the UK and then in Winnipeg, Manitoba, Canada. Singh received Christ and returned to be an apostle to India, just as Sung was to China and East Asia. In fact, Singh's New Testament church-planting model multiplied to over five hundred congregations in India and two hundred congregations in Pakistan, in addition to a number in Europe and North America.[3]
- Informants and "instructors" who may advance the missions movement. Two mega shifts in missions in the nineteenth and twentieth centuries were spurred on by the informants' role provided by international students. First, in the third week of the July-long Moody student conference at Mt. Hermon, Massachusetts, in 1886, a special "meeting of the ten nations" was held in which students from ten countries shared briefly about the need for missionaries in their part of the world. Those "Macedonian calls" fueled a response that resulted in a hundred of the 251 students signing a pledge of willingness and desire to be missionaries. The missionary passion coming out of the conference was the initial thrust that led to the formation of the Student Volunteer Movement for Foreign Missions (SVMFM) in 1888. The SVMFM produced over 20,500 missionaries on the field, and thousands more who supported the missionary movement.[4] The second mega shift was Dr. Ralph D. Winter's

---

3. Jonathan Bonk, "Thinking Small: Global Missions and American Churches," *Missiology: An International Review* 28, no. 2 (Apr. 2000): 149–61.

4. David Howard, *Student Power in World Evangelism* (Downers Grove: InterVarsity Press, 1970).

development of the Unfinished Task of World Evangelization in relation to the "hidden peoples"/unreached peoples concept, which effected a paradigm shift in mission understanding and strategic planning. What contributed to the emerging "people groups" worldview of Dr. Winter? According to him, the Fuller Seminary School of World Missions, where he taught, had ten students and a hundred faculty. He explained that he was a student learning about church growth and evangelism among the world's great diversity of cultural subgroups, from one hundred "teachers" – his international student informants.

- Gifts of God to the host nation and church. An African seminary student was instrumental in the missional conversion of a veteran Episcopal priest, who later became a bishop and played a significant role in the emerging evangelical renewal within the American Episcopal Church. The renewal or reformation is now evident in the new and growing Anglican Church in North America that comprises many former Episcopal congregations. It was my privilege to be invited to join the board of trustees of Trinity Episcopal (now Anglican) School for Ministry to specifically help develop the Stanway Institute for World Mission and Evangelism at the seminary in the early 1990s. The transformative seeds for renewal and missions were planted by an African seminarian.

As a Christian international student coming to America, Dr. Ted Yamamori can testify to how studying and living in another country may allow a student to grow, thrive, serve, and minister in a foreign land, and contribute to the host country, its church, and the global church.

Local churches are also discovering how enriching it is to have a ministry among international students, as exemplified in the following points:[5]

- Great benefits and significant global impact are possible with a modest ISM budget; they are high yield, but low cost. Some churches' outreach among international students has no budget or funding but is wholly financed by volunteer finances.
- ISM provides a tangible dimension to a church's mission vision, with engagement options for the congregation to participate beyond

---

5. These are adapted from Leiton Chinn, "Global Missions at Home," *Mission Maker Magazine*, 2008.

- prayer, care, and financial support of overseas missionaries and ministries.
- ISM incorporates the broad range of church members available for involvement, from children to retirees, and utilizes their varied gifts for service, such as hospitality, helps, administration, teaching, mercy, evangelism, and leadership.
- Returned or retired missionaries back home are extending their cross-cultural mission service by ministering among international students from the country or cultural-linguistic group they served overseas. We had several missionaries and other returned expatriate government or business people regularly involved in our church-based ISM.
- Many people who have a desire to serve abroad but are not able to are having a fruitful ministry with international students from the country or region of the world they had intended to go to. It is not unusual to hear volunteers say that they had a desire to be a missionary when they were younger, but circumstances changed their direction in life, and they are now being global missionaries at home, and sometimes in their homes.
- International student friends are ready-made language and cultural teachers for anyone going to the students' countries for long-term or short-term missions, study abroad, work, or simply a visit.
- International students may provide a critical linkage for ministry/mission in their homeland, either personally after they return home or by giving a positive introduction and endorsement of missionaries to their family, friends, and networks. Returnees can be gatekeepers who open the door for ministry by foreigners in their country.
- The reality is that most Christians are not "called" to serve as long-term professional missionaries or to be self-supporting "tentmaker" or BAM missionaries in another country. But staying home does not mean we cannot engage in cross-cultural, global ministry. ISM is one avenue for participating in world missions at home.

John R. Mott is well known for being an extraordinary mission mobilizer, leader, and strategist, and he saw the need for ISM. Mott attended that first international student Christian conference at Mt. Hermon, heard the plea for missionaries by students from the ten nations, signed the missionary pledge, and was one of four who traveled across the country to spread the missionary challenge that gave birth to the SVMFM. According to Mary Thompson, "it was undoubtedly at this conference that the idea of a student volunteer organization to assist foreign students in the US grew in the mind of Mott . . . but it was not to come to fruition for more than 25 years."[6]

Mott was the first chairman of the SVMFM, first general secretary of the World's Student Christian Federation, chair of the International Missionary Council, chair of the 1910 World Missionary Conference in Edinburgh (which was celebrated at Lausanne's Cape Town 2010, Edinburgh 2010, Tokyo 2010, and other events), the national secretary of the Intercollegiate YMCA for twenty-seven years, and a recipient of the Nobel Peace Prize.

What most people do not know is that in 1911 Mott organized and led the US's first organization designed to aid foreign students – the Committee on Friendly Relations among Foreign Students (CFR). The CFR spawned and encouraged many programs and structures to service international students, including NAFSA (initially the National Association of Foreign Student Advisors, later changed to "Foreign Student Affairs," and now Association of International Educators). One of the greatest missionary advocates and leaders of the last century was also the visionary to pioneer the first ISM organization in America 111 years ago.

A tipping point indicating that the global church is embracing the ISM vision as a strategic mission methodology equal to the sending forth of missionaries to other countries was the inclusion of ISM as an integral component of the Lausanne Movement at the Lausanne Leadership meetings in Budapest, Hungary, in 2007. Lausanne's Global ISM Leadership Network became an official linked network of the World Evangelical Alliance Mission Commission in 2014, and the Lausanne Global ISM Leadership Forum: Charlotte'17 convened a hundred participants from seventy organizations and twenty-five countries.

Gradually, with gaps and growth spurts in the process over the past century, blindness to international student ministry is becoming sight by the church.

References

Bonk, Jonathan. "Thinking Small: Global Missions and American Churches." *Missiology: An International Review* 28, no. 2 (Apr. 2000): 149–61.

Chinn, Leiton. "Global Missions at Home." *Mission Maker Magazine*, 2008.

---

6. Mary Thompson, *Unofficial Ambassadors: The Story of International Student Service* (New York: International Student Service, YMCA of Greater New York, 1982), 18.

Howard, David. *Student Power in World Evangelism.* Downers Grove: InterVarsity Press, 1970.

Load, Sudeep, and Anip Sharma. "Global Student Mobility Trends – 2021 and Beyond." LEK, 29 June 2021. https://www.lek.com/insights/ar/global-student-mobility-trends-2021-and-beyond.

Thompson, Mary. *Unofficial Ambassadors: The Story of International Student Service.* New York: International Student Service, YMCA of Greater New York, 1982.

4

Church Growth in the Japanese Context of Complex Disasters

By Masanori Kurasawa

I met Dr. Ted Yamamori in 1990 at Tokyo Christian University (TCU), where I was teaching. When he published his book *God's New Envoys*,[1] he became a TCU special professor, lecturing on the integral ministry of Christian missions.

In those days, he was involved in working toward the eradication of hunger at Food for the Hungry International (FHI) and strengthening special ties with Japan International Food for the Hungry (JIFH), which I was connected with at that time. TCU is a university with an ambitious theology department equipping committed Christians not only for clergy positions, but also for lay ministry positions as "workers charged in Christian missions" who become the "salt of the earth" and "light of the world." That was why Dr. Yamamori's book was very attractive to our students.

As I became a board member of JIFH, I was given many opportunities to interact with Dr. Yamamori, and I learned a lot from him about the integral ministry of the gospel. At that time, he didn't talk much about his book *Church Growth in Japan*.[2] However, I recall that in one of our conversations he asked me about the situation of the church in Japan and commented that Donald A. McGavran's theory of church growth was not well understood in Japan.

Because I had studied missiology at the School of World Mission at Fuller Theological Seminary, I had read McGavran's book *Understanding Church*

---

1. Tetsunao Yamamori, *God's New Envoys: A Bold Strategy for Penetrating "Closed Countries"* (Portland: Multnomah, 1987), 131.
2. Tetsunao Yamamori, *Church Growth in Japan* (Pasadena: William Carey Library, 1974).

Growth[3] and I had been taught his idea by C. Peter Wagner. So, when I read Dr. Yamamori's book, I found that his analysis of church-growth factors in the major prewar Japanese Protestant denominations accurately reflected McGavran's theory of church growth. Yamamori's book described his steady empirical analysis and method for considering church-growth factors from the major prewar Japanese Protestant denominations.

Following his prewar research, I remember Dr. Yamamori appealing eagerly for someone to take charge of research on the growth of Japanese churches after the war. While due to the word limit it is not possible to cover in this Festschrift all of the postwar church growth and stagnation, or provide a detailed analysis of contributing factors, I would like to express my tribute to Dr. Yamamori for his many years of ministry by introducing the recent data on the trends and growth of the Protestant church in Japan over the ten years since the Great East Japan Earthquake of 2011.

Recent Church Trends and Growth after the Great East Japan Earthquake in 2011

Before considering the trends and growth of Protestant churches after the Great Earthquake, I would like to address the statistical trends of postwar Japanese churches. It is uncertain whether the "number of communicant members" used by Dr. Yamamori as a measuring device for the analysis of growth factors is strictly reflected, but figures from the *Christian Yearbook 2021–2022* will be a rough guide.[4]

From 1948 to 2021, the Christian population (Protestant, Catholic, Orthodox) increased from 331,087 (0.423 percent of the total population) to 987,621 (0.789 percent). Until 1972, the proportion of the Christian population doubled, from 0.423 percent to 0.809 percent. This is believed to be due to (1) the Christianity boom (when many people were attracted to American Christianity) in the turmoil of defeat and (2) evangelism directed at young, urbanized people due to Japan's strong economy. However, from 1974 to 2021, the Christian population remained relatively flat, from 0.764 percent minimum (in 1978) to 0.891 percent maximum (in 2008). Moreover, it is undeniable that there has been a gradual downward trend since 2010.

---

3. Donald A. McGavran, *Understanding Church Growth: Fully Revised* (Grand Rapids: Eerdmans, 1980).

4. *Kirisutokyo Nenkan 2021–2022* [Christian Yearbook 2021–2022] (Tokyo: Kirisuto Shinbunsha, 2021), 55.

In 2021, the total number of Protestants (536,857), Catholics (428,582), and Orthodox (11,261) believers was 976,700, and the total number of Japanese Christians, including 10,921 clergy, was 987,621 believers (0.789 percent of the population). Yet this shows a decrease from the 1,108,101 Japanese Christians of ten years before (2010). This shows that the Great Earthquake has not necessarily led to numerical growth for the church in Japan. On the contrary, with the declining birth rate and aging population, the number of church members is visibly decreasing due to the aging of the church itself.

In 2016, the "Data Book of the Japanese Church" was published. The "Christian Yearbook 2016" revealed that when it came to the ratio of current active members to registered church members, there was a lower ratio of active members for more traditional churches, whereas the ratio of active members was relatively high in newly established churches.[5]

In terms of the number of baptized people in 2014, when using the United Church of Christ in Japan and other denominations for sampling, the total number of Protestant churches was 7,921, and the number of baptized people per church was 0.97.[6] Furthermore, regarding the aging clergy, the average age was calculated based on a questionnaire by *Kirisuto Shinbunsha* in 2015; that number was 67.8 years of age.[7] So, the number of churches without a pastor had increased, and according to the 2014 survey, about a thousand churches had another pastor helping, accounting for 13 percent of all churches.[8] The aging of congregations was also significant, with the United Church of Christ in Japan, the largest Protestant denomination in Japan, having an average age of 62.9 years.[9] As a forecast for the future, with the declining birth rate and aging population continuing, and if the future assumption value was 1.5 percent based on the 2016 mortality rate of 1.04 percent in Japan, the number of Japanese Protestant church members would decrease from 610,000 to 575,000 within the next thirty years.[10]

By 2021, however, this number was already at 537,000, which was lower than expected.[11] The COVID-19 pandemic from 2020 to 2022 will have greatly

---

5. JCE6 Japan Mission Project, Data Book, *Nihon Senkyo no Korekara ga Mietekuru: Kirisutokyo no 30 Nengo wo Yomu* [The Future of Japanese Evangelization: Understanding Christianity in Japan after Thirty Years] (Tokyo: Inochi no Kotobasha, 2016), 36.

6. JCE6 Japan Mission Project, Data Book, 33, 39.

7. Data Book, 50.

8. Data Book, 46.

9. Data Book, 52.

10. Data Book, 57.

11. Christian Yearbook 2020–2021, 55.

impacted Japanese churches. According to the United Church of Christ in Japan's 2020 statistics, the number of current active members had decreased since 2019 by two thousand to 75,087, worship attendees had decreased by 11,111 to 36,973, and baptized persons had decreased by 195. There were 743 baptized people, 0.45 people per church (in 1,666 Japanese churches). According to the statistics of the Japan Baptist Convention, which is the second-largest denomination, the number of current active members in 2020 decreased since 2019 by 311 to 13,435, and the number of worship attendees decreased by 1,625 to 9,698. The number of baptized persons decreased by 118 to 157, reaching 0.49 per church (318 Japanese churches).[12]

During the COVID-19 pandemic, gathering together was restricted, and the number of worship attendees changed drastically, which has had a great impact on the economy of the church. In this way, the statistical trend of decline in Japanese Protestant churches in the 2010s did not stop, and the church has been forced into further stagnation.

New Waves of Church Growth in Japan

Despite this dire situation, new waves of revitalization have come to the church in Japan. The first wave came with the commemoration by three Protestant groups (ecumenical, evangelical, and revival) of the 150th anniversary of Protestant mission in Japan (2009) with the slogan "One in Christ – As a Witness of the Lord Jesus." Furthermore, the theme of the fifth Japan Congress on Evangelism (Sapporo) of the evangelical churches held in the same year was "Mission Cooperation in Times of Crisis: Wider and Deeper," which was focused on instilling the gospel in various areas of modern society. It was confirmed that church and missionary cooperation needed to be broader and deeper. To remove the wall of sectarianism, "*Kyokyohashugi*" (interdenominational cooperation) was called for. And while promoting interdenominational cooperation such as social work collaboration with the aging of the church and missionary cooperation for the next generations, there was also a focus on the local level. Two years later, the church in Japan encountered the triple disasters of an earthquake (the Great East Japan Earthquake), a tsunami, and a nuclear accident.

The church was the first to support the areas impacted by the earthquake. Church relief and supporting volunteers from around the world gathered in

---

12. *Japan Mission Research* (JMR), Nihon Senkyo Nyusu (Japan Mission News). No. 22 February 2022. Tokyo Christian University, 10–12.

Japan to continue to provide physical and mental support to the afflicted. Under such circumstances, the "Tohoku Help" was launched in collaboration with various denominations and churches in the disaster areas of Iwate, Miyagi, and Fukushima Prefecture. Especially, through the "Miyagi Mission Network" activities, mission cooperation became more practical.[13] In addition, the nationwide "Disaster Relief Christian Liaison Committee" (DRCnet) and the "Kyushu Christian Disaster Support Center" (called *Kyukisai*) were established to help those affected by the 2016 Kumamoto earthquakes.

During heavy rain and flood disasters, the church-based disaster prevention network was also established. In this way, interchurch cooperation at the regional level was beginning to be promoted. Through such support for the disaster-stricken areas, in collaboration with various churches in those areas, those afflicted put their trust in Christian volunteers, calling them "Mr. & Ms. Christ" (*kirisuto-san*), and the churches began to be regarded as open to the community rather than seen as only "preaching churches." Many came to regard the church as a "church that lives with the community." Both clergy and laypeople began to understand the integral ministry of Christian mission to convey the gospel in both word and deed.

The people in the Tohoku region have a very strong closed character due to their traditional Japanese culture and customs, regarding outsiders as "foreign." However, through the suffering caused by the earthquake and Christians supporting and rebuilding, many Japanese began to listen to stories in "community cafés" set up by Christian support groups. As a result, some churches have been formed and have become familiar to those living in these areas.

In addition, Christians who volunteered from throughout Japan learned how to express the gospel to meet the needs of people through support for the disaster areas. They also began bringing that experience back to their own areas and developing new ministries. According to the Sample Spiritual Response Rate in Tohoku, the number of churches before the earthquake was ten, but after the earthquake, the number rose to twenty, and the number of baptisms increased from twenty-six to sixty-four, decisions from ten to 178, and seekers from thirty-four to 461. According to John Mehn, "Christian ministry and church planting has greatly expanded throughout the region affected by the disaster."[14]

---

13. Data Book, 205–15.
14. John Wm Mehn, *Multiplying Churches in Japanese Soil* (Littleton: William Carey Library, 2017), 87.

The Great Earthquake also encouraged laypeople's efforts to evangelize. After World War II, the mobilization of lay believers was called for as a necessary factor in the progress of world missions. Hendrik Kraemer's description of the laity as "frozen credits" of the church was applied to the church in Japan.[15] When Kraemer spoke about this issue in his "Criticism of the Japanese Church" during his visit to Japan, he sharply criticized Japan's clergy-centered principle.

Dr. Yamamori presents two contrasting patterns of prewar church growth, defining the former as the "school approach pattern" and the latter as the "conversion approach pattern." The former is described as "the intellectual and individual response to the Christian faith," and the latter as "the experiential and group-oriented way into the church." In the former, the clergy play the key role, and the convert joins the church after a long time of learning. In the latter, the convert's decisive religious experience is joyfully shared with family, relatives, and friends. Dr. Yamamori concludes that the growing Holiness Church adopted the latter.[16] The "school approach pattern" was used as a model for church growth for forty-five years after World War II, but the effects of this method have been questioned.

Based on the research and practice of church planting in Japan over the past thirty years, John Mehn presented six models of effective church reproduction: (1) Target Penetration Missional Model, (2) Network Church Planting, (3) Simple Church Networks, (4) Cell Church Reproduction, (5) Multisite Churches, and (6) Sending Churches.[17]

What these six models have in common is the ministry of evangelism, which includes small groups emphasizing relationship-building and the utilization of lay leadership in daily life. Lay leaders need to receive coaching and encouragement. These six models are dedicated to evangelism, discipleship, and leadership development for the reproduction of the church. Since the models have been put into practice in Japan, and their characteristics and effective factors summarized, they will be helpful for those doing church planting in the future. And although we need to remember regional diversity, these six models are generally applicable and effective in church reproduction throughout Japan.

The 2021 statistics of Japan Alliance Christ Church (JACC), to which I belong, showed 261 churches, 9,380 current communicant members, 434

---

15. Hendrik Kraemer, *A Theology of the Laity* (Philadelphia: Westminster Press, 1958), 34, 176.

16. Yamamori, *Church Growth in Japan*, 120–33.

17. Mehn, *Multiplying Churches*, 97–116.

pastors, 190 baptized, and 8,040 worship attendees (adults).[18] Under the vision of "Alliance Churches in All Prefectures," JACC has been carrying out a church-planting project throughout Japan at three levels: the denominational level, the mission parish level, and the local church level. The church-planting model, however, is connected primarily to the traditional "school model."

Today, JACC recognizes two types of church growth in which lay believers take leadership and share Christ with non-Christian people. One type is multi-ministerial churches that seek to meet the various needs of the people around them through ministries of a church school from kindergarten to junior high school, a day-care service of support for the elderly and people with disabilities, and funeral support with an ossuary facility. They are trying to fulfill the rites of passage of life from the cradle to the grave for the needy, and the gifts and skills of lay believers are heavily applied in these ministries. The other type of church growth is like the "cell church" reproduction model (see below) but is within an institutional church such as through the practice of celebration. Many house churches operate under the same missional philosophy and budget, making them multisite and sending churches. By eating, sharing, and praying together once a week, believers and nonbelievers pray for and support one another with Christ at the center. Through it all, lay believers take up leadership roles, which promotes discipleship and training of leaders.

Toward Church Growth and Sustainable Church Reproduction

When Dr. Yamamori was working at Food for the Hungry International, he described the relationship between evangelism and social ministry as "symbiotic."[19] Symbiosis is a biological term that means "living in a state where different creatures interact with each other." The question is which one will be the main body.

In the case of earthquakes, the focus is on providing physical supplies and mental support. In the process of meeting needs, the hearts of the afflicted gradually become calmer, and people become open to Christian supporters as they know their motives and see their kind acts. Mutual trust is key. At the time of the Great Earthquake, both churches and local communities were affected by the triple disaster so that solidarity resulted. The churches thus had the opportunity to walk with the local people. The church was renewed through

---

18. Japan Alliance Christ Church (JACC), *2021 Nendo Jitsujo Houkoku* (The Actual Situation Report in 2021), 73rd JACC General Assembly Statistical Data, 16 March 2022.
19. Yamamori, *God's New Envoys*, 131.

the suffering of the triple disaster, being transformed from having a unilateral preaching focus to being open-hearted and collaborating with the community.

By affectionately calling church members *Kirisuto-san*, non-Christians began to listen to the gospel more readily. As mentioned earlier, however, disaster relief activities are not always directly linked to the numerical growth of a church. Instead, they bring about an increase in the church's influence in the community and bring trust and peace to suffering people. This is the blessing of God's kingdom and it gives us an opportunity to reconsider the devices that have been used to measure the growth of the church.

There are four biblical guidelines for measuring the growth of a church, according to Acts 2:41–47: growing up to maturity (Christlike way of life), growing together in community (*koinonia*), growing outward in service (*diakonia*), and growing more in numbers. It is important – and necessary – that the four indicators for the growth of the church are nurtured in a well-balanced symbiotic relationship between the church and the local community. As Japan continues to endure complex disasters of earthquakes, floods, volcanic eruptions, and the COVID-19 pandemic, the concepts of Christian mission and the church itself need to be reconsidered.

Another factor to be considered is that worship and communion services could not be held face-to-face during the pandemic but moved online. Additionally, with the advent of Internet churches, multibased and polycentric churches have begun to transcend time and space, and church services have emerged in the meta-world where physical space and cyberspace are fused. Considering these factors, the principle of the church in mission needs to be readdressed in a symbiotic manner as Dr. Yamamori proposes, and during times of great crisis and given the new social norm of online worship services, the church in Japan needs to play an integral role in the community, both serving urgent needs and bringing the hope of the gospel to suffering people.

Finally, we must also consider the "house church" network and the "cell church" reproduction model, of which there are many independent or simple churches that do not belong to a specific denomination or organization.[20] These groups are second to the ecumenical church group in terms of the number of churches and members. They have focused on aggressive evangelism by using the lay leadership and the relationship-building method through small groups. At the same time a system of organization for sustainable reproduction of these churches is needed. Whether it is through cooperative networking or multisite, new church formats will need to be considered.

---

20. *Data Book*, 33.

In any case, the church will be responsible for the final passage of people's lives in Japan's multireligious environment as the birth rate declines and the population ages. As the church grows, sustainable factors are needed moving forward.

Conclusion

We have gained great insight from Dr. Yamamori into the defining factors affecting postwar Japanese church growth. His ideas for an integral ministry of Christian mission in a symbiotic manner and conversion models in church planting have had a major impact on the growth of postwar Japanese churches.

Although the triple disaster of the Great East Japan Earthquake in 2011 did not lead to the numerical growth of Japanese churches, the influence of churches in their communities has been steadily increasing in the disaster-hit islands of Japan. The Christian service of love speaks to people through "deed." Each lay believer is used in times of crisis and can preach the gospel. Furthermore, church planting is being carried out using various conversion models by lay leadership.

When many people have not been able to gather for face-to-face worship services due to COVID-19, the occurrence of fellowship-centered ministry led by lay believers through small groups has expanded. In addition, the number of foreigners living in Japan is 2.88 million (2 percent of the Japanese population), and the number of Protestant international churches and ethnic churches is 118.[21]

World evangelization is at the door in Japan, and churches are mission partners responsible for church planting. Japanese churches and international and ethnic churches need to work together in church planting, and fortunately this collaboration has already begun. The complex disasters in Japan have brought united prayer and cooperation. In that sense, the evaluation index to measure the growth of the church is not only a numerical factor, but also a qualitative one: that is, the degree of its contribution to the local community (providing the ethical and social norms that embody being the "salt of the earth" and "light of the world"). The planting and formation of a "holy catholic and apostolic" church is our common indicator of the being and arrival of the kingdom of God in Christ.

---

21. *Kurisuchan Shinbun* (Christian newspaper), 5 May 2019.

References

Kirisutokyo Nenkan 2021–2022 [Christian Year Book 2021–2022]. Tokyo: Kirisuto Shinbunsha, 2021.

Dai 6 kai Nihon Dendo Kaigi Nihon Senkyo 170 - 200 Purojekuto Hen [JCE6 Japan Mission 170–200 Project, eds.]. *Nihon Senkyo no Korekara ga Mietekuru: Kirisutokyo no 30 Nengo wo Yomu* [The Future of Japanese Evangelization: Understanding Christianity in Japan after Thirty Years]. Tokyo: Inochi no Kotobasha, 2016.

Kraemer, Hendrik. *A Theology of the Laity*. Philadelphia: Westminster Press, 1958.

McGavran, Donald A. *Understanding Church Growth: Fully Revised*. Grand Rapids: Eerdmans, 1980.

Mehn, John Wm. *Multiplying Churches in Japanese Soil*. Littleton: William Carey Library, 2017.

Yamamori, Tetsunao. *Church Growth in Japan*. Pasadena: William Carey Library, 1974.

———. *God's New Envoys: A Bold Strategy for Penetrating "Closed Countries."* Portland: Multnomah, 1987.

5

Kingdomization through Integral Mission of House Church Networks

By David S. Lim

I got to know Dr. Ted Yamamori as the head of Food for the Hungry International during my PhD days at Fuller Theological Seminary from 1983 to 1987 as I had become a member of the International Fellowship of Evangelical Mission Theologians (INFEMIT, now renamed International Fellowship of Mission as Transformation). At that time, most evangelicals were still learning how to actualize the church's social responsibility, so Dr. Ted's writings gave words to the voice that I was seeking to articulate on this theology and practice of holistic mission.

    I became involved with the Lausanne Movement in 1989 during the Second International Congress in Manila, and I finally met Dr. Ted personally in 2004 during the Lausanne Global Forum in Chiang Mai, when I represented the Filipino Missions Movement. We were offering to shift missions mobilization to using the Filipino diaspora (especially overseas Filipino workers, OFWs) as tentmakers in order to reach unreached people groups globally. Dr. Ted was recently appointed as international director of Lausanne and was very receptive to this development.

    In 2006, when the Philippines hosted the Sixth Asia Lausanne Congress, I invited Dr. Ted to be one of our speakers. Lausanne Philippines was birthed as the Philippine delegation planned and hosted the First Philippine Congress on World Evangelization in 2007. Since that time, we have kept in touch via email. I consider Dr. Ted to be one of the most innovative and influential leaders in the Lausanne Movement and beyond, and his writings have inspired me to be more creative and entrepreneurial in my missiological journey.

Here, I share about the Integral Mission (IntM) paradigm that I have developed and advocated for in the Philippine Missions Association (PMA), where I served as national director from 2011 to 2014. I started as its member when I founded the China Ministries International-Philippines in 1995, which has sent 120 tentmakers to make disciples in China. In 1997, I began to serve on the PMA board, leading its Tentmakers Task Force in 2000. This became its flagship program as the Philippine Missions Mobilization Movement (PM3) in 2003.

How did we understand and implement the Great Commission to make disciples of all nations (Matt 28:18–20) to actualize the kingdom of God on earth (Matt 6:9–10)? What has been our biblical vision and our mission strategy as we have mobilized OFWs for IntM?

PMA gradually clarified this IntM missiology. We have realized that global missions has not been very fruitful among the unreached primarily because the church had devolved and been reformatted into the Christendom (clergy-centered, cathedral-based) system. We knew we needed to transform the church back to the original "servant-church" format found in the book of Acts (2:41–47; 8:4; 19:10). We believe that our mission should be *kingdomization*: to equip the royal priesthood of all believers (1 Pet 2:9–10; Eph 4:11–13) to effectively multiply Jesus's disciples who enthrone him as Lord over all those in our (common) neighborhoods/communities and (secular) workplaces.

We believe that God has a *simple* plan for world evangelization and transformation. The Bible clearly says that God desires all people to be saved (2 Pet 3:8–9) and to know the truth (1 Tim 2:3–5). To achieve this, the all-wise God must have devised the *simplest* master plan to get this good news out to the whole world (of fallen humanity) in the quickest possible time. This he did by sending his Son Jesus Christ not just to provide the way of redemption (cf. Gal 4:4), but also for Jesus to model this strategic plan (Luke 4:18–21; 7:20–23) and to train his disciples in how to implement this plan (Luke 9:1–6; 10:1–20) by the power of the Holy Spirit across the Roman Empire and the world (Acts 1:8; 8:4; 11:19–21; 19:1–10; Rom 15:18–20).

So how do we view the Great Commission in terms of its goal, structure, strategy, and methodology? We have seen that instead of the predominant Christianization (to fill the world with church buildings and facilities), God's *simple* plan is kingdomization (to transform the world's buildings and facilities to serve him). Our mission is to convert the secular to the sacred by incarnating Jesus in all societal institutions (starting with families) by implementing prayer to God in Jesus's name and obedience to his word (1 Tim 4:4–5) anytime and anywhere (including workplaces and residences) from the inside out (infiltratively and subversively) and from the bottom up (Luke 12:32).

Simple Goal: Kingdomization (Not Christianization)

We believe God desires to bless all peoples to inherit his eternal kingdom/reign in heaven and experience his abundant life on earth as they obey him as their Creator and King through their faith in his Son Jesus Christ. His goal is *kingdomization* or "societal transformation," by which individuals, families, communities, and institutions are enabled to relate with each other and with other communities with biblical norms and values. We do this not perfectly, but substantially and significantly. This translates into building Christ-centered transformational communities that are growing in righteousness and justice and are marked by self-giving love (*agape*) where every household (*oikos*)[1] will be blessed (cf. Gen 12:1–3). *Righteousness* refers to just/right relationships (usually using one word: "love" or peace/shalom) with God, with self, with all people (esp. those already in the kingdom, Gal 6:10), and with creation.[2]

My favorite text to depict God's kingdom is Isaiah 65:17–25 (popularly called the "Isaiah 65 vision"), which envisions "new heavens and a new earth." The first three verses describe the New Jerusalem as a "city of joy" where life is celebrated, and God is delighted. Verse 20 sees people living long lives, presumably with healthy lifestyles, clean environments, and good governance (cf. 1 Tim 2:1–2), implying that the leaders are also godly and competent. Verses 21–22 show a society where social justice prevails, where each one's labor is rewarded accordingly, following the prophetic ideal of "every man [sitting] under his vine and under his fig tree" with nothing to fear (Mic 4:4 ESV) and with the Mosaic laws of gleaning and the year of Jubilee in force (so none will be poor, Deut 15:1–11; Lev 25). The next verse depicts prosperity passed on from one generation to the next, and the last verse describes harmony among animals, humans, and the whole creation. Additionally, verse 24 hints at a

---

1. *Oikos* is best translated as "household" for it is composed not just of the family, but also of friends, tenants, and slaves, as seen in the instructions given in Eph 5:22 – 6:9 and Col 3:18 – 4:1 (cf. David Lim, "God's Kingdom as *Oikos* Church Networks: A Biblical Theology," *International Journal of Frontier Mission* 34, no. 1–4 [Jan.–Dec. 2017]: 25–35). This means that each *oikos* church crossed many cultural barriers – particularly gender, age, class, and ethnicity – as they gathered and broke bread together around the same table as equals (cf. Gal 3:28).

2. On transformational mission, see Vinay Samuel and C. Sugden, *Mission as Transformation* (Oxford: Regnum, 1999).

mature form of faith in the gracious God whose blessings do not need to be earned or pleaded for, religiously or otherwise (cf. Rev 21:22–27).

However, historically, the church diverted into the "Christianization" vision, particularly in conceiving of its mission as a religious undertaking and its goal as a religious institution building (in short, to establish Christendom).[3] Rather than infiltrating and subverting institutions and cultures, the Christian mainstream sought to establish its own institutions, thus maintaining subcultures separate from the allegedly pagan, religio-cultural, and social orders in the world. This was based on three major shifts in their understanding of the kingdom of God, namely in their concepts of holy people, holy places, and holy practices.

Holy People

First, God's kingdom is a royal priesthood of all believers (1 Pet 2:9–10; cf. Exod 19:5–6; Rev 5:10), but this was changed to the prevailing Christendom practice in which only ordained clergy are "holy people" who can administer the sacraments. The New Testament church was a lay movement. There is really no need for "ordained pastoral workers."[4] The task of Spirit-gifted leaders is to equip "all the saints" to do the ministry, which is disciple-making or "spiritual reproduction/fruitfulness" (Eph 4:11–13). Each Christ-follower can be discipled to become an "elder of the city" who can be used by God to bless and transform his or her neighborhood and workplace where Jesus can reign as Lord; and where Jesus reigns, God's kingdom (on earth) is realized.

This concept is important for effective kingdom expansion, as well. Kingdomization is best actualized through a flat (nonhierarchical) structure of empowered individuals and families through "zero-budget missions" (Luke 10:4a; Acts 3:6). There is no need to collect regular tithes, but only offerings as specific needs arise and as the Spirit leads. The focus is on the glory of God (not any gifted human being) in the name of Jesus and by the power of the Holy Spirit (cf. Zech 4:6). Christ-followers can develop a simple (yet mature) faith where they understand that they have direct access to God and can represent him in whichever community, profession, and situation God places them.

---

3. On the contrast between Christendom and "servant church," see David Lim, "The Servant Church," *Evangelical Review of Theology* 13, no. 1 (Jan. 1989): 87–90.

4. On the historical development of ordination and clericalism in the post-apostolic church, see David Lim, "The Development of the Monepiscopate in the Early Church," *Studia Biblica et Theologia* 15, no. 2 (Oct. 1987): 163–95.

Holy Places

Second, these Christ-followers know that they rule with Christ in the heavenlies (Eph 2:6), yet they are grounded and rooted as salt and light (and stars) in the sociocultural structures of their times (Matt 5:13–16; Phil 2:14–16), without having to build structures of their own. All secular things – including natural (God-created) places, assets, and talents, and cultural (human-made) ideas, artifacts, gadgets, traditions, customs, worldviews, etc. – can be redeemed and sanctified through faith expressed in prayer to God in Jesus's name and obedience to his word (1 Tim 4:4–5). There is no need to build religious facilities, for all properties of Christ-followers belong to (and can be used for) his kingdom (John 4:21–24; Acts 7:48; 17:24–28).[5] Worship, therefore, can be done anytime and anywhere (cf. Rom 12:1–8)!

The goal is for all peoples to accept the kingdom's worldview and follow its lifestyle, which can be (and have been) contextually institutionalized into laws, policies, and structures. This can be achieved through the processes of evangelization and disciple-making – forming Christ-centered communities in any place, mainly in residences (neighborhoods), and places of work or study (schools, factories, government offices, banks, stores, etc.) – where God's word is prayerfully discussed and applied to daily life (1 Cor 10:31; Col 3:17), usually in weekly group devotions. Any section of creation can be sanctified and transformed into "holy ground" when people consciously and constantly live for his glory.

Holy Practices

Finally, there is the other distinctive kingdom feature of faith ("worship") expressed in "loving God through loving neighbors" (Matt 22:37–39; 7:12), instead of doing religious rituals and ceremonies (Matt 15:1–20; cf. Isa 58:1–12; Amos 5:21–24; Hos 6:6).[6] The proof of faith is "love and good works" (Heb 10:24; Eph 2:8–10; Jas 2:14–26 ESV), and living the Micah 6:8 lifestyle: "to act justly and to love mercy and to walk humbly with your God." In his inaugural address in Nazareth, Jesus taught that his mission was "to proclaim good

---

5. Israel had only one temple, not one in each village, city, or region. On the multiple functions of the synagogues, see David Lim, "The Origin, Nature and Organization of the Synagogue," *Studia Biblica et Theologia* 15, no. 1 (Apr. 1987): 23–51.

6. On a biblical theology of "worship," see David Lim, "Biblical Worship Rediscovered: A Theology for Communicating Basic Christianity," in *Communicating Christ through Story and Song: Orality in Buddhist Contexts*, ed. Paul De Neui (Pasadena: William Carey Library, 2008), 27–59.

news to the poor . . . [and] proclaim the year of the Lord's favor [= Jubilee]" (Luke 4:18–19 ESV), so he had come to realize this IntM so that people could experience Jubilee everyday (v. 20), and showed such good works as proof of his messianic identity to John the Baptist and his disciples (Luke 7:20–23).

Hence, the visible expression of God's kingdom is simply to "love one another . . . as I have loved you" (self-sacrificially) (John 13:34–35 ESV; cf. 1 John 3:16–18) in the form of social services rather than religious services. In Matthew 25:31–46, Jesus taught that in the final judgment, God's only standard for sheep to find eternal life is whether their faith worked itself out in love (cf. Gal 5:6), particularly to the least of his family (the hungry, thirsty, strangers, naked, sick, prisoners). His is a "bottom-up" kingdom, where his blessings are generously shared, so no one is left behind poor (Matt 6:19–33; 19:21; Luke 6:20–26; cf. Acts 2:44–45; 4:34–37; 2 Cor 8:11–15).

Simple Structure: Cellular Networks of House Churches

What outcome will have been established when God's kingdom is realized in any segment of the world? As the "Second Adam," Jesus modeled what a perfect person could be and what vocation a godly/righteous human being should do for the kingdom (Acts 10:36–38). Thus, to expand the kingdom, he trained his disciples to transform the villages of Galilee by going out two by two without bringing outside resources into the community (Luke 10:4a), and to find a "person of peace/shalom" (vv. 5–6) and disciple that person to disciple his or her family, kin, friends, and neighbors (vv. 4b–9). If there was no such person in a community, they could just leave and go to another one (vv. 10–15).

Small (Oikos) Size

Jesus called twelve men to be his disciples; these he turned into *apostles* ("missionaries" = disciple-makers; Mark 3:13–15) to be sent out to make disciples (eventually to all nations). That is how the apostles and the early church extended the kingdom in and through house churches across the Roman Empire and beyond. The formation of house churches was the practical outworking of the "priesthood of all believers" in the early church as all Christ-followers were empowered to use their homes to serve and bless their neighbors where they lived and worked (cf. 2 Tim 2:2).

This is simply discipling every believer to become "perfect/mature in Christ" (Col 1:28–29), with the confidence to serve as a priest (minister) in his or her house. (The Reformation recovered the doctrine of the "priesthood of all believers," but failed to implement it.)[7] Disciples are made in small groups, never in big meetings. Each person must grow in love so that he or she can practice and experience intimate relationships as "best friends," as disciples teach, correct, and confess their sins to one another.

Cellular System

Jesus did not set a formal structure but introduced a cellular system that subsists in the constant reproduction of "new wineskins" (Mark 2:22) in the structures of society. This is a different outworking and structure of his body on earth. It is different from the denominational hierarchies of local churches with episcopal, presbyterian, or congregationalist structures.[8] The early church had a cellular order whereby the church existed whenever a small group (even as small as two or three) gathered for mutual edification (cf. 1 Cor 14:26) in order to scatter to share Christ's love through good works in the world (cf. Heb 10:24; Matt 5:13–16).[9] Each cell forms a part of a house church network (HCN), which is similar to the decentralized system of volunteer leaders that veteran (ex-pagan) priest Jethro advised Moses to form (Exod 18:21), where

---

    7. For instance, Martin Luther wrote in his preface to the *German Mass*: "Those who really want to be Christians and to confess the gospel in deed and word would have to enroll by name and assemble themselves apart in some house to pray, to read, to baptize, to receive the sacrament, and to do similar Christian works. For in such a regime it would be possible to discover and punish and correct and exclude those who do not behave as Christians and to excommunicate them according to Christ's rule in Matthew 18. Here, too, a common collection of alms could be enjoined on Christians to be given voluntarily and distributed to the poor following Paul's example in 2 Corinthians 9. . . . Here, baptism and the sacrament could be administered in a brief and simple manner, and everything directed to the word and prayer and love. . . . In short, if one had people and individuals who really wanted to be Christians, the rules and forms could soon be drawn up. But I cannot and will not order or establish such a community or congregation yet, for I do not yet have the people and individuals to do this nor, so far as I can see, are there many pressing for this." "The Preface of Martin Luther" in "The German Mass and Order of Divine Service, January 1526," in B. J. Kidd (ed.), *Documents Illustrative of the Continental Reformation* (Oxford: Clarendon Press, 1911), 193–202; scanned by Monica Banas, 1995 at https://history.hanover.edu/texts/luthserve.html.

    8. Perhaps best articulated in Wolfgang Simson, *Houses That Change the World* (Carlisle: Paternoster, 2001), ch. 5.

    9. Cf. David Lim, "The Servant Nature of the Church in the Pauline Corpus" (PhD diss., Fuller Theological Seminary, 1987); Rodney Stark, *The Rise of Christianity: How the Obscure, Marginal Jesus Movement Became the Dominant Religious Force in the Western World in a Few Centuries* (New York: HarperCollins, 1996); Rodney Stark, *Cities of God: The Real Story of How Christianity Became an Urban Movement and Conquered Rome* (New York: HarperCollins, 2006).

authority rests on the lowest units ("leaders of tens") which are assisted by the "higher" coordinating units.[10]

Network (Flat) Structure

The kingdom's organic structure is also *decentralized* in the form of networks of friendships among the disciples and servant leaders. No hierarchy gives permission or controls the church, for only Jesus is the Lord and foundation of his church through the Holy Spirit. All leaders in HCNs see themselves as "servants of God" whose only job description is to "equip the saints to do the ministry" of disciple-making (Eph 4:11–13; 2 Tim 2:2), each according to the spiritual gifts that the Holy Spirit sovereignly distributes to build up the one body (1 Cor 12:1–13), one temple (1 Pet 4:10–11), and one kingdom. It is a flat structure where leaders view themselves as "first among equals" and empower others to become better than themselves (Phil 2:3–4).

Moreover, HCNs are lay movements, and their leaders serve in various sectors of society – not in the clergy-led structures of Christendom. Each Christ-follower is discipled to be self-supporting through a means of livelihood (Eph 4:28). HCN leaders in Christendom (and Buddhist) contexts will have to gradually phase out the need for the clerical (and monastic) order as they learn about the "priesthood of all believers." Although they may continue to be supported by "tithes and offerings" at the start,[11] they will each transition to a livelihood or trade (to serve as models, 2 Thess 3:6–12), most probably for many as teachers of philosophy and ethics. Those who have leadership qualities will naturally rise into management and governance positions in the community and marketplace.

Simple Strategy: Insider Movements (InsM)[12]

What then is the mission strategy to set up HCNs in the world – one which has multicultural and multireligious contexts? Jesus trained his disciples to do

---

10. Roman Catholics call this the "subsidiarity" principle.

11. Like Jesus, some may go full-time when they have well-to-do disciples in their HCN (Luke 8:1–3) to take care of their needs.

12. For more detailed biblical missiology of InsMs, see Harley Talman and J. J. Travis, eds., *Understanding Insider Movements: Disciples of Jesus within Diverse Religious Communities* (Pasadena: William Carey Library, 2015); Kevin Higgins, "The Key to Insider Movements: The 'Devoted's' of Acts," *International Journal of Frontier Missiology* 21, no. 4 (Winter 2004): 156–60; David Lim, "Catalyzing 'Insider Movements' among the Unreached," *Journal of Asian*

his simple strategy effectively (Luke 9:1–6; 10:1–17), which he also illustrated cross-culturally among the Samaritans (John 4) and in gentile Decapolis (Mark 5:1–20; 7:31 – 8:10). When entering other cultures, Paul practiced "becoming all things to all people" (1 Cor 9:20–23), in fact "making himself a slave [*doulos*]" among them (v. 19). As for the local converts, his simple strategy – now called "Insider Movements (InsM)"[13] – comprised three dimensions: incarnational (1 Cor 7:11–17, 20, 24), contextual (vv. 18–20), and transformational (vv. 21–24).[14]

Incarnational

Through the home of the person of peace in each community, people begin their faith journey by contextually adapting to the majority religion (or nonreligion) in their family and community. They develop their faith with a simple religiosity, with each one learning how to live a "love God and love everyone" lifestyle (Matt 22:37–39; Col 3:17) in their society. Jesus did not train his disciples to establish a structure separate from the communities and contexts in which they lived and worked.

Kingdomization is an occupation plan, not an evacuation plan (1 Cor 15:24–25; Phil 2:9–11), because Christ is ruler over all things (Col 1:16–17).[15] Christ-followers sanctify the nonbelievers (1 Cor 7:14) and food offered to idols (10:20–26), because all things can be purified (Titus 1:15) by prayer and the Word (1 Tim 4:4–5). Jesus Christ entered European pagan cosmologies and transformed them Christ-ward. New Christ-followers can continue to join in the activities and festivities of their communities with a clear conscience. When they are confronted and asked about their motivation, they can then explain and witness to Christ, even if doing so may result in persecution. Meanwhile, they should have been trained to make disciples (see below) already before such conflict arises.

Mission 10, no. 1–2 (Mar.–Sep. 2008): 125–45; David Lim, "Missiological Framework for the Contextualization of Christ-Centered Communities," *Asian Missions Advance* 44 (Jul. 2014): 20–22; Lim, "God's Kingdom."

13. For more elaboration on the InsM of Jesus, Paul, and the early church, see Lim, "God's Kingdom."

14. This seems to be a universal principle, since Paul says he teaches this in all the churches (v. 17b).

15. David Taylor, "Contextualization, Syncretism, and the Demonic in Indigenous Movements," in *Understanding Insider Movements*, eds. H. Talman and J. J. Travis (Pasadena: William Carey Library, 2015), 377.

InsMs may thus be called "incarnational missions," which contrasts with the disastrous effects of Christendom's "imperial missions" in making Jesus look very bad (aggressive, foreign, and irrelevant), especially in the Global South.[16] Perhaps worst is the heavy burden that the latter has been imposing on new believers and churches (esp. those among the poor) as they need to invest their very limited resources in supporting the salaries and theological studies of their clergymen, buying property, constructing cathedrals, and financing their religious activities – all of which make them look insensitively rich (and irrelevant) in relation to the houses and facilities in their poor(er) neighborhoods. Most of these projects have been highly subsidized from abroad, especially their denominational partners, up to this day. Nearly all of them don't even have small budgets for community services unless they partner with some Christian development organizations.

In contrast, the rich harvest that Jesus expected from his disciples is being reaped nowadays through the simple incarnational approach by HCNs. By just following the instructions of Jesus in his "zero-budget missions" (Luke 10:4a), every disciple just leads someone (usually a relative or new friend, called a "person of peace") to trust and obey Jesus in love and good works. As they serve one another, the people (especially community leaders) around them will take notice of "how they love one another" (and the neighborhood) and will soon ask for their help. They then naturally rise to become leaders in the community.

Contextual

Christ-followers should be allowed to develop contextualized religious practices, retaining most of them and redefining them as Christ-centered and Christ-ward customs, while finding "functional substitutes" for those beliefs and values that are idolatrous and occultic. For instance, most popular practices in karmic cultures, including ancestral and merit-making practices, will be simplified and some may eventually be phased out as they live out the logic of nonsamsaric and post-animistic worldviews as they reflect on the word.[17]

---

16. On incarnational missions, see David Lim, "Towards Closure: Imperial or Incarnational Missions?," *Asian Missions Advance* 33 (Oct. 2011): 20–22.

17. David Lim, "Appreciating Rituals and Festivals from within Buddhist Christward Movements," in *Sacred Moments: Reflections on Buddhist Rites and Christian Rituals*, ed. Paul De Neui (New Delhi: Christian World Imprints, 2019), 105–21; Mitsuo Fukuda, *Developing a Contextualized Church as a Bridge to Christianity in Japan* (Gloucester: Wide Margin, 2012), 183–92.

They may even become more biblical and Christ-centered than the tradition-laden and liturgy-oriented denominations in today's uncontextualized and Westernized Christendom. They will gradually learn how to get rid of anything that is sinful: idolatry, individualism, immorality, and injustice. They will not do this all at once, as none of us have been totally rid of such sins (e.g. Elisha permitted Naaman to perform ceremonial worship to pagan gods, 2 Kgs 5:17–19; and Paul permitted the Corinthians to eat foods offered to idols, 1 Cor 8 and 10). Almost all our present Christian practices (in liturgies, weddings, Christmas, Easter, Halloween, etc.) were adapted from pagan customs of pre-Christian European tribes anyway.[18]

Contextuality should also mark the house church meetings, with the free mixture of activities according to the needs and gifts of the participants, as set by the leader(s) in close consultation with all the members. Following the 1 Corinthians 14 pattern of meeting, all members come prepared to "consider one another to provoke unto love and good works" (Heb 10:24 KJV) in their body-life together. In literate cultures, Christ-followers can go through any biblical text according to the needs and interests of the people present. In oral cultures, they can learn about Jesus and his teachings through storying, singing, and drama, which can lead to worldview change.[19] Today, they can also download the *Jesus* movie and film clips, with translations available in over 1,600 languages.[20]

Transformational

And what will be the outcome of fulfilling Jesus's InsM to realize Jubilee every day? The HCNs will ultimately help their societies to have a simple yet profound religiosity marked by "loving one another" as members of one big family as Christ loves us (John 13:34–35; 1 John 3:16–18), most concretely expressed in the "common purse" of the earliest church's "caring and sharing economy" (Acts 2:42–47; 4:32–37; 6:1–7; cf. 2 Cor 8–9), for sustainability and socioeconomic development (cf. 1 Cor 7:21–24), where no one is left behind.

As disciples grow in Christlikeness, they will be liberated from sin to become more generous, more caring toward and sharing with their neighbors,

---

18. See Andrew Walls, *The Missionary Movement in Christian History* (Maryknoll: Orbis, 1996), 15–54.

19. Steven Evans, "From the Biblical World to the Buddhist Worldview: Using Bible Narratives to Impact at the Heart Level," in *Communicating Christ through Story and Song: Orality in Buddhist Contexts*, ed. Paul De Neui (Pasadena: William Carey Library, 2008), 128–50.

20. *Jesus* film at www.jesusfilm.org and www.indigitube.tv.

which is the "*agape*" law of Christ (Gal 5:13–23; 6:1–2; Rom 13:8–10). They are discipled to do acts of kindness and justice, which has been called "integral mission" or "transformational development."

This spirituality translates into discipling and transforming the global economic system, as well. Many house church leaders are involved in Christian development organizations that are already leading in building the third (other than capitalism and socialism) alternative economic order called the Solidarity Economy, which equips and empowers the poor through social entrepreneurship and fair trade so that each person can have his or her own land (Lev 25) and own "vine and fig tree" (Mic 4:4) passed on to the next generations (Isa 65:21–23).

For instance, the HCNs that have had "gospel explosion" in six big provinces in China spread from village to village through the witnessing lifestyles of ordinary Christ-followers who were known for their serving, caring, and hard work in their neighborhoods. Even Communist cadres and leaders became "secret believers" in these HCNs.[21]

Simple Methodology: Disciple Multiplication

Like what Jesus did in equipping and sending each of his disciples out into their world (Mark 3:13–15),[22] "disciple multiplication" is HCN's simple method to "disciple all nations." All believers (family, tribe, and nation) can be mobilized and equipped to multiply disciples where they live and work.[23] Anything less – or more – is a diversion from God's *simple* plan to evangelize and transform the world speedily.

Disciple-Making

House churches (HCs) are actually "disciple-making groups," which may also be called "simple (or organic) churches," "basic ecclesial communities" (BEC),[24] "kingdom cells," or "care groups." It is any *small* (not more than ten couples, preferably as "two or three" for intimate sharing) Christ-worshiping and Scripture-honoring body of believers who have covenanted to meet

---

21. See Paul Hattaway et al., *Back to Jerusalem* (Carlisle: Piquant, 2003).
22. On Jesus's disciple-making strategy, see Robert Coleman, *The Master Plan of Evangelism* (Old Tappan: Revell, 1964).
23. This was first popularized through Dawson Trotman and the Navigators in 1933.
24. Leonardo Boff, *Ecclesiogenesis* (London: Collins; Maryknoll: Orbis, 1986).

regularly and are willing to be held accountable to one another for their Christ-centered lives.

Life is relationships; the rest is just detail. To *disciple* means to equip Christ-followers with just three relational habits: (1) hearing *God* through prayerful meditation to turn his word (*logos*) into a word (*rhema*) to be obeyed (2 Tim 3:16–17); (2) making disciples through leading a HC in Bible-and-life sharing, whereby each one learns how to do personal devotions (or Quiet Time = *lectio divina*) with *fellow believers* (Heb 10:24; 1 Cor 14:26); and (3) doing friendship evangelism to share what they learn of God and his will with their *nonbelieving* networks.

The HCs may be (1) residential, where members meet in homes, living out their faith in their neighborhood (Eph 5:21 – 6:4), or in urbanized and industrialized centers; or (2) professional, where members meet in their places of work or study, and witness to their faith in the marketplace (6:5–18), for the transformation of all sociocultural structures.

Spiritual Reproduction

Disciples are those who are willing not just to be mentored to form a more Christlike character and equipped to discover and minister with their spiritual gift(s), but also to be trained to do evangelism and lead their own HCs. They should become disciple-makers, empowered (given authority) to lead their own HCs and HCNs as soon as possible. They will seek to turn their contacts into friends and into converts through "friendship evangelism," and then also into disciple-makers by equipping them and sending them to form their own HCs and HCNs.

Disciple-making should be finished in less than a year, so that the discipler can make more disciples and start more HCs. This should happen intentionally, as HC members are encouraged to disciple new believers in new (their own) HCs, or to pair up and start new HCs in other contexts as soon as possible. At the start of each HC (say, the first month), it is best that they meet as often as possible (perhaps daily). After several months (maximum of one year), HCs can meet less regularly (monthly), and then quarterly, and later annually or even just through correspondence and social media.

Minimal Religiosity

InsMs will result in HCNs whose spirituality will require fewer and fewer religious practices. Following Christ does not require public displays of religiosity – in fact, Jesus literally discouraged such (Matt 6:1–18), which included almsgiving, praying, and fasting. As Christ-followers walk humbly and simply for God's glory (1 Cor 10:31; Mic 6:8), their community leaders will establish shalom where their constituents enjoy life with love and justice (1 Tim 2:1–2). Their spirituality does not need to develop elaborate theologies, ethics, liturgies, and hierarchies (cf. Amos 5:21–24; Ps 131).

As our world modernizes and globalizes and science and technology advance rapidly, and as Christ-followers form HCNs organically, their inherited socioreligious traditions will be reduced and/or transformed into simpler forms. They will have overcome fears and feelings of guilt that have been the roots of superstitious practices, lucky charms, and elaborate rituals.

If a community already has good community services, HCs just need to aim to become part of the leadership and introduce devotions (prayer and the Word) into the existing structures. If the community lacks such ministries, Insider Movement (InsMs) practitioners can start serving informally as volunteers and later help set up people's organizations or nongovernment agencies to address needs with the blessing of the community leaders.

Kingdomization Today

By God's grace, in the past thirty years most HCNs in all continents, especially Asia,[25] North America, and Australia, have been catalyzing InsMs. Among the better known writers are Wolfgang Simson (*Houses That Change the World*), Neil Cole (*Organic Church*), Tony and Felicity Dale (*Simply Church*), Frank Viola and George Barna (*Pagan Christianity*), and Rad Zdero (*The Global House Church Movement*).[26] Most significant in promoting InsMs are Frontier Ventures (formerly the US Center for World Mission), its organ *Mission Frontiers* and its publishing arm William Carey Library, as well as the International Society of Frontier Missions and its organ *International Journal*

---

25. On HCNs in Asia, see David Lim, "Asian Mission Movements in Asia Today," *Asian Missions Advance* 41 (Oct. 2013): 29–36; David Lim, "The House Church Movements in Asia," *Asian Missions Advance* 38 (Jan. 2013): 3–7; David Lim, "Asia's House Church Movements Today," *Asian Missions Advance* 52 (Jul. 2016): 7–12, www.asiamissions.net/asias-house-church-movements-today/; Mitsuo Fukuda, "Incarnational Approaches to the Japanese People Using House Church Strategies," in *Sharing Jesus Effectively in the Buddhist World*, eds. David Lim, Steve Spaulding, and Paul De Neui (Pasadena: William Carey Library, 2005), 353–62; and Yalin Xin, "The Role of the Host Families in the Missional Structure of a House Church Movement," in *Evangelism and Diakonia in Context*, eds. Rose Dowsett et al. (Oxford: Regnum, 2016), 315–24.

26. Rad Zdero, *The Global House Church Movement* (Pasadena: William Carey Library, 2004).

of Frontier Missions (*IJFM*). In Asia, since 1999, the Asia Society of Frontier Missions has been meeting annually, too.

In China and the Philippines, HCNs have been sending multitudes of disciple-makers as "ants, bees and (earth)worms,"[27] ordinary people using ordinary/organic ways to bless (develop, enrich) the lives of others.[28] HCNs are spreading the gospel of Christ simply – through "nameless, faceless and (apparently) powerless"[29] servants of the Most High God.

The HCNs in China have sent seventeen- and eighteen-year-olds to go (with one-way tickets) and help in the farms and tell stories of Jesus. In the Philippines, we're setting up training centers for organic farming and marketing hubs for social enterprises to sell their products beyond their communities. Since 2005, the PMA's flagship mobilization program has focused on equipping and sending overseas Filipino workers (OFWs) to be tentmakers who catalyze simple disciple multiplication movements (DMMs) to bless the nations.[30]

In India, they're going from village to village to enrich farmers with organic farming technology. In Japan, businessmen are leading fellow businessmen and their employees to follow Jesus through "business coaching." The top leader of the Japanese HCN is now getting a PhD in Urban Engineering in order to position himself to catalyze an InsM among the Parliament (Diet) members in his district. In Thailand, the main leader of the Thailand HCN produced a satellite TV program that offered sociocultural commentary on issues in various sectors of society.

Conclusion

Across the world today, most HCNs are doing IntM to form transformational communities that are led by local Christ-followers who have not been extracted

---

27. On China's HCNs' Back to Jerusalem movement, see Hattaway et al., *Back to Jerusalem*. In the animal kingdom, these insects are "small yet terrible" in terms of enriching the harvests as they help in fertilizing the soil and the plants of the land where they subsist.

28. David Lim, "History and Ministry of Philippine Missions Association: Leading the Global Shift to Tentmaker Missions," *Asian Missions Advance* 41 (Oct. 2013): 2–6.

29. The self-definition of the HCNs in China and the Philippines.

30. Lim, "History and Ministry of Philippine Missions Association." The main model used by PMA is the formation of "Company-3," whereby Christ-followers are trained just to make two (local) disciples who will in turn be equipped to make two disciples; see Robert Claro, *A Higher Purpose for Your Overseas Job* (Makati City: Church Strengthening Ministry, 2003). Another model is "Effective Tentmaking Made Simple." See David Lim, "Effective Tentmaking Made Simple," in *Blessing OFWs to Bless the Nations*, ed. Ana M. Gamez (Makati: Church Strengthening Ministry, 2012), 108–11 (first used in 2001).

from their relational and religio-cultural communities. Empowered by the Holy Spirit, HCNs will continue to catalyze InsMs in Asia and beyond, for they believe that the harvest has always been ripe for reaping (John 4:35). Our King Jesus is indeed building his church and the gates of hell will not prevail against it (Matt 16:18–19).

InsMs aim to form HCNs to simply multiply Christ-followers who can disciple and transform societies into Christ-following communities and workplaces – contextualized, holistic, and transformational "indigenous churches" that are truly replicable: self-governing, self-supporting, self-propagating, and self-theologizing. We will be "planting churches" that will be copied by future generations of Christ-followers, so we should avoid transplanting denominational churches (= complex Christianity) which are often decontextualized (= foreign-looking, if not actually foreign) and have almost always produced marginalized Christ-followers who have been extracted and separated from their communities.

Our call is to focus on making disciples and multiplying HCs, for where two or three believers are gathered prayerfully, the church emerges. We should encourage all Christ-followers to "gossip Jesus" and multiply small disciple-making groups among their friends and kin in their neighborhoods and workplaces. We are all called to do this spiritual network marketing of the gospel from village to village, city to city, region to region, and nation to nation, until every home and workplace in the world knows and obeys Jesus as King. May God find us faithful in working together in IntM and through InsMs to actualize the kingdom of God effectively (not perfectly, yet substantially), so that all families on earth will be blessed (cf. Gen 12:1–3) in our generation.

I'm sure that Dr. Ted would gladly say "Amen" and "Hallelujah" to this paradigm of kingdomization through integral mission. Thank you very much, Dr. Ted, for being our inspiration.

References

Boff, Leonardo. *Ecclesiogenesis*. London: Collins; Maryknoll: Orbis, 1986.
Claro, Robert. *A Higher Purpose for Your Overseas Job*. Makati City: Church Strengthening Ministry, 2003.
Coleman, Robert. *The Master Plan of Evangelism*. Old Tappan: Revell, 1964.
Evans, Steven. "From the Biblical World to the Buddhist Worldview: Using Bible Narratives to Impact at the Heart Level." In *Communicating Christ through Story and Song: Orality in Buddhist Contexts*, edited by Paul De Neui, 128–50. Pasadena : William Carey Library, 2008.

Fukuda, Mitsuo. *Developing a Contextualized Church as a Bridge to Christianity in Japan*. Gloucester: Wide Margin, 2012.

———. "Incarnational Approaches to the Japanese People Using House Church Strategies." in *Sharing Jesus Effectively in the Buddhist World*, edited by David Lim, Steve Spaulding, and Paul De Neui, 353–62. Pasadena: William Carey Library, 2005.

Hattaway, Paul, et al. *Back to Jerusalem*. Carlisle: Piquant, 2003.

Higgins, Kevin. "The Key to Insider Movements: The 'Devoted's' of Acts." *International Journal of Frontier Missiology* 21, no. 4 (Winter 2004): 156–60.

Lim, David. "Appreciating Rituals and Festivals from within Buddhist Christward Movements." In *Sacred Moments: Reflections on Buddhist Rites and Christian Rituals*, edited by Paul De Neui, 105–21. New Delhi: Christian World Imprints, 2019.

———. "Asian Mission Movements in Asia Today." *Asian Missions Advance* 41 (Oct. 2013): 29–36.

———. "Asia's House Church Movements Today." *Asian Missions Advance* 52 (Jul. 2016): 7–12. www.asiamissions.net/asias-house-church-movements-today/.

———. "Biblical Worship Rediscovered: A Theology for Communicating Basic Christianity." In *Communicating Christ through Story and Song: Orality in Buddhist Contexts*, edited by Paul De Neui, 27–59. Pasadena: William Carey Library, 2008.

———. "Catalyzing 'Insider Movements' among the Unreached." *Journal of Asian Mission* 10, no. 1–2 (Mar.–Sep. 2008): 125–45.

———. "The Development of the Monepiscopate in the Early Church." *Studia Biblica et Theologia* 15, no. 2 (Oct. 1987): 163–95.

———. "Effective Tentmaking Made Simple." In *Blessing OFWs to Bless the Nations*, edited by Ana M. Gamez, 108–11. Makati: Church Strengthening Ministry, 2012.

———. "God's Kingdom as *Oikos* Church Networks: A Biblical Theology." *International Journal of Frontier Mission* 34, no. 1–4 (Jan.–Dec. 2017): 25–35.

———. "History and Ministry of Philippine Missions Association: Leading the Global Shift to Tentmaker Missions." *Asian Missions Advance* 41 (Oct. 2013): 2–6.

———. "The House Church Movements in Asia." *Asian Missions Advance* 38 (Jan. 2013): 3–7.

———. "Missiological Framework for the Contextualization of Christ-Centered Communities." *Asian Missions Advance* 44 (Jul. 2014): 20–22.

———. "The Origin, Nature and Organization of the Synagogue." *Studia Biblica et Theologia* 15, no. 1 (Apr. 1987): 23–51.

———. "The Servant Church." *Evangelical Review of Theology* 13, no. 1 (Jan. 1989): 87–90.

———. "The Servant Nature of the Church in the Pauline Corpus." PhD diss., Fuller Theological Seminary, 1987.

———. "Towards Closure: Imperial or Incarnational Missions?" *Asian Missions Advance* 33 (Oct. 2011): 20–22.

Samuel, Vinay, and C. Sugden. *Mission as Transformation*. Oxford: Regnum, 1999.

Simson, Wolfgang. *Houses That Change the World*. Carlisle: Paternoster, 2001.

Stark, Rodney. *Cities of God: The Real Story of How Christianity Became an Urban Movement and Conquered Rome*. New York: HarperCollins, 2006.

———. *The Rise of Christianity: How the Obscure, Marginal Jesus Movement Became the Dominant Religious Force in the Western World in a Few Centuries*. New York: HarperCollins, 1996.

Talman, Harley, and J. J. Travis, eds. *Understanding Insider Movements: Disciples of Jesus within Diverse Religious Communities*. Pasadena: William Carey Library, 2015.

Taylor, David. "Contextualization, Syncretism, and the Demonic in Indigenous Movements." In *Understanding Insider Movements*, edited by H. Talman and J. J. Travis, 375–83. Pasadena: William Carey Library, 2015.

Walls, Andrew. *The Missionary Movement in Christian History*. Maryknoll: Orbis, 1996.

Xin, Yalin. "The Role of the Host Families in the Missional Structure of a House Church Movement." In *Evangelism and Diakonia in Context*, edited by Rose Dowsett et al., 315–24. Oxford: Regnum, 2016.

Zdero, Rad. *The Global House Church Movement*. Pasadena: William Carey Library, 2004.

6

Church Planting in All Seasons: A Personal Reflection

By Sadiri Tonyvic Tira Jr.

Introduction

I first met Dr. Ted Yamamori in 2016 when he visited Edmonton, Alberta, for meetings, and I am honored to contribute to this Festschrift in light of his life and work for the body of Christ. Here I share how Supper Club in Edmonton was started at the height of the COVID-19 pandemic.

"The pandemic wrote the menu!" the restaurant owner said to me. Because of the global pandemic, he had adjusted his menu and rebranded the restaurant (from "The Local Omnivore" to "Gravy"). He further explained that to meet the needs of a community that relied on food but could no longer consume it as they had done, he needed to change his method of delivery, his staffing model, and his menu. And while the essence of his menu remained, he needed to tailor it to meet the needs of those to whom he was trying to connect.

During the past couple years, various studies have illustrated the challenges and effects of COVID-19 on our global society. Regardless of geography or station in life, the pandemic has affected how people work, gather, speak, and relate to one another. For many churches, this has meant expanding their digital services. In fact, prior to COVID-19, "only around 1 in 4 (27%) [of Protestant pastors surveyed] said they livestreamed either the entire service or just the sermon." Today, however,

> 85% of Protestant churchgoers said their congregation offered livestreamed worship services, and 76% said their church posted a video of the worship service to watch later. Additionally, 53%

of churchgoers said they watched online worship services at their church more in 2020 than in 2019, while 21% said they watched more online services at a different church in 2020.[1]

In other words, the pandemic has affected how churches connect with people, while simultaneously changing how people connect with churches. Furthermore, while churches enjoyed an initial boost in reach through online delivery, recent studies have challenged the quality of those connections. *Christianity Today* reported on data collected by Barna Group in April and May 2020 that "one in three practicing Christians dropped out of church completely at the beginning of COVID-19. Moreover, church membership in the US dropped below 50 percent for the first time in 2020, according to Gallup data dating back to 1940."[2]

In Canada, these statistics have been practically observed by many. Here, the issues of change and rapid decline are not new, although they have been greatly exacerbated during the pandemic. An April 2022 report by Global News revealed that the fastest-growing religious classification in Canada is the "nones" or nonbelievers (19 percent or 1 in 5 Canadians), while the largest religious group (46 percent) identifies as "spiritually uncertain." The Angus Reid Institute survey referenced in the article found that among those surveyed, "evangelical Christianity – which encompasses dozens of denominations such as Baptist, Pentecostal and Mennonite – was the only religion seen as more damaging than beneficial by every other self-identified religious group."[3]

In Edmonton, pandemic restrictions sparked great debate over the integrity and obligation of churches to meet in person. Some made international headlines, claiming "persecution" and encouraging active defiance of local governance as a moral, ethical, and spiritual responsibility of the church. These arguments brought to the fore the efficacy of the local church in my context and questions about both the delivery of our ministries and the essence of what we are offering. Many today are asking, "How can we connect with people in a society where the church is seemingly disconnected?"

---

1. Aaron Earls, "Online Services Expanded Reach of Churches during Pandemic," Lifeway Research, 14 October 2021, https://research.lifeway.com/2021/10/14/online-services-expanded-reach-of-churches-during-pandemic.

2. Wendy Wang and Alysse Elhage, "Here's Who Stopped Going to Church during the Pandemic," *Christianity Today* online, 20 January 2022, https://www.christianitytoday.com/ct/2022/january-web-only/attendance-decline-covid-pandemic-church.html.

3. Ashleigh Stewart, "Canadians Consider Certain Religions Damaging to Society: Survey," Global News, 18 April 2022, https://globalnews.ca/news/8759564/canada-religion-society-perceptions.

Disciples Eat Together

> And they devoted themselves to the apostles' teaching and the fellowship, to the breaking of bread and the prayers. . . . And day by day, attending the temple together and breaking bread in their homes, they received their food with glad and generous hearts, praising God and having favor with all the people. And the Lord added to their number day by day those who were being saved. (Acts 2:42, 46–47 ESV)

In 2015, I started working as a pastor for young adults. It was my belief that if people were educated, exposed, and experienced in mission they would naturally take the next steps in full-time kingdom service and ministry. For three years, we intentionally pursued active mission engagement. We went on short-term mission trips both nationally and internationally, and many of our core group of forty joined mission ventures through work in inner-city Edmonton. Others joined with mission organizations leading their own mission trips. This group met for weekly fellowship and Bible study, and served people experiencing homelessness by delivering hot dogs. After three years of experiencing numerical growth and emphasizing missional living, many of those serving desired to be more focused and aligned with the heart of Jesus. In the summer of 2018, we embarked on a study and reflection on heart and purity issues. Unfortunately, over the course of five weeks, our attendance declined to under five people.

This experience caused me to reflect on "the menu." After a year of honest reflection, I concluded that while we were connecting with people, the essence of that connection – Jesus – was not as primary as I had believed. Rather, it seemed secondary to missional service. This focus had led people not to a richness of abiding that resulted in bearing "much fruit," but instead to a focus on human endeavor, utilitarian relationships, and obligatory programming.

In the summer of 2019, after intentionally discerning and prayerfully asking "How can our community meet Jesus in a more profound, genuine, and powerful way?," we started a monthly gathering focused on facilitating an intentional yet simple atmosphere that initiated intimate fellowship, free worship, and authoritative prayer. This was centered around the person of Jesus and the exercise of communion (typically through a potluck meal). By January of 2021 (during the pandemic) this monthly fellowship began meeting weekly online. By September 2021 we were incorporated as a church and recognized as a church plant of the SEND Network one month later. We named this gathering the "Supper Club."

Preparing for Presence (Before Power)

> Jesus said to them, "I am the bread of life; whoever comes to me shall not hunger, and whoever believes in me shall never thirst." (John 6:35 ESV)

"How do I do that?" or "I don't hear anything" were common responses when I had asked others to discern and ask the Holy Spirit for direction. Some responded that they didn't believe the Holy Spirit spoke to people directly. I must admit that for most of my life as a PK (or pastor's kid) and now as a pastor, these were my responses too. My prayer life was akin to picking up a cup on a string, speaking into it, putting it to my ear to hear a response, and frequently hearing nothing. This resulted in me pulling on the string to check if the connection was working. Unfortunately, many in our churches also lack this confidence. Most prayers I heard were desires for an exhibition of God's power, but many lacked an equally, if not significantly greater, fervor for God's presence.

The summer of 2021 was a historically dry and hot season in Edmonton. The weather fluctuated from extraordinarily hot to unbearably smoky (due to forest fires hundreds of kilometers away). At the beginning of July 2021, the provincial government revised restrictions and the Supper Club was allowed to meet in person. However, we needed to reduce the potential size of the gathering by two-thirds to keep within lawful occupancy. After prayerful consideration, we decided to meet outdoors in a different backyard or park each week.

Interestingly, on the Sunday afternoons we would gather, the forecast would often show that inclement weather was expected. On one occasion when rain was forecast, our people began to pray for good weather and no rain. The prayer was rooted in the idea that the preferred weather would result in the gathering being more impactful. Challenged by this, we began to pray a prayer of surrender, that regardless of the weather (rain or shine), what we wanted most was God's presence. Interestingly, the weather turned out to be delightful.

On another occasion, a local advisory for smoke inhalation was lifted to a suitable amount a couple hours before our fellowship was to begin. Another time, while meeting in a busy, centrally located park, the sky darkened and it began to rain heavily, thus forcing strangers into the gazebo where we were worshiping. It felt like an Old Testament story: the rain fell all around us, stopping only several meters away. When the days looked too hot, the weather cooled, or when it looked gloomy, the weather warmed. Week after week, from

July to October, we were never forced indoors due to weather. As we prioritized God's presence, we began to experience and grow in awareness of his power.

In John 15, Jesus's disciples are encouraged to abide in Christ. The passage reminds us that the place of abiding is where fruit manifests, and that apart from Christ, we can do nothing. But how much do we really believe that? As a pastor, I was often asked to pray for people in the congregation. The vast majority of times it related to cars or health or home or career. Rarely did churchgoers pray for the manifest presence of God in their homes, work, or relationships. It should not have been surprising that people did not have confidence to speak to the Holy Spirit themselves. As a church, are we preparing for presence before power? If not, it shouldn't be a surprise that the fastest-growing belief in Canada among those who grew up in churches is that God does not exist – and if he does, he is not within earshot of people.

So, as a community, we have been prioritizing intentional stillness. Adopting a posture of humility, our goal has been to be in God's presence and stay there. The idea is that if we are to partake in meaningful mission, it'll be God's initiative and not our own. In a practical way, the extent of our "church programs" has been prayer. Through a divine appointment, our church was provided a mentor to teach us to pray. Dr. David Chotka of Spirit Equip Ministries taught a weekly class on discernment, partnering with us to teach the Lord's Prayer to fifty-nine individuals representing eight churches from three denominations. We also invested in three months of weekly meetings to relearn how to pray (taking the Transform! Prayer Course). The initial members of the church have also read or been to Soul Care conferences and have had at least an introduction to deliverance ministry. We believe that to pursue God, we must learn how to hear from him first.

By prioritizing listening to the Holy Spirit, we've intentionally addressed and surrendered many corporate and individual barriers to kingdom advancement. Throughout the year, the corporate practice of prayer walking led us through the city. We are learning to trust God in new ways, and to be comfortable being still in his presence.

A Data-Informed (Not Intended) Menu

> Now when it was evening, the disciples came to [Jesus] and said, "This is a desolate place, and the day is now over; send the crowds away to go into the villages and buy food for themselves." But Jesus said, "They need not go away; you give them something

to eat." They said to him, "We have only five loaves here and two fish." And he said, "Bring them here to me." Then he ordered the crowds to sit down on the grass, and taking the five loaves and the two fish, he looked up to heaven and said a blessing. Then he broke the loaves and gave them to the disciples, and the disciples gave them to the crowds. And they all ate and were satisfied. And they took up twelve baskets full of the broken pieces left over. And those who ate were about five thousand men, besides women and children. (Matt 14:15–21 ESV)

From the creation account in Genesis to the New Jerusalem in Revelation, the Bible shares data. As churches, we are encouraged to gather data before we embark on a task. And yet, the extent to which churches gather and communicate data is often limited to monthly finances, Sunday attendance, membership, and/or professions of faith. While this data is useful, it only highlights one part of the story. Imagine the feeding account without knowing either that five thousand people were fed, or that the initial meal was from five loaves and two fish. The story and its impact would be incomplete. We could not know that God feeds abundantly from a meager initial offering. Likewise, when churches limit data to "bucks, butts, and baptisms," we fail to encourage further action. Instead, we reward established behavior based on how much people give rather than the joy of their worship, their weekly commitment rather than their daily witness, and their initial decisions rather than their growth as disciple-makers.

In a disciple-making study of US churches in March 2020, Grey Matter Research found that 73 percent of all churches had either plateaued or were in statistical decline, 27 percent of churches reported short-term growth through programs, while only 5 percent of churches were "numerically growing churches... also characterized as churches that are reproducing disciples and disciple making." Five percent of churches "weren't even scored because no one in their church was making disciples."[4]

Discipleship.org defines a disciple-making movement this way:

> gospel activity, that has abundant fruit among the lost, that multiplies these disciples (people growing in obedience to all of Jesus' commands), who in turn replicate themselves in others, so

---

4. Grey Matter Research & Consulting, *National Study on Disciple Making in USA Churches: High Aspirations amidst Disappointing Results*, sponsored by Discipleship.org and Exponential.org, March 2020, https://discipleship-org.s3.amazonaws.com/text/ebooks/Final+2020_National_Study_Report.pdf.

that we can see at least four generations regularly produced in multiple streams of disciple-making activity and these streams multiply consistently into churches.

What are we counting as a church, and how are we reporting it? And is it having the intended impact? If we were to gather data based on what we wanted to accomplish, are we doing it? Oftentimes, faith leaders are reluctant to collect or communicate data, insisting that the value it provides cannot be counted; it is intangible. Being a leader without measurables is akin to taking people on a journey without a destination. To steward without accountability is to risk resources without development. Churches have a responsibility to not only gather data, but to communicate it in a way that encourages forward progress.

Prior to launching weekly gatherings, we used data to further understand and strategize connection points in the community and to begin praying for the individuals and families in our target community. When studying potential church-planting communities, we prayed for areas with (1) a low ratio of established churches to people (i.e. the lost); and (2) a greater number of diverse people groups with the potential to impact exponential communities in addition to the target community (i.e. the kingdom). These variables led us to an intersection community in central Edmonton which bordered downtown and a new community with the potential for growth equal to the size of downtown (which, due to its age, was completely unchurched). Afterward, we completed several demographic studies, looking at individual and family makeup, culture, and career. These have allowed us to tailor "the menu" according to the identity, belonging, and (desired) purpose of the people we are trying to reach. Furthermore, these studies allowed us to identify not only needs and service opportunities, but also pre-existing barriers to Christ-centered community.

At Supper Club, we've looked for practical ways to communicate engagement. Based on the philosophy that introduced vehicle-activated speed indicator devices, our desire is to intentionally collect all points of data and simply tell people how "fast" they are currently traveling in a certain direction at a fixed point in time. It is not intended to police or govern behavior; rather, it is to encourage reflection and personal assessment, thus leading individuals to ask, "Is it my intention to be moving in this direction at this current rate in this season of life?"

Quarterly, we communicate the impact of what we have accomplished. Simple questions are presented according to our stated mission, vision, and values. We ask things such as whether we have eaten a meal with our neighbors, whether we are exercising life-giving spiritual disciplines, or whether we have served a community need. The questions are intended to be simple, encouraging yes or no responses. Based on the responses, we encourage a single point of action for the upcoming quarter. Our desire is purposeful, integrated, missional living rather than seasonal practices where mission can be switched off or assigned to a selected few instead of undertaken by the church as a whole. We want to have community impact for Jesus through integral disciple-making in all seasons.

Offering Relationship (Instead of Religion)

> A man once gave a great banquet and invited many. . . . [He] said to his servant, "Go out quickly to the streets and lanes of the city, and bring in the poor and crippled and blind and lame." And the servant said, "Sir, what you commanded has been done, and still there is room." And the master said to the servant, "Go out to the highways and hedges and compel people to come in, that my house may be filled." (Luke 14:16, 21b–23 ESV)

People are not looking for a church. This is the reality of the community we are church planting in. In fact, the mere mention of church or religion is considered so off-base that it is essentially the simplest way to end a conversation. However, while many people are disinterested in organized church, COVID-19 has articulated a great hunger for genuine, inclusive, and meaningful relationships. In a 2019 City of Edmonton video, people were encouraged to simply begin with, "Hello, how are you?" As a church plant, we've prioritized a culture that models itself on Jesus through the simple invitation to eat with others.

Over Christmas 2021, several volunteers were cleaning up Supper Club and setting up a tree. Noticing a trespasser inside one of our volunteer's vehicles, I informed the owner, who came out to speak with the person. After the trespasser left, I spoke with the owner, who shared that the person was probably in the car because of the cold, and if possible he would like to invite the person in to warm up. On cue, the trespasser returned because he had forgotten his phone in the car. We invited him in to not only warm up, but to eat with us. As we shared a meal, he shared his life with us. We asked if we could pray with him. Afterward, he said, "I thought I was in trouble when you wanted to talk to me. I didn't know there was a church here, but I am thankful that this church is here [now]."

Often, we can become so preoccupied with programs and outcomes that it is easy to forget that we are called into relationship (first) with God, then with his body, followed by the communities he has sent us to. As we've embarked on this season of church planting, we want to be intentional about developing relationships. Not only have we encouraged intentional simplicity in mission, but we have done so in community also. It can be tempting in this season of statistical church decline to prioritize the growth of our local church plant; however, one of the great opportunities we see in our community is not only being able to reach the lost, but also to work together for the kingdom.

A 2019 Barna study reported that among lapsed Christians, 31 percent would be more interested in learning about Christianity if they "saw various churches in [their] community working together more."[5] While we ask how we will connect with the community of unbelievers, we must also ask how we will connect with the community of believers. After all, through our love for one another, people will know that we are Jesus's disciples.

At Supper Club, we've attempted to work with other churches by encouraging Christians of different traditions and cultures to pray together and lead worship in central Edmonton. In October of 2021, when we moved into our location, we hosted a worship night. The goal was both to facilitate and to invite other churches to lead in this space. That evening, we worshiped with fifty-nine people from eight congregations in two languages. Encouraged, we did the same thing for Christmas Eve, with almost ninety people. This past Good Friday (April 2022), we worshiped with 128 people from thirteen churches representing three denominations in English, Mandarin, and Swahili (while being livestreamed via Zoom in mainland China)! At the communion table, Jesus calls all disciples to love and serve one another. In this way, we show and share the gospel to the world.

Conclusion

"Farm to Table" is a food concept that encourages healthy and sustainable eating through local produce and consumption. As church planters, are we promoting healthy practices which encourage others in our churches not only to serve but also to grow? Jesus encourages his disciples to participate in the harvest (Mark 9:37) and to be reminded that it is God who plants the seeds (Mark 20:1). For Supper Club, we have been learning that it is indeed

---

5. Alpha USA, *Reviving Evangelism*, Barna, 2019, https://barna.gloo.us/reports/reviving-evangelism.

God who prepares the harvest. During the worship night in October 2021, a pastor shared with us how nine pastors had previously committed to praying for a church to start in the specific community we planted in. Unbeknown to us, they started praying on 26 November 2013, almost eight years prior. Even in seasons of great challenge, God is reminding us that "the harvest is plentiful." Let's keep praying for planters to move according to God's agenda, to act according to their actual impact (not simply their intentions), and to prioritize people over programs.

References

Alpha USA. *Reviving Evangelism.* Barna, 2019. https://barna.gloo.us/reports/reviving-evangelism.

Earls, Aaron. "Online Services Expanded Reach of Churches during Pandemic." Lifeway Research, 14 October 2021. https://research.lifeway.com/2021/10/14/online-services-expanded-reach-of-churches-during-pandemic.

Grey Matter Research & Consulting. *National Study on Disciple Making in USA Churches: High Aspirations amidst Disappointing Results.* Sponsored by Discipleship.org and Exponential.org. March 2020. https://discipleship-org.s3.amazonaws.com/text/ebooks/Final+2020_National_Study_Report.pdf.

Stewart, Ashleigh. "Canadians Consider Certain Religions Damaging to Society: Survey." Global News, 18 April 2022. https://globalnews.ca/news/8759564/canada-religion-society-perceptions.

Wang, Wendy, and Alysse Elhage. "Here's Who Stopped Going to Church during the Pandemic." *Christianity Today* online, 20 January 2022. https://www.christianitytoday.com/ct/2022/january-web-only/attendance-decline-covid-pandemic-church.html.

7

Business as Mission: Roots, Scope, and Future

By Mats Tunehag

She was amazed and perplexed at the same time.[1] She was treated with respect and dignity. She was a woman challenged with disabilities, but her life had changed. Having had little or no prospect of ever getting a job, she was now working in a manufacturing company. She was creative, she had made friends, and she made money.

Women in this country and religious context were treated as second-class citizens. If they had mental or physical disabilities they were often further down. But the company she worked for employed and offered jobs with dignity to women with disabilities. It was unheard of, and it made a huge difference not only in her life, but also for the other women who worked there. It even had a transformational impact on families and the community.

This woman asked herself: *Why is this workplace so different?* It changed lives on many levels. She knew that the founder and CEO was a follower of Jesus. So, she told herself: *If that's what it means to be a follower of Jesus, I will also follow him.* It was a huge and risky step for a woman with disabilities in a conservative Muslim environment.

What brought her to Christ? A gospel tract? A *Jesus* film? A Bible study? No, it was human resource management informed by biblical values and underpinned with prayer. Ultimately, it was, of course, God's doing.

---

1. This chapter can also be found online: https://businessasmission.com/deeply-rooted-business-as-mission-looking-back/.

Concept, Practice, Movement

This story from the Middle East points toward three aspects of Business as Mission (BAM), which is about serving God and people in and through business, with a Great Commission perspective. BAM is a biblical *concept* which is *practiced and applied* by people around the world with a wide variety of backgrounds, who together form a global *movement*.

Since 2002, BAM Global has engaged around five hundred significant leaders in business, church, missions, NGOs, and academia from about fifty countries in global conversations about the concept and the practice. This has resulted in about thirty peer-produced and peer-reviewed think tank reports, and two manifestos which summarize our findings.[2] The global and participatory nature of the think tank processes has created an unprecedented spread and ownership of the BAM concept.[3]

Global Trends

But the BAM concept did not emerge in a vacuum. The backdrop to the global BAM movement can be found in the business world in general, but also in our Jewish roots, as well as in church councils and consultations[4] in recent generations.

In business and economics there has been a shift in recent decades from maximizing profit for shareholders to creating value on multiple bottom lines for multiple stakeholders. Terms such as *social enterprises*, *creative capitalism*, *corporate social responsibility*, and *impact investment* indicate a trend toward a more holistic and sustainable approach to business.

The Second Vatican Council (1962–65) renewed the call for a holistic engagement in society,[5] and the Lausanne Congress (1974) articulated our responsibility to take the whole gospel to the whole world.

---

2. BAM, "BAM Global Reports," https://bamglobal.org/reports/. See especially the "BAM Manifesto" and the "Wealth Creation Manifesto." https://bamglobal.org/lop-manifesto/.

3. See this article where the think tank is briefly described and put into a wider church context: Mats Tunehag, "The Global BAM Think Tank and the 2nd Vatican Council," 16 November 2012, http://matstunehag.com/2012/11/16/the-global-bam-think-tank-and-the-2nd-vatican-council/.

4. The following article briefly describes four major Lausanne-related consultations (2004, 2009, 2014, 2017) dealing with Business as Mission: Mats Tunehag, "Wealth Creation Manifesto," 10 May 2017, http://matstunehag.com/2017/05/10/wealth-creation-manifesto/.

5. It would be a costly mistake to neglect the intellectual wealth generated over the centuries in both Jewish and Christian traditions. Please allow me to recommend one of the better books I've read: *Papal Economics* by Maciej Zieba. He gives an insightful overview and critical analysis of a dozen papal encyclicals published over a hundred-plus years. They deal with issues such as work, business, wealth, property rights, democracy, market economy, socialism,

In BAM, we talk about the quadruple bottom line: financial, social, environmental, and spiritual. BAM is not about doing business with a touch of "churchianity." BAM is not Christians just doing social enterprise. BAM recognizes God as the ultimate stakeholder who has a vested interest in the multiple bottom lines and multiple stakeholders. BAM is about serving *people*, aligning with God's *purposes*, being good stewards of the *planet*, and making a *profit*.[6] Jo Plummer writes,

> BAM is a response to at least three God-given biblical mandates:
>
> - The *cultural mandate* given in Genesis 1 and 2 to develop flourishing human society and care for creation
> - The *great commandment* given in Matthew 22 to love God above all else and love our neighbour as ourselves, and
> - The *great commission* given in Matthew 28 to share the gospel and make disciples of Jesus in all corners of the earth.
>
> Thus we have *a definition of BAM* that is "intentional about Kingdom of God purpose and impact on people and nations" and "concerned about the world's poorest and least evangelized peoples."[7]

Our Roots

The BAM concept is deeply rooted in Judeo-Christian tradition.[8] The late Rabbi Lord Jonathan Sacks, an intellectual giant, wrote an essay which helps us understand our Jewish roots when it comes to a worldview conducive to problem-solving and innovation, the sanctity of work, and the role of business for human flourishing.[9]

---

and human dignity and freedom (Maciej Zieba, *Papal Economics: The Catholic Church on Democratic Capitalism, from* Rerum Nevraum *to* Caritas in Veritate [n.p.: Intercollegiate Studies Institute, 2014]).

6. See introduction and summary by my BAM colleague Jo Plummer: "4 Things You Need to Know about Business as Mission," 28 February 2022, https://businessasmission.com/4-things-you-need-to-know-about-business-as-mission/.

7. Excerpts from Plummer, "4 Things You Need to Know." For infographics and short texts regarding the three mandates and the four bottom lines, see also Mats Tunehag, "A Brief Introduction to Business as Mission, BAM," 15 January 2020, http://matstunehag.com/2020/01/15/bam-1-2-3-4-beyond/.

8. I elaborate on the Judeo-Christian roots of BAM in the article "Deeply Rooted for the Future," 23 December 2020, http://matstunehag.com/2020/12/23/deeply-rooted-for-the-future.

9. Jonathan Sacks, "Markets and Morals," *First Things*, August 2020, https://www.firstthings.com/article/2000/08/markets-and-morals. I am indebted to Sacks's books, articles, and lectures.

The BAM movement aims at transforming the world. It is related to what the Jews call *tikkun olam*, which means "repairing the world." *Tikkun olam* is co-creating with God and bridging the gap between the world that is and the world as it ought to be.[10] The Lord's Prayer is in a sense a *tikkun olam* prayer: May your kingdom come on earth, may your will be done among us.

Work Is Worship

Professor Angelo Nicolaides expresses an Orthodox Church perspective on work, worship, and mission: "In Old Testament times work was the way in which one worshipped God." He goes on to say: "Christians should thus view work as a mission."[11]

Work, creativity, and human dignity are related because we are created in God's image. Rabbi Sacks contrasts animals and human beings: "Work . . . has spiritual value, because earning our food is part of the essential dignity of the human condition. Animals find sustenance; only mankind creates it."[12]

This relates to the Hebrew word *avodah* which means to "work, worship, and serve." Thus, BAM pursues a seamless integration of work, worship, and service. The thirteenth-century commentator Rabbenu Bachya said, "The active participation of man in the creation of his own wealth is a sign of his spiritual greatness."[13]

Wealth Creation

The value of creating different kinds of wealth through business is endorsed in both rabbinic and Christian traditions. As Pope Francis says, "Business is a noble vocation, directed to producing wealth and improving the world. It can be a fruitful source of prosperity for the area in which it operates, especially if it sees the creation of jobs as an essential part of its service to the common good."[14]

---

10. See Mats Tunehag, "Tikkun Olam: Repair the World," 4 October 2020, http://matstunehag.com/2020/10/04/tikkun-olam-repair-the-world.

11. Angelo Nicolaides, "Ethics and the Dignity of Work: An Orthodox Christian Perspective," *Pharos Journal of Theology*, online Volume 101 (2020), https://www.pharosjot.com/uploads/7/1/6/3/7163688/article_22_vol_101__2020__unisa.pdf.

12. Sacks, "Markets and Morals."

13. Sacks.

14. Pope Francis, "Encyclical Letter *Laudato Si'* of the Holy Father Francis on Care for Our Common Home," #129, 24 May 2015, https://www.vatican.va/content/francesco/en/encyclicals/documents/papa-francesco_20150524_enciclica-laudato-si.html.

BAM Global, together with the Lausanne Movement, organized a global consultation in 2017 around the issue of wealth creation for holistic transformation. Our findings were documented in seven papers, a summarizing manifesto, and an educational video series.[15]

The Wealth Creation Manifesto[16] is deeply rooted in Judeo-Christian thought but also adds to a firm foundation for our day and age. The first three affirmations are as follows:

1. Wealth creation is rooted in God the Creator, who created a world that flourishes with abundance and diversity.

2. We are created in God's image, to co-create with Him and for Him, to create products and services for the common good.

3. Wealth creation is a holy calling, and a God-given gift, which is commended in the Bible.

This is also mentioned within the Orthodox Church tradition. God gives "wealth to serve His purposes."[17]

Why Is There a BAM Movement?

Each generation has to review and highlight age-old concepts and truths and see how they apply to today's context. That includes various arenas and constituencies such as business, church, and academia.

While acknowledging our roots, we also recognize the emergence of the BAM movement in our generation. Today, we can talk about a *global* BAM movement – we could not do that twenty-five years ago. Today, there are tens of thousands of businesses on all continents on a BAM journey. Today, there are churches and denominations embracing Business as Mission. Today, most of the oldest and biggest evangelical mission agencies in the world are pursuing BAM. Today, there are many academic institutions teaching BAM and producing masters' and doctoral theses on Business as Mission. This was not the case just a few decades ago.

Thus, we may ask: *Why is there a global BAM movement? How did that come about?* First and foremost, we recognize that God is the ultimate initiator and

---

15. Mats Tunehag, "Wealth Creation," 22 July 2017, http://matstunehag.com/wealth-creation.

16. BAM Global, "Wealth Creation Manifesto," last modified 2022, https://bamglobal.org/report-wealth-creation-manifesto/.

17. Nicolaides, "Dignity of Work."

conductor of the movement. But I must also mention three essential building blocks: *common language, communication,* and *collaboration.*

Without a common language you cannot communicate. If you cannot communicate you cannot collaborate, and it will lead to disconnected initiatives with limited impact.

BAM Global Think Tank

Since 2002, BAM Global has focused on creating and sharing intellectual and social capital. What does that mean? An underlying principle is the belief that there is wisdom in the counsel of many. To that end, we have been facilitating global listening processes, whereby voices from both history and today's world can be heard, and discussions be held and documented.[18] These inclusive and participatory conversations have created ownership of the concept, which continues to be discussed and shared in many languages and contexts. We have also brought people together not only to listen, share, and learn, but also to connect and act. The BAM Manifesto and the Wealth Creation Manifesto are essential for establishing a common language for communication and collaboration, to create greater impact. See the BAM A–Z booklet which also expresses the common BAM language.[19]

The Second BAM Global Think Tank (2011–13) started over thirty national, regional, and international working groups, dealing with BAM in a particular country or region, or BAM related to issues such as poverty, human

---

18. The preamble of the BAM Manifesto shows the ethos of our modus operandi over twenty years and counting: "The Lausanne 2004 Forum Business as Mission Issue Group worked for a year, addressing issues relating to God's purposes for work and business, the role of businesspeople in church and missions, the needs of the world and the potential response of business. The group consisted of more than 70 people from all continents. Most came from a business background but there were also church and mission leaders, educators, theologians, lawyers and researchers. The collaboration process included 60 papers, 25 case studies, several national and regional Business as Mission consultations and email-based discussions, culminating in a week of face to face dialogue and work." Business as Mission Issue Group, "The Business as Mission Manifesto," October 2004, http://matstunehag.com/wp-content/uploads/2011/04/BAM-MANIFESTO-2.pdf.

19. "The BAM A–Z booklet communicates the concepts of Business as Mission, BAM, with graphics, single words and short texts. Using the 26 letters of the English alphabet, Tunehag has identified 26 key words and concepts related to BAM. They are accompanied by a brief explanation and a graphic. 66 pages." Mats Tunehag, *Know Your BAM A–Z: Business as Mission – BAM* (Sweden, April 2001), http://matstunehag.com/wp-content/uploads/2021/05/BAM-A-Z-Booklet-25-April-2021.pdf.

See also the A–Z of Business as Mission, BAM, in 26 short videos: "A–Z of BAM Videos," Vimeo, https://vimeo.com/showcase/9233513.

trafficking, unreached peoples, metrics, funding, and incubation. Many of these groups produced a report, but the ongoing conversations also catalyzed BAM initiatives around the world, which further propelled the global movement. Today, there is a growing number of BAM Global Ambassadors serving regions and issues.[20]

"Poly-" x 3

A movement is different from an organization. The latter is registered, has a board and a budget, and it hires (and fires) staff. It is defined and operates under some kind of legal and management control. A movement, on the other hand, consists of many independent initiatives and organizations which share a vision and are aligned in mission and values. Examples are the abolitionist movement, the civil rights movement, and the charismatic movement.

Nobody has executive control of or power over a movement; rather, it is held together by a common cause, and it grows through collaboration built on trust relationships.

BAM is a global movement with numerous initiatives on all continents, in business, missions, church, and academia. The glue is our common vision, our aligned mission and values, as briefly expressed in the two manifestos.

A movement can be served by an SMO, a societal movement organization. BAM Global is such an entity. An SMO facilitates communication and collaborations within and outside a movement, and it catalyzes new initiatives. BAM Global exists to invigorate, serve, strengthen, and equip the global BAM movement.

The global BAM movement can also be described with three words which start with the prefix "poly-," which means "many":

- *Polycentric*: BAM does not have a global headquarters. You can find BAM centers, initiatives, and networks from Seoul to São Paolo, from Sydney to St. Petersburg, from Bucharest to Birmingham (Alabama), from China to Cuba, from Egypt to England, from South Africa to Sweden, from Nepal to the Netherlands, from Myanmar to Mongolia – and beyond.

---

20. See the minute-and-a-half video introducing BAM Global Ambassadors (BAM Global, "Mats: Introduction to BAMbassadors," https://vimeo.com/618984120), and a three-part blog: Business as Mission, "BAM: A Global Glimpse," 16 September 2021, https://businessasmission.com/bam-a-global-glimpse/.

- *Poly-directional*: BAM is not a Western idea or an initiative which goes from the West to the rest. It goes from everywhere to everywhere.
- *Polyglot*: BAM operates in many languages. In fact, the biggest BAM networks in the world are not using English. Today, there are many BAM websites, books, conferences, blogs, podcasts, and YouTube channels in different languages. The BAM Manifesto, the Wealth Creation Manifesto, and other key BAM documents are available in twenty-plus languages.

BHAGs: Big Hairy Audacious Goals

We have briefly reviewed the BAM concept's historical roots, and painted a picture, albeit incomplete, of the scope and nature of the global BAM movement. Now, let's look ahead. What are some of the challenges facing us?

Over the years and through the global conversations we've had, three major challenges have been identified. We call them BHAGs: Big Hairy Audacious Goals. These are major issues that can be dealt with only if we continue to stay on course and grow the strength of the movement. These are macro issues, which force us to think and act intergenerationally, and to intentionally build an ecosystem to optimize holistic impact. They will not be achieved by one company, organization, or network alone, but through collaborative effort.

Here I briefly describe them, in no particular order.[21]

Aligning Views of Business with Biblical Principles

BAM is not a technique, but a worldview and a lifestyle. Or as BAM Global puts it, "Business as mission is not simply a method or strategy; it encompasses a worldview and business praxis based on biblical principles and the church's teaching."[22]

The sacred-secular divide has been an issue throughout the history of the church. But Pope John Paul II stated,

---

21. For the full text of the BHAGs identified by BAM Global, see "BAM Global Goals," April 2019, https://www.bamglobal.org/wp-content/uploads/2019/10/BAM-Global-BHAGs.pdf.

22. See "About BAM Global," https://bamglobal.org/about/; and "BAM Global Goals," April 2019, https://www.bamglobal.org/wp-content/uploads/2019/10/BAM-Global-BHAGs.pdf.

> There cannot be two parallel lives in [people's] existence: on the one hand, the so-called "spiritual" life, with its values and demands; and on the other, the so-called "secular" life, that is, life in a family, at work, in social relationships, in the responsibilities of public life and in culture.... This split between the faith which many profess and their daily lives deserves to be counted among the more serious errors of our age.[23]

Back to BAM Global's BHAG statement:

> Thus, we want to change the thinking of the global church on business. BAM Global will positively engage with leaders in business, church, missions, and academia to influence attitudes about business, wealth creation, work, and economics, and affirm business as a God-given gift and calling. Business as mission is about realising this new paradigm in the marketplace.

In the words of the Business as Mission Manifesto:

> We call upon the church worldwide to identify, affirm, pray for, commission and release business people and entrepreneurs to exercise their gifts and calling as business people in the world – among all peoples and to the ends of the earth.
>
> We call upon business people globally to receive this affirmation and to consider how their gifts and experience might be used to help meet the world's most pressing spiritual and physical needs through Business as Mission.

Creating a Critical Mass

We thank God for the exponential growth of the BAM movement in our generation. We see more and bigger BAM businesses, and various supporting initiatives in a growing ecosystem. But we need to work toward a critical mass,

---

23. Pope John Paul II, "Post-Synodal Apostolic Exhortation *Christifideles Laici* of His Holiness John Paul II on the Vocation and the Mission of the Lay Faithful in the Church and in the World: To Bishops, to Priests and Deacons, to Women and Men Religious, and to All the Lay Faithful," 30 December 1988, https://www.vatican.va/content/john-paul-ii/en/apost_exhortations/documents/hf_jp-ii_exh_30121988_christifideles-laici.html.

to reach a tipping point, for macro transformation on an intergenerational scale.[24] The BAM Global BHAGs again:

> [To] reach a tipping point for macro impact through BAM businesses: The global BAM movement has grown rapidly in the last 20-plus years. There are now thousands of BAM businesses, and countless BAM-related initiatives in businesses, churches, missions, and academia.... However, now we need to go further, to build on this growth and better "connect the dots" of BAM to enable greater impact. Transformation on a macro level is yet to emerge; on cultures, industries, cities and nations. To create momentum for macro transformation we need to scale up, multiply and reach a critical mass of business as mission initiatives in cities, nations, and industries.... BAM Global will facilitate communication, connection and collaboration among BAM leaders and practitioners. BAM Global will nurture networks and communities focused around industries, geographical areas and special interests. We will also provide forums, tools, resources, and case studies that support the growth of the BAM ecosystem as a whole.

Developing BAM Solutions to Global Issues

Businesses are strong transformational agents and have a good track record of enabling humanity to flourish:

> The biggest lift out of poverty in the history of mankind has taken place in our generation. This has happened not through aid but trade – through businesses – especially small and medium sized companies. Financial wealth has been created through business, but so has physical wealth (health, medicines, etc.), cultural wealth (books, theatres, museums, etc.), and many other kinds of wealth. Wealth creation through business and job creation has been and continues to be a key driver for welcome progress in society....

---

24. Here is a helpful report by Deloitte about scaling for impact and building ecosystems: Harvey Koh, Nidhi Hegde, and Ashish Karamchandani, *Beyond the Pioneer: Getting Inclusive Industries to Scale* (Deloitte, April 2014), https://www2.deloitte.com/bg/en/pages/public-sector/articles/beyond-the-pioneer.html.

BAM Global focuses attention on BAM solutions to strategic global issues on every continent. These issues are global and transnational, and they affect nations and peoples around the world. As a global BAM movement, we are addressing some of these challenges, but we need further reflection and action. Thus, BAM Global focuses on strategic issues such as:

- Unreached peoples: The role of business in bringing the whole gospel to the whole world
- Poverty: The need for job creation and providing essential goods and services
- Slavery: The role of business in prevention and restoration of victims of human trafficking.
- Corruption: Encouraging Christian business leaders as they model and multiply ethical business practices
- Creation care: The opportunity for businesses to take a lead in good stewardship of earth's resources, and to innovate and find business solutions to environmental issues.

Staying Mission True

The BHAGs above are external challenges. As a movement, we also have an internal issue we need to constantly be aware of and always address: how to avoid mission drift and stay mission true.

No organization or church plans for mission drift. It happens by default if you fail to have systems to stay mission true. Historical examples abound, and I strongly recommend the book *Mission Drift* by Peter Greer. Money and the wrong people are often two factors which cause organizations to drift from intended mission and values.

No organization or movement is immune from the risk of mission drift, and this applies also to the global BAM movement. This brief chapter on BAM – its roots, scope, and future – does not allow for a lengthy elaboration on the subject. But a particular danger is that the Great Commission is downplayed, neglected, or lost. As a movement, and as an SMO, we can only exercise what I call "gentle quality control" based on relationships and ongoing conversations. If we lose the global thrust – to all peoples – and the aim of making Christ known and God glorified, then we have lost the plot.

Stay Rooted and Be Tenacious

It can take up to twenty-five years before an olive tree produces olives that can be eaten. But once the tree starts bearing fruit, it can produce olives for two thousand years or more. Olive trees are an example of intergenerational blessing.

The modern BAM movement is still young; we are in some ways still within the first twenty-five years of the life of an olive tree.[25] We do see some fruit but we are eagerly awaiting more. We need to nurture and care for the BAM olive tree in these early days of the movement. We want to build a movement that can bring good and lasting transformation, and we know it takes time. But we need tenacity, and we must hold on to our vision and mission, and maintain our values, as we build BAM communities around the globe.

Our worldview and business practice must be thoroughly infused and constantly informed by a few millennia worth of Judeo-Christian thought.[26] BAM and faith-driven entrepreneurship did not start with us, even though it is experiencing a global surge in our generation. But it will only have a lasting impact if we are deeply rooted for the future.

We embrace the promise that God will bless us so we can be a blessing – in and through business – in our generation and for many generations to come. All for the greater glory of God. *Ad maiorem Dei gloriam.*

---

25. To learn more about the olive tree, and lessons learned from other movements of societal transformation, see Mats Tunehag, "BAM & the Olive Tree," 8 May 2013, http://matstunehag.com/2013/05/08/bam-the-olive-tree/.

26. All truth is God's truth! We mustn't be afraid of or instinctively reject statements just because they come from sources we are less familiar with or skeptical of.

> BAM Resources
> - The world's most extensive BAM resource library: businessasmission.com
> - BAM Global: BAMglobal.org
> - BAM in 22 languages: matstunehag.com
> - BAM book: Gea Gort and Mats Tunehag, *BAM Global Movement: Business as Mission – Concepts and Stories*. Peabody: Hendrickson, 2018. http://matstunehag.com/2018/04/25/bam-global-movement-business-as-mission-concept-and-stories/
> - BAM booklet: The *BAM A–Z* booklet communicates the concepts of BAM with graphics, single words, and short texts. Using the 26 letters of the English alphabet, Tunehag has identified 26 key words and concepts related to BAM. They are accompanied by a brief explanation and a graphic. Free download: http://matstunehag.com/bam-material-in-different-languages/

References

Francis (Pope). "Encyclical Letter *Laudato Si'* of the Holy Father Francis on Care for Our Common Home." 24 May 2015. https://www.vatican.va/content/francesco/en/encyclicals/documents/papa-francesco_20150524_enciclica-laudato-si.html.

John Paul II (Pope). "Post-Synodal Apostolic Exhortation *Christifideles Laici* of His Holiness John Paul II on the Vocation and the Mission of the Lay Faithful in the Church and in the World: To Bishops, to Priests and Deacons, to Women and Men Religious, and to All the Lay Faithful." 30 December 1988. https://www.vatican.va/content/john-paul-ii/en/apost_exhortations/documents/hf_jp-ii_exh_30121988_christifideles-laici.html.

Koh, Harvey, Nidhi Hegde, and Ashish Karamchandani. *Beyond the Pioneer: Getting Inclusive Industries to Scale*. Deloitte, April 2014. https://www2.deloitte.com/bg/en/pages/public-sector/articles/beyond-the-pioneer.html.

Nicolaides, Angelo. "Ethics and the Dignity of Work: An Orthodox Christian Perspective." *Pharos Journal of Theology*, online Volume 101 (2020). https://www.pharosjot.com/uploads/7/1/6/3/7163688/article_22_vol_101__2020__unisa.pdf.

Sacks, Jonathan. "Markets and Morals." *First Things*, August 2020. https://www.firstthings.com/article/2000/08/markets-and-morals.

Zieba, Maciej. *Papal Economics: The Catholic Church on Democratic Capitalism, from Rerum Nevraum to Caritas in Veritate*. [n.p.]: Intercollegiate Studies Institute, 2014.

8

Brewing All the Good You Can: Discovering the Prophetic Calling of Kingdom Business

By Cody Lorance

It Didn't All Start One Day in Memphis

Heroes rarely survive face-to-face meetings with the admiration of their fans intact. Rarer still is the hero who risks being really known by those whom he or she has previously influenced only through protective layers of lectures and publications. It requires a special kind of brazenness to share meals, bathrooms, and conversations with ordinary folk. Such people either don't care what others will think of them should the veil be removed, or else they want to be exposed for the earthen vessels they know themselves to be.

Tetsunao Yamamori began influencing me long before either of us knew it. I am, after all, a member of that generation who stood weeping in a field near Memphis in the summer of 2000 as John Piper, Louie Giglio, Beth Moore, and others charged us to lay down our lives to reach the unreached in faraway and hostile lands that were closed to traditional forms of evangelism and mission.[1] As Piper told stories of saints and seashells, Katherine looked up at me with

---

1. This is a reference to an event organized by Passion Conferences on 20 May 2000 called "One Day." Since that day, much has been written to both celebrate and critique what happened there. See Sarah Eekhoff Zylstra, "How John Piper's Seashells Swept over a Generation," TGC, 20 March 2017, https://www.thegospelcoalition.org/article/how-john-pipers-seashells-swept-over-a-generation/; Keith Daukas, "The Tragedy of John Piper's 'Shell Collection' Illustration," 27 August 2021, https://medium.com/outside-the-box-inside-the-book/the-tragedy-of-john-pipers-shell-collection-illustration-c8d240ecf145; Tim Challies, "Why John Piper's 'Shells' Illustration Transformed a Generation," *@Challies* (blog), 24 April 2018, https://www.challies.

long braids framing a tear-tracked face. I glanced down at her left hand where a crudely crafted assemblage of twist ties stood in for what would soon be a cheap engagement ring and then down further to lovely sandaled feet which have since carried the hope of Jesus to people and places all over the planet. We wept in reaffirming God's call on our lives.

It would be years before I realized that the messengers in Memphis didn't invent the call to what we have come to know as the "third era of world missions."[2] Preceding them was the historic work of missiologists such as Donald McGavran, Ralph Winter, C. Peter Wagner, Tetsunao Yamamori, and others. It was their genius which had been helping the church to understand where exactly the gospel wasn't, what the ethno-cultural barriers constituting the frontier of mission advance were, and just who were the sorts of missionaries required for finishing the unfinished task.

Tucked surreptitiously between the acknowledgments and the introduction of Yamamori's 1987 classic *God's New Envoys* is a wanted ad that would have fit in well in Memphis:

> WANTED:
> 100,000 New Envoys
> To serve in countries
> Closed to traditional missionaries.
> No salary. No security.
> Hardship, danger expected.
> Special training, new strategies required.
> Immediate Need![3]

From New Envoys to Kingdom Entrepreneurs

I first met Dr. Yamamori at the airport in Paris in 2011. By then, I was beginning to realize that he was a missiological giant whose work had greatly influenced me, and so, greeting him as he arrived, I extended a nervous hand. He shook it and then said simply, "Call me Ted."

---

com/vlog/why-john-pipers-shells-illustration-transformed-a-generation/; "The Rise and Fall of Mars Hill" (podcast), https://www.christianitytoday.com/ct/podcasts/rise-and-fall-of-mars-hill/.

2. Ralph Winter, "Three Mission Eras: And the Loss and Recovery of Kingdom Mission, 1800–2000," in *Perspectives on the World Christian Movement*, ed. Ralph D. Winter (Pasadena: William Carey Library, 2013), 263–78.

3. Tetsunao Yamamori, *God's New Envoys: A Bold Strategy for Penetrating "Closed Countries"* (Portland: Multnomah, 1987).

I think I've done that twice – called him Ted. It never felt respectful enough. He told me "Dr. Yamamori" was too stuffy. Eventually, I followed the example of some friends and settled on "Uncle Ted" as a compromise. It was the first lesson he would teach me in person – to not let anything overshadow the humanity of another. In his academic work too, Uncle Ted always seems more inclined to talk about people than about mere strategy, phenomena, or theology. People need the gospel and we have it; all Yamamorian missiology fundamentally flows out of solving this conundrum.

When talking about "new envoys," he was solving it with the idea of sending out "independently operating, self-supporting" missionaries who were also professionals – doctors, teachers, engineers, and more.[4] These people, Uncle Ted wrote, were the answer to what he had identified as ineffective evangelism, particularly among those who most needed the gospel: "Put simply, we're not succeeding at the task of bringing the gospel to those who need to hear it; and even when we do, we're not bringing enough of those who do hear the Word to faith and obedience in Christ."[5]

Why this ineffectiveness? *God's New Envoys* points to two problems:

"Closed" Countries

God's New Envoys was written in the 1980s when Ronald Reagan had yet to tell Mikhail Gorbachev to "tear down this wall." Significant space in the book is dedicated to maps and charts listing and analyzing the world's inaccessible nations, many of which were behind the "Iron Curtain." Seventy-seven countries were classified as restricted to missionaries as *God's New Envoys* went to print.[6]

Cultural Barriers

Here *God's New Envoys* leans on the work of Ralph Winter who describes "unreached people groups" as a function not merely of geography but also of

---

4. Yamamori, *God's New Envoys*.
5. Yamamori, 31–32.
6. Yamamori. Today, there are multiple entities which study the persecution of Christians and attempt to measure how open or hostile a nation is to missionaries. Open Doors lists seventy-four countries on its 2021 World Watch List and maintains a list of the fifty nations most hostile to Christians (see World Watch Research, *Complete World Watch List Methodology* [Open Doors International, Nov. 2021], https://odusa-media.com/2022/01/Complete-WWL-Methodology-November-2021.pdf).

cultural and language barriers. Proximity, in the case of unreached peoples, is less relevant than these barriers of understanding and acceptance. As *God's New Envoys* went to print, it was estimated that seventeen thousand of the world's twenty-four thousand people groups were unreached with "no viable, indigenous, evangelizing church."[7]

The new envoys were an answer to these barriers of access, understanding, and acceptance because they would combine standard cross-cultural missions training with "passport skills" – a professional area of expertise which would make them "valuable commodities" to countries whose governments would normally decline to give visas to missionaries. Science, medicine, engineering, agriculture, and the like were attractive skill sets that even "closed" countries would welcome; this was an "admissions ticket to the missions theater."[8]

Yamamori's concept would greatly influence the ultimately more popular term "tentmaking," which still commonly describes missionaries who either support themselves financially with "secular" work or at least use their professional experience and training to acquire visas to countries that are closed to more traditional missionary approaches. Reflecting on this in the preface of his 2003 book *On Kingdom Business*, co-edited with Kenneth Eldred, Yamamori acknowledges the most obvious shortcomings of the tentmaking model as it was commonly practiced:

> Tentmaking has borne some fruit, although there have been many failures along the way. Some tentmakers have been kicked out of the countries they were attempting to reach. Why? Because they were not doing the work their visa said they would do. Instead, their secular job was merely a cover for the "real" work of evangelism they hoped to do.[9]

God's New Envoys, of course, never suggests that such a bifurcation should exist between spiritual and professional work, but the rift formed nonetheless. Yamamori thus suggests a new model called "kingdom entrepreneurs," which he defines as "cross-cultural business owners, called by God, to do ministry

---

7. Yamamori, *God's New Envoys*. The methodology for how people groups are defined and counted has evolved since the publication of *God's New Envoys*. Joshua Project now puts the total number of people groups in the world at 17,413, with 7,387 of these considered "unreached" (see Joshua Project, "Global Statistics Dashboard," 2022, https://www.joshuaproject.net/people_groups/statistics).

8. Yamamori, 82–83.

9. Tetsunao Yamamori and Kenneth A. Eldred, "Preface," in *On Kingdom Business: Transforming Missions through Entrepreneurial Strategies* (Wheaton: Crossway, 2003), 7–10.

through business in restricted-access countries."[10] The kingdom entrepreneur, like the tentmaker, remains focused on reaching the unreached with the gospel of Jesus Christ and on strategically overcoming barriers of access and culture to make disciples of all nations. However, added to this is the function of starting companies that create jobs and meet needs. The business is not a front but is itself a means by which mission is done.

Missions Scattered, Smothered, Covered, Bifurcated, and Transformed

I was often told that I was a "tentmaker." I don't know if that was ever true. My job at Waffle House was secular enough and made it financially possible for me to work in ministry, but rural Oklahoma wasn't exactly what Uncle Ted had in mind when he spoke of "closed countries." Tentmaking, along with its cousin "bivocational ministry," always seemed to me more like an attempt to spiritually justify underpaying me for church work. Kenneth Eldred said that most of the church considered people in business or the workplace to be "second-class" citizens compared with traditional ministers and missionaries.[11] That's how I felt from having to supplement my paltry $25-per-week youth pastor job with a full-time second life scattering, smothering, and covering hash browns.

John Cragin argues that a kind of bifurcation often takes place even in kingdom businesses. Often, companies become divided practically into "true business" and "true missions" departments.[12] Business, says Cragin, "is seen as an unfortunate but necessary evil, required to provide support for the ministry."

I understood my true ministry to be what I did in and around the church and I failed to recognize what God was doing all around me at Waffle House. Preparing sermons and worship services and planning for church camp was God's work, not flipping eggs and baking waffles. Looking back, I can see that it was at the restaurant that God surrounded me with people who needed Jesus – folk who willingly came to me every day for coffee, conversation and "good food fast." I didn't need to invite them or beg them to come. They wanted to come. They wanted to talk. Many of them even wanted to talk about God.

---

10. Yamamori and Eldred, "Preface," 7–10.

11. Kenneth A. Eldred, "Introduction," in Yamamori and Eldred, *On Kingdom Business*, 19–27.

12. John Cragin, "The Business of Missions – The Missions of Business," in Yamamori and Eldred, 169–80.

I didn't have eyes to see. My life as a "Master Grill Operator" was just a necessary evil. It paid the bills so I could do real ministry. I prayed daily that God would deliver me from "secular" work and allow me to be in "full-time ministry." Once I had a chance to hang up my apron, I left the kitchen and never looked back.

Years go by. I get married to Katherine and we have some kids. We start working with immigrants and refugees. We baptize some unreached peoples and plant some churches among them. I study and write some stuff. In 2010, I find myself at the Third Lausanne Congress in Cape Town. There, I meet crazy people like Gloria Katusiime and "Kuyya Joy" Tira. I marry and bury. I am blessed. I am betrayed. I ordain some leaders and watch others walk away from the faith. Life is filled with "true ministry," extreme joy, and excruciating pain. There is stress, anxiety, and depression. I find myself occasionally missing Waffle House.

And then it's 2013 and I'm in Kampala in a little café called Endiro Coffee. I'm on a prescribed vacation. Fellow Cape Town alum and covenant sister Gloria Katusiime owns the place. I'm sitting at a table with a cappuccino, a gecko, and my copy of *Transforming Mission*. I've been trying to read *Transforming Mission* for years and have barely made a dent, but I find this: "Mission is understood as an enterprise that transforms reality. . . . Mission, in this perspective, is that dimension of our faith that refuses to accept reality as it is and aims at changing it."[13]

It's breakfast time. Or it was when I ordered. Things move more slowly in Uganda than I'm used to. The first attempt at my meal featured drastically overcooked eggs. The second was also overcooked but less impressively so. The server was approaching me with round three and I was silently prophesying an overcorrection – these eggs would still be in shell, if not in the chicken. I wasn't far off.

And now, with Gloria's permission (this may have been her plan all along), I'm in the kitchen teaching American egg cookery to the chef and his compatriots. This is probably my "White Savior" moment, but I just really want two eggs over-medium so I'm forgiving myself. Cooking lessons give way to prayer and ultimately to me resigning from my "true missions" post with my denomination and joining the Endiro team full-time.

As I write this, Gloria and I are co-CEOs of Endiro Coffee. It has become a group of five companies which represent operations across the value chain

---

13. David Bosch, *Transforming Mission: Paradigm Shifts in Theology of Mission* (Maryknoll: Orbis, 1991), xv.

including farming, processing, exporting, importing, roasting, wholesaling, and retailing. That one coffee shop in Kampala has now given birth to more than a dozen cafés in three countries. We are on an airline and on the shelves of a major US retailer. A few hundred people are counted among our farmers, roasters, baristas, cooks, servers, managers, and administrative staff.

We've nearly gone under many times and the COVID-19 pandemic didn't make things easier. Often, I feel that our biggest accomplishment is that we still exist. Too many businesses cannot say that.

In a recent report published by the United Nations Development Programme, Gloria wrote about Endiro:

> Today we own [many] coffee shop locations in Uganda and the United States of America, and we plan to expand. Our vision as a company is to create that experience many times over, and to be a company that partners with others to end child vulnerability.... We aim to work globally through the utilization of coffee and its related products, profits, services, and spaces. We are a tree-to-cup coffee business committed to changing lives at every step of our supply chain.[14]

So, there's a measure of success. The eggs are fantastic, and the coffee is incredible, but would Bosch say we are transforming reality? Is this missions?

Rewind.

It's 2010 and the Lausanne Congress is wrapping up. It has been an intense week. I have been called a cult leader by most of a certain nation's leaders. I have forcibly introduced myself to espresso to stay awake around the clock and fulfill my responsibilities as an "official blogger" and table group leader. I have been welcomed by Joy Tira into the newly born Global Diaspora Network. I have feasted on learning from the Bible and from God's people. I have a new sister, Gloria, who is sitting at the opposite end of the table. I am listening to Lindsay Brown give the closing address of Cape Town 2010. I have run out of tissue and am wiping my tears with my socks.

Lindsay Brown is quoting John Wesley:

> Do all the good you can,
> By all the means you can,

---

14. Gloria Katusiime, "The Bean That Transforms Communities and Nations: How Agro-Production and Value Addition Can Be Enhanced in Africa's Coffee Chain," in *Which Value Chains for a Made in Africa Revolution: The Futures Report 2021* (New York: United Nations Development Programme/AfCFTA Secretariat, 2021), 95–99, https://www.africa.undp.org/content/rba/en/home/library/reports/futures-report-2021.html.

In all the places you can,
At all the times you can,
To all the people you can,
As long as ever you can.

I commit to God: from that day forward, I will always only do, as a career, the most important thing I can imagine for the sake of his kingdom. I am helping lead Endiro today because of that commitment, and it might be mission.

Coffee as Mission or as Oppressor – It's One of Those

A few years into my journey with Endiro, I began asking tough questions about the company we were building. To that point, we had been making a little bit of money and were faithfully giving as much as we could to projects that helped children in need. They were good, Christ-centered, and missional projects. It was lovely, but it was still bifurcated. The business was *for* mission but wasn't *itself* mission.

João Mordomo distinguishes business *as* mission ventures (BAM) as "the doxologically-motivated strategic development and use of authentic business activities to create authentic ministry opportunities leading to the transformation of the world's least-reached people and peoples spiritually, economically, socially, and environmentally."[15] BAM is an "instrument of God's holistic ministry." Indeed, two decades after *On Kingdom Business* and more than thirty years since *God's New Envoys*, the prevailing missiological attitude is that business itself can be mission without the previously assumed necessary bifurcation. In Lausanne Movement vernacular, business itself can take the whole gospel to the whole world. Echoing Bosch, business itself can transform reality.

I was having these kinds of conversations with João, Uncle Ted, Art Medina, and others as Gloria and I were discovering that the "Fair Trade Certified" (FT) coffee we had been sourcing wasn't what it seemed. The well-known system which had been developed to ensure that farmers were earning livable wages had become in practice, at least in certain areas of Uganda, a shell game in which people several steps away from farming coffee were getting the

---

15. João Mordomo, "Business as Mission (BAM) to, in and through Diaspora," in *Scattered and Gathered: A Global Compendium of Diaspora Missiology*, eds. S. J. Tira and Tetsunao Yamamori (Carlisle: Langham Global Library, 2020), 281–96.

certified price premium while the actual growers were earning only a small fraction of that.

The problem, we found, lay in the fact that the minimum FT price of US$1.40 per pound was set at the green coffee transaction point.[16] Most coffee farmers in Uganda, however, don't produce green coffee. They sell coffee cherries to middlemen who either process it themselves to green or sell to others who will. The "farmer" who receives the FT price and related premiums often has had nothing to do with actually growing the coffee. Coffee researcher Karl Wienhold cited a study which confirmed that in East Africa, "workers on Fair-Trade-certified farms earned generally less than those working on uncertified farms."[17]

Our company was making money for missions but in the process was perpetuating a system keeping coffee farmers in poverty and, moreover, destroying God's creation in ways that would eventually mean they would not be able to grow anything at all. The curtain was being pulled back on our BAM endeavor. Missiological definitions were not lining up and it was beginning to look like we were doing more harm than good. Mission, business-related or otherwise, isn't God's mission if it relies on harming one group of people to help another.

Here's Wienhold again:

> If something is cheaper than it's worth, either someone else is subsidizing it, or someone is getting a raw deal. . . . If you like cheap coffee and don't care if it's bad, or if it is half-burnt rice and chickpeas, then have at it. But if coffee is both good and cheap, it's probably because a producer was swindled.[18]

The Problem with Coffee Is That It Is Drunk Only by Sinners

Let's zoom out a bit and consider the global coffee industry.

First, it's big – very big. Annually, coffee revenues exceed US$200 billion. The industry employs twenty-five million people. Coffee is grown in fifty nations and is consumed in all of them.[19]

---

16. Peter Kettler, "We Love Coffee. Are We Willing to Pay the Price?," Fairtrade America, 6 June 2019, https://www.fairtradeamerica.org/news-insights/we-love-coffee-are-we-willing-to-pay-the-price/.

17. Karl Wienhold, *Cheap Coffee: Behind the Curtain of the Global Coffee Trade* (n.p.: Roast Magazine, 2021), 180.

18. Wienhold, *Cheap Coffee*, 5.

19. Wienhold.

Second, injustice is inherent. All the coffee is produced by 12.5 million farms, and 84 percent of these are smaller than two hectares,[20] but just five companies buy half of all the world's coffee exports.[21]

How much bargaining leverage does a farmer with an acre of coffee trees have against a company that has billions in purchasing power and has designed products so that a crop in Uganda is 100 percent interchangeable with that of a similar coffee farmer in Brazil, Papua New Guinea, or India? Is it any wonder that less than 10 percent of the US$200 billion makes its way to coffee-growing countries and, as we've already seen, only a fraction of that makes it to the growers themselves?[22] The overall trend of the past few decades has seen the total global value of the coffee industry increasing while the compensation of coffee growers has steadily decreased. In Cameroon, as many as 44 percent of coffee farmers live below the extreme poverty line of US$1.90 per day,[23] and in Nicaragua, it is as much as 50 percent.[24] One study conducted in Uganda's Bududa district, where our company's coffee is grown, found that the average household of six to ten persons earned only around US$100 per year.[25]

We first started visiting coffee farms ourselves in 2015 and discovered levels of poverty and cases of exploitation that absolutely shook us. We were selling coffee as "Fair Trade" that was being produced in villages where large households lived in extreme poverty. Children lacked adequate nutrition and access to education. Health care was nonexistent. Women and young people were socially marginalized and silenced.

I remember my first walk among the coffee trees. I found a fungus known as coffee leaf rust on nearly every tree. Many coffee cherries had tiny surface holes indicating that pests known as coffee borers had infested the plants. I am no agronomist, and was less of one then, but I knew enough to know that even the few trees these farmers had were in danger of disappearing completely. I quote the authors of the 2020 *Coffee Barometer*:

---

20. Sjoerd Panhuysen and Joost Pierrot, *Coffee Barometer* (n.p.: Coffee Collective, 2020).
21. Panhuysen and Pierrot, *Coffee Barometer*; Wienhold, *Cheap Coffee*.
22. Wienhold.
23. Extreme poverty is defined in the United Nations "Sustainable Development Goals" as living on less than US$1.90 per day. See United Nations, "Sustainable Development Goals," https://www.un.org/sustainabledevelopment/poverty/.
24. Panhuysen and Pierrot, *Coffee Barometer*.
25. Kelly Austin, "Brewing Unequal Exchanges in Coffee: A Qualitative Investigation into the Consequences of the Java Trade in Rural Uganda," *Journal of World-Systems Research* 23, no. 2 (Aug. 2017): 326–52.

> The growing economic inequality and deteriorating living and working conditions are aggravated by environmental problems and the impacts of climate change and the destruction of biodiversity. . . . It is well documented that climate change is increasingly impacting the livelihoods of coffee producers. For instance, coffee pests and diseases, which are already troublesome under the current climate, are aggravated by the effects of higher temperatures. . . . What is less well documented and reported is that changes to land suitability for coffee production is increasingly driving deforestation and forest degradation in coffee landscapes.[26]

Coffee-growing methodology that prioritizes the production of high volumes of undifferentiated commodity coffee degrades forests and destroys soils. Year by year, coffee production encroaches upon virgin forest, accelerating deforestation and climate change, and eradicates native biodiversity. Harvest by harvest, there is less land for coffee growing, less coffee to sell, and less money for coffee-growing communities and households to live on.

No business built on such a status quo can consider itself to be a kingdom business. Even if such a business produced millions of dollars to support ministries around the world and had its own internal discipleship program that saw many employees and customers come to faith in Jesus every year, it could not be classified as a true BAM enterprise if it was built upon unchecked systemic sin and exploitation. Mission, we must not forget, is God's mission by which he establishes and advances his kingdom in every aspect of life, in every sphere of society. We have no permission to be insular in our thinking. It is not just a cup of caffeine that powers us through sermon prep or a Sunday school class. It is a product that we consume and thereby align ourselves with all the forces which have resulted in its production.

I can sip my coffee and say that I didn't personally exploit the farmer or destroy God's creation. But I cannot ignore the echo of my forebearers who said that they never saw Jesus naked, hungry, oppressed or imprisoned. "Truly I tell you," Jesus answered, "whatever you did not do for one of the least of these, you did not do for me" (Matt 25:45). This is the King of kingdom entrepreneurship who defined his own ministry as preaching "good news to the poor" and liberating the oppressed (Luke 4:18).

This is a gospel issue.

---

26. Panhuysen and Pierrot, *Coffee Barometer*.

Going further, the apostle Paul tells us that all creation is groaning and longing for freedom from its decay (Rom 8:19–23). The degradation of the environment is contrary to the will of God who wants to see creation enjoying redemption alongside his children. This too is a gospel issue and thus an integral part of what it means to be on mission with God.[27]

I look down at my cup of coffee – it's 2016 and now I prefer it black. Is this a cup of exploitation of people and the planet? I had been asking if our business was really mission. Now I had to go further and ask if the business itself was sin. I hesitantly raise the cup to my lips. The hot liquid flows down my throat and into my stomach. It warms my body. It fills my fingertips. I shudder and feel like Balzac: "Ideas quick-march into motion like battalions of a grand army to its legendary fighting ground, and the battle rages. Memories charge in, bright flags on high. . . . The artillery of logic rushes up with clattering wagons and cartridges; on imagination's orders, sharpshooters sight and fire."[28]

I set down my cup and begin writing questions:

1. What if our coffee company created jobs and professional development all along a fully integrated tree-to-cup value chain? What if we exemplified career mobility, egalitarian information access, democratic decision-making for all stakeholders, and long-term sustainability? What if we ended child vulnerability and extreme poverty? What if coffee meant prosperity for everyone in the business?

2. What if we formed strategic partnerships to address local and global injustices in contextualized and eschatological ways wherever we operated? What if we prayed and worked toward actualizing the reign of Jesus in every part of our company and in every community we touched?

3. What if we created spaces (coffee shops, roastery facilities, coffee washing stations, etc.) which encouraged redemptive relationships, church-outside-the-walls-style gatherings, and bases for holistic community engagement, and which otherwise facilitated and multiplied local disciple-making?

---

27. Lausanne Global Consultation on Creation Care and the Gospel, "Creation Care and the Gospel: Jamaica Call to Action," November 2012, Lausanne Movement, https://lausanne.org/content/statement/creation-care-call-to-action.

28. Honoré de Balzac, "The Pleasures and Pains of Coffee," 1830s, tr. Robert Onopa, https://urbigenous.net/library/pleasures_pains_coffee.html.

4. What if we approached agriculture as co-creators with God, intelligently practicing and modeling regenerative agriculture? What if we were absolutely bent on revealing God's glory in creation? What if we redesigned our operations to serve this creation care mandate in all our operations?

5. What if we paired coffee as a positive, sustainable, and profitable business presence with mission mobilization – training up world-class coffee professionals who were also effective disciple-makers? What if we looked intentionally at "closed countries," diasporic movement of unreached peoples, and emerging situations of human crisis around the world as we strategically planned our corporate expansion?

In the years since I first considered these questions, we have spent a great deal of time and what was left of our youth trying to answer them – to make them put on flesh and dwell in every part of Endiro. We are not done yet and it might be better to let another generation judge the results of our efforts. For now, however, let them be our missiological contribution.

Ted Yamamori's Underwear and the Prophetic Responsibility of Kingdom Business

There's a story here about the time Uncle Ted made me his plus-one in the business class lounge at Ninoy Aquino International Airport in Manila. At this point, we had been to a few countries together and I was getting used to the idea that this missiological legend was my friend. I was not a person who got to hang out in airport lounges so the cheap Filipino beer and cold egg salad sandwiches might as well have been champagne and caviar as far as I was concerned. I'm forever grateful for an experience that Uncle Ted most likely doesn't even remember; it made me feel seen, appreciated, and accepted by a personal hero. That's a lot for someone who honestly still feels like a second-class citizen in God's kingdom.

As we waited for our flights, I asked Uncle Ted about his single small carry-on bag. I had checked in a big suitcase and was additionally lugging around a cumbersome bulging backpack. I couldn't understand how this man, who had far more important responsibilities than myself on this trip, had managed to pack so lightly. Well, Dr. Tetsunao Yamamori taught me travel secrets that day, including some almost magical underwear hacks, that blew my mind. I will save those stories for when you're my plus-one in a lounge somewhere. Here's the lesson he taught me that I will share: Don't accept that the way things have always been done is the way things always must be done. Be willing to rethink and reimagine everything.

The atheistic but empathetic science fiction writer Octavia Butler left us these verses in her *Parable of the Sower*:

> All that you touch
> You Change.
> All that you Change
> Changes you.
> The only lasting truth
> Is Change.
> God is Change.[29]

Strictly speaking, that's heretical. But all the best heresy has a way of taking some forgotten orthodoxy out of a dusty corner and shining new light on it. In this case, Butler was giving words of hope to a fictional movement of people who were trying to escape a society of widespread oppression, exploitation, and violence. It's true that those who face every day as another day of suffering and hopelessness will find refreshment in the notion that change is coming, that they have a part in it, and that God is all about it.

That's the orthodoxy we too often forget.

To be sure, God is the same, yesterday, today, and forever (Heb 13:8), but he is not keeping things the same. We do not serve the mission of God when we are so entrenched in our social conservatism that we refuse to reject the systemic sin and convenient corruptions upon which much of our comfortable lives are built. Bosch said that mission "refuses to accept reality as it is and aims at changing it."[30] He may be more biblically sound than Butler, but he is not disagreeing with her sentiment. Change must happen and mission must be marked by a distinct witness to an ever-encroaching kingdom that will wrinkle your trousers, upset apple carts, flip over tables, and break every chain. Uncritically accepting the status quo in a world of suffering, oppression, sin, poverty, and environmental exploitation cannot be said to have anything to do with the kingdom. Again, the mission of Jesus was clear: to preach good news to the poor, to proclaim liberty to the captives, to open the eyes of the blind, to release the oppressed, and to proclaim the year of the Lord's favor (Luke 4:18–19).

---

29. Octavia Butler, *Parable of the Sower* (London: Headline, 2019), 75.
30. Bosch, *Transforming Mission*, xv.

In other words, *missio Dei* transforms reality. *God's New Envoys* awakened us to the opportunity of work and business to provide gospel access across barriers to the world's least reached. *On Kingdom Business* taught us that we needed to build companies that were profitable, legitimate, ethical, and beneficial to the society at large to be effective agents for mission. The wider BAM missiological literature demonstrates that business *itself* can be mission and not just a way to fund "true ministry."

But a missionary, of the kind Jesus has sent, is necessarily a prophet of the coming kingdom. Therefore, kingdom businesses have an inescapable prophetic duty. We must bear witness in our governance, operations, labor practices, and environmental stewardship to the truth of a gospel which reconciles all peoples and all of creation to God in Christ. We must proclaim good news to the poor and warn of pending judgment to the greedy and corrupt. Kingdom businesses and the envoys and entrepreneurs who lead them must be willing even to fail economically rather than to fail in faithfulness, knowing they are not building a company but a kingdom which is always advancing and will ultimately arrive in full.

In *God's New Envoys*, Uncle Ted asks us to dream with him about Zechariah 14:9 and the day when "the LORD shall be King over all the earth" (NKJV). This is the metric of our success in kingdom business and the last line of any true BAM business plan: God will prevail in the end. Until then, we keep brewing all the good we can.

References

Austin, Kelly. "Brewing Unequal Exchanges in Coffee: A Qualitative Investigation into the Consequences of the Java Trade in Rural Uganda." *Journal of World-Systems Research* 23, no. 2 (Aug. 2017): 326–52.

Balzac, Honoré de. "The Pleasures and Pains of Coffee." 1830s. Translated by Robert Onopa. https://urbigenous.net/library/pleasures_pains_coffee.html.

Bosch, David. *Transforming Mission: Paradigm Shifts in Theology of Mission*. Maryknoll: Orbis, 1991.

Butler, Octavia. *Parable of the Sower*. London: Headline, 2019.

Challies, Tim. "Why John Piper's 'Shells' Illustration Transformed a Generation." *@Challies* (blog), 24 April 2018. https://www.challies.com/vlog/why-john-pipers-shells-illustration-transformed-a-generation/.

"The Rise and Fall of Mars Hill" (podcast). https://www.christianitytoday.com/ct/podcasts/rise-and-fall-of-mars-hill/.

Daukas, Keith. "The Tragedy of John Piper's 'Shell Collection' Illustration." 27 August 2021. https://medium.com/outside-the-box-inside-the-book/the-tragedy-of-john-pipers-shell-collection-illustration-c8d240ecf145.

Joshua Project. "Global Statistics Dashboard." 2022. https://www.joshuaproject.net/people_groups/statistics.

Katusiime, Gloria. "The Bean That Transforms Communities and Nations: How Agro-Production and Value Addition Can Be Enhanced in Africa's Coffee Chain." In *Which Value Chains for a Made in Africa Revolution: The Futures Report 2021*. New York: United Nations Development Programme/AfCFTA Secretariat, 2021. https://www.africa.undp.org/content/rba/en/home/library/reports/futures-report-2021.html.

Kettler, Peter. "We Love Coffee. Are We Willing to Pay the Price?" Fairtrade America, 6 June 2019. https://www.fairtradeamerica.org/news-insights/we-love-coffee-are-we-willing-to-pay-the-price/.

Lausanne Global Consultation on Creation Care and the Gospel. "Creation Care and the Gospel: Jamaica Call to Action." November 2012. Lausanne Movement. https://lausanne.org/content/statement/creation-care-call-to-action.

Mordomo, João. "Business as Mission (BAM) to, in and through Diaspora." In *Scattered and Gathered: A Global Compendium of Diaspora Missiology*, edited by S. J. Tira and Tetsunao Yamamori, 281–96. Carlisle: Langham Global Library, 2020.

Panhuysen, Sjoerd, and Joost Pierrot. *Coffee Barometer*. N.p.: Coffee Collective, 2020.

United Nations. "Sustainable Development Goals." https://www.un.org/sustainabledevelopment/poverty/.

Wienhold, Karl. *Cheap Coffee: Behind the Curtain of the Global Coffee Trade*. N.p.: Roast Magazine, 2021.

Winter, Ralph. "Three Mission Eras: And the Loss and Recovery of Kingdom Mission, 1800–2000." In *Perspectives on the World Christian Movement*, edited by Ralph D. Winter, 263–78. Pasadena: William Carey Library, 2013.

World Watch Research. *Complete World Watch List Methodology*. Open Doors International, November 2021. https://odusa-media.com/2022/01/Complete-WWL-Methodology-November-2021.pdf.

Yamamori, Tetsunao. *God's New Envoys: A Bold Strategy for Penetrating "Closed Countries."* Portland: Multnomah, 1987.

Yamamori, Tetsunao, and Kenneth A. Eldred, eds. *On Kingdom Business: Transforming Missions through Entrepreneurial Strategies*. Wheaton: Crossway, 2003.

Zylstra, Sarah Eekhoff. "How John Piper's Seashells Swept over a Generation." TGC, 20 March 2017. https://www.thegospelcoalition.org/article/how-john-pipers-seashells-swept-over-a-generation/.

9

Mobilizing Thousands to Move in among the Urban Poor: A Brief History of MoveIn

By Nigel Paul

The vision of the global MoveIn movement is this: "To see thousands of regular Christians prayerfully moving in among the unreached, urban poor." This is the story of how MoveIn came to be.

I spent just four months on the *Logos II* ship, but it changed the direction of my life. I was twenty-two, and two hundred of us from all over the world lived in close quarters on that floating piece of metal. We docked in various countries in the Caribbean, and thousands of people came every day to buy books and Bibles at cut-rate prices in the ship's bookstore and to experience the novelty of the curious missions vessel in their port.

To me, the ship felt like a foretaste of heaven. We were passionate believers from forty or so countries, worshiping and serving in different ways and languages and seeking the Lord together. It felt like Revelation 7:9.

If we ever thought we were in heaven, we were quickly brought back to earth by the inevitable frictions of intense community. But we were learning together, experiencing God together, and spending hours a day in the combination of prayer, the Word, worship, and service.

Even as we were experiencing such life-giving, Spirit-filled community, God was *using* us as well. The visitors who came aboard each day were blessed. Many received Christ. Local churches were encouraged. And when work crews went out from the ship – for example, to repair homes after a devastating hurricane – communities were helped.

The beauty of it all was – and is – this: The needs in our world are immense, but those willing to *go* can make a difference and experience God powerfully in so doing. "Go into all the world," Jesus said in Matthew 28, "and make disciples of all nations." Jesus couples this commission with a promise: "And surely I am *with you* always, to the very end of the age."

When I left the ship in the spring of 2004 and returned to my home city of Toronto in Canada, I wanted everyone I met to go to the ship or something like it; to meet big needs in the world; and to see God at work in breathtaking ways. By this time, God had begun to show me two of the biggest areas of need in the world: the unreached and the poor.

Unreached peoples are Muslims, Hindus, Buddhists, and people from other faiths and traditions whose families may not have encountered someone who loves Jesus. There are more than two billion unreached people in our world today, and taking the gospel to them is our great unfinished task.

The second group of people the Lord was teaching me about was the global poor. Four billion people in our world today are poor and have not yet broken into the middle class. Of these, one billion are so poor that even an untreated toothache could end their life.

The more the Lord showed me these needs, the more it broke my heart, and the more I wanted to *go* and mobilize my peers to do the same. I used to carry small cards around to give away. On one side, the card said, *G.O.* On the other it explained: *Love God. Love Others. Go.* Without intending to, I became an unofficial mobilizer not only for Operation Mobilization (OM), on whose ship I served, but for many other mission agencies as well. I viewed them as the vehicle through which my peers could "go into all the world."

I had some success in getting people to join an agency and embark on global mission work, but I began to see how very few would go in this way: quit their jobs, raise support, and travel to a foreign land to serve. I came to realize that as few as 1 in 1,000 believers would do this. It was then that I began to ask God for something that would help mobilize the other 999.

Although my life-changing experience on the ship happened in my early twenties, I was born into a missionary legacy reaching back more than a hundred years. My great-grandfather moved with his young family to what was then Southern Rhodesia in 1905. They, then their children – my grandparents and my parents – were all missionaries in southern Africa. I was born in Zambia in 1981, the fourth of five children. I grew up there, as well as in Canada (my passport country), Kenya (at the Rift Valley Academy boarding school), and Pakistan (where my parents felt called to serve for a four-year period along the way).

After high school, I returned to Canada and, in 2003, completed a degree in Internet Business at the University of Waterloo. I chose Internet Business because I had been a hopeless entrepreneur since Grade One (when I successfully sold gravel in sandwich bags to my classmates). And – sensing global missions work in my future – I wanted to be able to work from anywhere in the world, hence the Internet focus.

As I reached adulthood, I attempted to support myself through entrepreneurship. By the age of nineteen, I had started a family-friendly website about the popular television show *Survivor* that garnered more than a million visitors and I had been interviewed about it live on America's largest morning TV show, the CBS *Early Show*. After my time on the ship, I ran an online book business.

Around this time, I applied to be the traveling assistant – or "gofer" – to OM founder George Verwer. I started in the fall of 2006. That year, I carried George's bags in three hundred meetings in twenty countries on six continents. It was a powerful window into the global church. I learned a great deal from his life – about loving others and the world, prayer, humility, brokenness, and grace. I also learned about vision: that it is possible to dream and develop a plan for something that – by God's grace and power – can impact thousands.

In 2003, my close friend Dave Sutherland – with whom I had shared many conversations about global missions – intentionally moved with his young family into the most Muslim neighborhood in Toronto, an intensely urban area where the local primary school had twenty-four kindergarten classes. Another young family joined Dave in 2007 and started a church-plant-based ministry in the neighborhood.

In 2008, after my year with George, I joined this group. Like my times with OM, it was a powerful time of community, service, and weekly prayer meetings. As George had done with me, I began to intentionally mentor younger men in this context. I also befriended and reached out to people of different faiths and backgrounds.

God was sending the nations to us in Canada, and I sensed a new opportunity for mobilization. Now, regular young believers could be cross-cultural workers without quitting their jobs, raising support, or going overseas. They would just need – prayerfully – to *move in*.

A Mission to Move In

John 1:14 says, "The Word became flesh and dwelt among us" (NKJV). *The Message* paraphrase puts it this way: "The Word became flesh and blood, and moved into the neighborhood." God walked with us in the garden, dwelled with us in the Israelite camp, and lived in our village before ultimately going to the cross. He is our example of moving in.

Another key passage for us in MoveIn is 2 Corinthians 8:9: "For you know the grace of our Lord Jesus Christ, that though he was rich, yet for your sake he became poor, so that you through his poverty might become rich." Also, Matthew 25, where Jesus identifies with the needy. And Galatians 2:10, where the pillar apostles of the New Testament church agreed that "the very thing" they should do was "remember the poor." In Luke 6:20, Jesus looked at his disciples and said, "Blessed are you who are poor, for yours is the kingdom of God."

I began to meet with people one at a time over coffee or lunch to share the new MoveIn vision God was giving me. I asked each person, "Would you be willing to move into a neighborhood that is unreached, urban, and poor? Might God be calling you to live and pray in one of these neighborhoods?" As Romans 10:14 says, how will people hear about Jesus if believers don't go?

The message was this: move into a patch with a small group of other regular people, work or study, pray weekly as a team, and follow the Lord's leading in forming relationships, sharing the good news, and serving.

To those considering moving in, I promised one other thing: there would be no paperwork. As this was something for regular people, we did not need paperwork to be a barrier.

The idea of moving in resonated with people and, one by one, they began to move in. Soon, I realized that I should probably think about sharing the vision with more than one person at a time – maybe share it at an event with a group of thirty or forty people. The idea grew. As plans began to materialize, God sent a few key helpers, including Valera (a young man from Kazakhstan who worked in information technology and had a heart to serve Muslims) and Rachel (who was working as a reporter for a daily newspaper).

The vision for the event grew to be a twenty-four-hour, Friday-to-Saturday event, and the dates were set for 8–9 May 2009. Wanting to blanket the event in prayer, we organized ten days of solid prayer leading up to and following the event, with people signing up for prayer slots throughout the day and night. During the event itself, with the help of the group called 24–7 Prayer, we rented a U-Haul to serve as an on-site, twenty-four-hour prayer room.

One of the people who most encouraged me as MoveIn was getting off the ground was Charles Price, pastor of the well-known missions church in Toronto called The Peoples Church. When Charles offered the church's sizable facilities for the MoveIn launch event, we jumped at the chance.

The day of the first MoveIn event arrived and, having initially conceived of something much smaller, we were thrilled when six hundred people came! Some who had recently moved in shared their testimonies. There was powerful worship music. I shared the MoveIn vision and spoke from Matthew 6 about "seeking first the kingdom." Toward the end of the night, I said, "Tomorrow is only for those of you who are seriously considering moving into one of these neighborhoods. If that's you, please come back tomorrow."

The next day, we were encouraged to see about a hundred people return. Through trusted friends, we interviewed participants one at a time. We had volunteers present twenty-five different MoveIn-qualifying neighborhoods, or "patches," as we sometimes refer to them. One of the volunteer presenters was a young woman by the name of Jessie. When I walked by Jessie's booth, I noticed how much work she had put into her presentation, the photos she'd taken herself, and her enthusiasm about all God was doing. I recalled how, the night before, her bright smile in the audience had caught my eye.

After lunch, the participants piled into cars and fanned out across the city to the different patches within driving distance. Afterwards, about thirty-five participants expressed a desire to move in and we commissioned them with prayer. Then the event was over. The building was empty, and whatever was in store was entirely in God's hands.

Over the course of that summer, many from the conference and others began to move in. By the end of that year, there were eight teams in eight patches, and the movement had spread to Hamilton, a city an hour or so from Toronto. By this time, we officially called the movement MoveIn and there were forty or so of us "MoveIners."

Before the conference, I had identified the neighborhood I would move into myself. Valera agreed to join me. It was Tower Park in east Toronto, a community of four 25-story high-rise buildings in a very small area known for its Bangladeshi community. What we didn't know about the neighborhood then was that there was a critical person already living there: a new believer from a Muslim background named Mama Hala.[1]

Ten days after the conference, Valera and I and a few others decided we would prayer-walk in Tower Park in preparation for moving in. Before we did so an email came in from a friend connecting us with Mama Hala. I called her and asked if we could come and pray with her that evening. At first, she was hesitant, but then she sensed the Lord leading her to say yes. At about 9 p.m. that night we found ourselves having our first prayer meeting in Mama Hala's

---

1. Some names have been changed for privacy or security reasons.

living room. Her spiritually fervent twelve-year-old daughter Sarah joined us. (We have continued to pray with Mama Hala every week since then, for thirteen years now at the time of writing.)

Valera and I moved into a three-bedroom apartment in Tower Park a few weeks after the conference, in July 2009. Somehow, we fit two bunk beds into each room, for a total of twelve beds in the apartment. The vision was to lead a discipleship center for young men that we called "the DC." Over the next few years, we would see forty young men from varied backgrounds live in this apartment for an average of a year each. By the time we initially moved in, a university student and relatively new believer of Iranian heritage named Farhad had joined us. There was also James, a student at Tyndale University who would go on to serve with Pioneers in Central Asia. Soon, an apartment for young women came together as well, including Rachel; my first administrative assistant, Joanna; Farhad's significant other, Heidi; and others. Farhad and Heidi would soon marry and be an instrumental couple on our team before later heading to Africa as missionaries.

We decided to plant a house church in our neighborhood. Wanting to set an example of accountability, I got credentialed with the Mennonite Brethren, one of the many denominations that was supporting us. As MoveIn was getting off the ground, many leaders, individuals, and groups supported us. Among them were Terry Wiseman, Gerry Dyck, Gord Martin, Gerry Organ, Harvey Thiessen, and Matthew Gibbins, who, with his wife, Rachel, joined one of the first MoveIn teams.

As we prayed weekly (late into the night in the early years) and served, we began to see people come to Christ.

One such person was Enam. I remember the day Mama Hala told us that an Israeli Muslim single mother and her three young children would be moving into Tower Park the next day and that we needed to help them move. We did not have a great attitude at short notice, but some of us found a way to help Enam move in. In the coming days and months, we spent quite a lot of time with Enam and her kids. Enam knew we were all Christians, but she was not initially open to the gospel, in part because she felt it was at odds with her faith identity. Over time, though, she found God's forgiveness and love for her irresistible, and surrendered her life to him. Enam even turned out to have the gift of evangelism, leading others in her extended family to Christ.

Meanwhile, the MoveIn vision continued to spread. In the early days we were speaking in different churches and groups on an almost daily basis. A few of these opportunities were key in the growth of MoveIn. These included the Mission Fest conferences in Toronto and Vancouver; the Moody Bible Institute

Missions Week; the Missio Nexus conference – the largest annual gathering of mission leaders in North America – where MoveIn was presented with that year's mission award for "Innovation in Mission"; the Amplify conference, hosted by the Billy Graham Center at Wheaton College and its director Ed Stetzer; and, later, the Lausanne Global Diaspora-themed conference in Manila organized by Sadiri Joy Tira.

Joy has been a champion for MoveIn since its inception, when George Verwer introduced us, and he and his wife Lulu have become close personal friends to us. In 2010 or so Joy brought a group of diaspora academics to my neighborhood, and I had the honor of hosting them for discussion and lunch. Among them were Dr. Ted Yamamori, Stanley John, Cody Lorance, Barnabas Moon, and other key people. Connected to this group, Micah Kim decided to do her PhD with Asbury Theological Seminary on MoveIn. Her dissertation was called "Missional Fidelity of MoveIn: An Intentional Christian Mission Movement to Unreached Immigrants to North America."

I had the opportunity to meet with Argentinian missiologist Dr. Luis Bush and his wife Doris. The Bushes – who coined the term "10/40 window" for the geographic swath of the world that is the most unreached – were speaking at The Peoples Church in Toronto, and I had the honor of taking them out for a Bangladeshi lunch in my neighborhood. They deeply encouraged us in MoveIn.

Another key event as MoveIn was getting going was the Lausanne Cape Town 2010 Congress, a globally representative gathering of four thousand or so Christian leaders. Many of us on the forming MoveIn staff team served behind the scenes there. It was then that I met Doug Birdsall, international director of Lausanne at the time, and Michael Oh, his successor – two vital advocates for us.

As MoveIn began, I faced a paradox in how to support the growing movement. On the one hand, this was a movement for regular people – a movement for "tentmakers" like the apostle Paul, who made tents to support himself. Yet the movement needed people to answer email enquiries, manage the logistics for resources such as Bibles and discipleship materials, help teams work through challenges, and so much more. We realized that some MoveIners would need to step out in faith to do this practical work, trusting the Lord for their financial support. Thus began our staff team, called to spread the vision, support the movement, and mobilize new teams. We call it the Vision Team.

A literal godsend in those early years was Mike Fischhoff, who joined one of the first MoveIn teams in east Toronto even before the launch conference in 2009. Mike had a pastor's heart and was gifted in logistics and management. Mike joined the Vision Team in 2010. Before long, he was the associate director, managing many of the team's activities. Mike served in this role for almost ten years, during which time the movement grew tremendously. MoveIn could not have grown as it did without Mike, Valera, and Rachel, whom I consider cofounders.

The Wedding Story

I mentioned earlier how I had noticed a young woman named Jessie at the launch conference of MoveIn. Valera had recruited her to volunteer for the conference, but our two families were already friends.

After the conference, I wanted to get to know Jessie more, so I "zoomed in on the target" (to borrow a phrase from George Verwer). She took a little while to come around, but eventually agreed to a relationship with me. Not long after, she moved into the girls' apartment in the MoveIn patch. (I lived in the next building, in the guys' apartment.) The neighborhood is predominantly Bengali, with Afghans and Sudanese – about four thousand people in total. Jessie picks up the story from here, lightly edited from when she told the story to a live audience:

> As our relationship progressed, Nigel brought up a crazy idea. He said, "Jessie, what if we got married in our neighborhood and invited all of our neighbors?" I was so excited. I could not sleep that night, mostly because Nigel had brought up the idea of getting married.
>
> I woke up the next morning and the challenges of a wedding in our neighborhood hit me. The only area that would work for the site was between two 25-story high-rise buildings beside a train track where the city train passes every two minutes. And so, I'm picturing myself getting married to Nigel, saying our vows, and a train comes, and we can't hear each other. And then the neighborhood gangs come and run off with our wedding gifts. And I'm thinking, ah, this is not a good idea.
>
> I got on my knees and had a moment of prayer about it. I opened the Bible and came across Luke 14:13–14. I just felt like the Word pierced my heart in a good way. To paraphrase it, the passage says, "When you give a banquet, invite the poor, the crippled, the lame, and the blind – those who won't repay you – and your reward will be in heaven." I just felt the Lord say, "This

is what the wedding in heaven is going to look like. And this is what I want your wedding to look like."

And so it was this beautiful moment of surrender where I just said, "OK, Lord, I give you this wedding. However it happens, I give it to you." And so, we started planning this crazy wedding.

As you can imagine, we ran into a few major obstacles. The first one was getting permission to get married in this neighborhood. We persistently asked the owner of the buildings, but he was not interested in the liabilities and everything else. So, we got on our knees, and we prayed and kept calling him. We nicknamed his secretary "the bouncer" because she would not let us through to him. We just kept praying, and by God's grace, I got through to him. I know it was the Lord because by the end of the phone call this powerful businessman said, "You know what, I don't know why I'm letting you do this but, yes, you can get married on my property. And you can name your first child 'Princess' after my company Princess Management." So, we always joked if we had a little boy named Princess, you'd know why! (But we did not use that name and we do have a little boy and we proudly named him Courage.) So, praise the Lord, we got permission.

The other big obstacle for me was that train. It's so loud and I was almost embarrassed to get married next to a train. I didn't have a solution, so I just gave it to the Lord and trusted him.

The day of our wedding came. Our neighborhood – which is in the bottom 1 percent in terms of income in the city and can be grungy – became beautiful. Our neighbors were thrilled about the wedding and hung huge paper flowers we had made over their balconies, all down the sides of the two buildings facing the wedding site. Someone described it as "buildings into bouquets." And so, the neighborhood became full of flowers.

Another part of the story is that the space was too small for everybody we wanted to invite, so we decided to have two weddings in one day! At our first wedding I walked down the aisle and looked around and there were as many as five hundred people there. The verse that came to mind was Revelation 7:9 about every tribe and nation worshiping the Lamb. We had songs and prayers in many different languages and there were people there representing probably forty different nationalities. It was a beautiful celebration. We shared our testimonies. We shared the gospel through our wedding, and it was an awesome morning.

Then it was time for the second wedding. We were on the balcony looking over at the wedding site. There were only a handful of people, and we were so embarrassed. Why did we plan two weddings in one day? Such a bad idea. We got on our knees again and we just said, "Lord, thank you for this morning. You did an incredible thing. We just give you the rest of the day. Do what you want through it. Our desire is to share your love with our neighbors."

Twenty minutes later, I walked down the aisle for the second wedding and there was no longer just a handful of people there, but several hundred! Such an encouraging answer to prayer. And we got to share the good news of Jesus with our neighborhood again.

It was awesome and we ended the day with a family-friendly dance party with fun music and hundreds of people dancing, including many kids.

To end the story, I'll tell you one answer to prayer. On the day of the wedding, there was construction at the subway station some distance from where we were getting married. Because of the construction, all the trains had to slow down just when they were passing our wedding site – so this solved the noise problem!

Praise the Lord! I am so grateful for Jessie and that the Lord caused me to notice her at the MoveIn launch conference. We often thank God for our marriage arranged in heaven!

We did not anticipate it, but our wedding story is something God has used to spread the MoveIn vision. One way is through a video that speaker and author Francis Chan produced on marriage called *You and Me Forever*. It was viewed more than two hundred thousand times online and helped spread the MoveIn vision farther.

Videos, social media, and monthly newsletters by the MoveIn Vision Team have kept the word spreading and supporters updated. There is also a weekly email called the "prayer sheet" that MoveIners receive for their encouragement, where one of the teams shares about what the Lord has been doing in their patch. MoveIners are also invited to pray for various things across the movement.

In addition to small regional gatherings for MoveIners, the Lord has given us annual events to make the movement stronger. Our annual conferences for

MoveIners began a couple of years after MoveIn began. Today, we have annual conferences in Canada and Europe, with a growing number of conferences in Latin America, the Philippines, and Indonesia. Over the years, we have been encouraged by keynote speakers such as Jackie Pullinger, Cheryl Nembhard, Peter Tarantal, Yonatan Hiruy, Viv and Iêda Grigg, Patrick and Jenny Fung, and Francis Chan.

Our largest global event is the Prayer Journey. On a single Saturday in mid-June each year, groups of believers prayer-walk, run, or cycle through MoveIn-qualifying neighborhoods, praying for more believers to move in. In 2020, the Prayer Journey had 591 participants in fifty-six locations in sixteen countries. Through this event, we raise up prayer, mobilization, and funds. In 2020 and 2021, we raised funds through the Prayer Journey to provide tens of thousands of meals for global poor families affected by the COVID-19 pandemic.

Another annual MoveIn event is Dollar-a-Day. This is a seven-day period when participants limit their spending on food and drink to just one US dollar a day, donating their savings to ministries led by MoveIners in their patches. There are daily devotionals and opportunities for reflection and prayer, especially in relation to the global poor.

Charisa's Story

The year MoveIn started, my sister Charisa was a teacher in a Southeast Asian country. She was teaching some of the wealthiest children in the country at an international school and was living in a luxury home, which was part of her remuneration package. There was a maid living there with her, and it was in a gated community.

Charisa was hearing about what God was doing as MoveIn was beginning back in Toronto and wondered what it meant for her. Our family from around the world came to spend Christmas in the country where Charisa lived. I was there and asked Charisa if we could visit a slum. She didn't know where one was, but she found a kind evangelist who took us to the poorest slum in the city – home to families who begged for a living.

As we walked into the slum, Charisa was worried about what God might ask her to do. When we entered, these beautiful people used what little they had to buy us bottles of Coke. We were treated so kindly by them.

Our family returned to our respective homes around the world. But Charisa went back to the slum the following Saturday. And then she went back again. And she even started to learn the language to the point of fluency as she sat on the floors of the people's homes. One day, Charisa asked the people in the slum a fateful question: "What would you think if I moved in here?" They responded that they would love for her to do that.

But Charisa needed the permission of the school that employed her, and the odds were not in her favor. Some of the kids at the school had three personal assistants: a nanny, a driver, and a bodyguard. So, before Charisa went to ask the principal of the school for permission to move into the slum, we mobilized prayer. She learned that the principal had to ask his boss, the superintendent of three sister schools. So, we prayed again. Amazingly, the superintendent said yes, so the principal felt free to say yes, and Charisa moved in!

Charisa was being paid about US$25,000 per year to teach at the school. She gave up her free housing, with the live-in maid, and rented a room in the slum with shared bathroom facilities for just US$50 a month. She decided to rent the next room over as well to use as a schoolroom for the children in the slum.

Charisa would get up every morning at 5:30 a.m. and drive her little motorbike through the busy streets of the city to the wealthy school where she taught. After a long, demanding day, she would return to her home in the slum. There, she was always greeted by the same sight. Outside the little schoolroom she had rented was a pile of children's dusty sandals and shoes. Inside, the children were waiting for their lesson from their only teacher in the world, Charisa.

Although she was exhausted after a full day of teaching at the wealthy school, Charisa gave what she had left to these children. And then the mosque call to prayer would ring out, and the children would scamper back to their homes. Charisa would fall into bed and wake up again the next morning at 5:30 and do it again.

After a year or so Charisa needed to leave the slum to return to Canada, where she would get married. Before leaving, she wanted to say goodbye to her many friends in the slum. She decided to rent a full-sized school bus and, with permission, took the children from the slum to the swimming pool of the wealthy school. The children had the time of their lives. When it was time to go, it was a tearful goodbye.

Back in Canada, Charisa married a wonderful young man with a heart for missions named Ben. Soon Charisa and Ben felt called to the mission field, now with a baby boy in tow. They felt called back to the same Southeast Asian country Charisa had lived in before. Eventually, the Lord led them as a family back into the very slum where Charisa had lived before!

Today, Charisa and Ben and their three kids live in the slum. Despite the hardships, the Lord has given them the joy of lifting up many of the people who live there, especially the children and teens. They have even begun to see people give their lives to Jesus. Furthermore, Charisa and Ben have had the joy of mobilizing others, mostly young national believers, to move into more slums there.

The Lord's Growth

The Lord has been faithful to grow MoveIn around the world. He raised up a Mexican young woman in Canada to take the vision back to Mexico when she returned there. The movement in Latin America has now spread to Guatemala, El Salvador, Brazil, Chile, Colombia, and Venezuela. A young man from a city two hours outside Toronto left Canada to pioneer MoveIn in the Philippines. He moved into a slum, learned Tagalog fluently, and married a Filipina. Together, they lead MoveIn Philippines. There are now several Filipino MoveIners on four different teams in three different regions of the Philippines.

MoveIn began in the UK and Europe in 2010. In the UK, students from Oxford University were among the first MoveIners, including my own brother, Ted. In Germany, a partnership with OM led to an OM-MoveIn team. Today, there are almost a hundred MoveIners in Europe, including in Portugal, Sweden, France, and Albania. We are indebted to leaders such as Evi Rodemann who support the movement in Europe.

In Canada and the US, MoveIn spans from Vancouver and Los Angeles through Edmonton, Calgary, Winnipeg, Toronto, Ottawa, Montreal, and Halifax.

Today, there are just shy of four hundred MoveIners on eighty-five teams in forty-five cities in sixteen countries. All told, we have seen about 1,100 move in over the thirteen years since MoveIn began.

The COVID-19 pandemic proved to be a headwind for our movement, slowing our growth for a period, even as the Lord continued to work powerfully in different ways. While he enables us to persevere through the trying times, we anticipate with excitement the seasons of flourishing ahead.

As a movement today, we recognize eighty-five thousand people in our patches and know twenty-two thousand by name. We believe hundreds have come to Christ and thousands have been helped.

The MoveIn story itself is one of God's faithfulness. Long ago, Jesus moved into the neighborhood. Today, we can do the same. In doing so, we are joining our Lord, who is always there before us, active and working. May thousands more move in to join him. And may thousands more encounter him through those who do.

10

Pentecostal Holistic Mission: Looking Back and Looking Forward

By Wonsuk Ma

The publication of *Global Pentecostalism*[1] by Donald Miller and Ted Yamamori occurred around the time when Pentecostal mission thinking was expanding to embrace what was called "holistic mission." The aim of this study is to explore areas to bring Pentecostal holistic mission, both in practice and in academic reflection, into the next level of maturity. Below I share an overview of the development of Pentecostal holistic mission, sample two contributions from outsiders, and identify challenges to further develop Pentecostal holistic mission. I conclude with several general issues for further attention. Through this study, I wish to express my appreciation for Ted's lifelong work for the poor.

Development of Pentecostal Holistic Mission
Intuitive Holism

It is now commonly understood that the Pentecostal movement has maintained a strong focus on its mission from inception. As Allan Anderson demonstrates, various global epic centers of Pentecostalism shared both revival and mission

---

1. Donald E. Miller and Tetsunao Yamamori, *Global Pentecostalism: The New Face of Christian Social Engagement* (Berkeley: University of California Press, 2007).

emphases.² For example, the Mukti Revival (1904) began at the children's homes founded and operated by the high-caste Pandita Ramabai (1858–1922). In this mission setting, a revival broke out among the girls, and naturally it continued its strong mission focus.³ The Azusa Street Mission (1906–9), led by William Seymour, shaped a critical theological impetus by bringing the baptism of the Holy Spirit, an eschatological urgency of the imminent return of the Lord, and a drive for mission to save as many souls as possible in the last hour. Gary McGee estimated that approximately two hundred missionaries had gone out from the United States by 1910.⁴ Although signs and wonders were celebrated, the sense of God's call, the Spirit's empowerment, and the sheer commitment of the missionaries to the Great Commission set the unique paradigm of Pentecostal mission.

In many mission settings, however, Pentecostal missionaries have been deeply involved in caring for those who suffer hardship. Their responses have depended on the presented needs, from caring for the sick to community development programs to lessening or alleviating poverty. Their intuitive empathy for the suffering may have come from their poorer status, as early Pentecostals were drawn from lower social strata.

Most Pentecostal missionaries regularly offered this care ministry as an integral part of their missionary work. From a theoretical point of view, this component of mission was often understood as a conduit to evangelism, the goal of mission. In fact, large and small "healing crusades" by Pentecostal evangelists have often dotted cities and towns of the world. Divine healing has been a popular theme when preaching evangelistic messages. In Pentecostal mission practice, from the start Pentecostals have embraced both supernatural healing and healing through loving care, although some earlier communities refused the use of medicine.

Some mercy operations have grown with the necessary institutional structure. For example, Mark and Huldah Buntain's Mission of Mercy in Calcutta evolved from church planting and now comprises nine hundred churches and more than a hundred schools with thirty-five thousand students each year. They feed twenty-five thousand people each day in schools and

---

2. Allan Anderson, *An Introduction to Pentecostalism: Global Charismatic Christianity* (Cambridge: Cambridge University Press, 2004).

3. Allan Anderson, "Pandita Ramabai, the Mukti Revival and Global Pentecostalism," *Transformation: An International Journal of Holistic Mission Studies* 23, no. 1 (Jan. 2006): 37–48.

4. Gary McGee, "Missions, Overseas (North American Pentecostal)," in *The New International Dictionary of Pentecostal and Charismatic Movements*, eds. Stanley M. Burgess and Eduard M. van der Maas (Grand Rapids: Zondervan, 2002), 888.

on the streets and have a hospital and clinics (with a nursing college) that provide much-needed medical care to the poor for free. At the 1989 funeral of Mark Buntain, twenty thousand people paid homage as his funeral procession passed various streets of Calcutta.[5] Ivan Satyavrata, the first national leader of the ministry, succinctly provides the biblical, theological, and philosophical framework for the integration of evangelism and social concern for Pentecostal mission.[6] Lillian Thrasher (1887–1961) in Egypt was another early heroic missionary who integrated care and evangelism with unrelenting devotion and effectiveness.

Academic Reflections

Although this care element had been an integral part of Pentecostal mission practice from its inception, it was only in the last quarter of the twentieth century that serious scholarly reflections began to appear, treating the "care" component as a valid mission agenda. This development almost mirrored the development of the holistic mission thinking among evangelicals from the 1970s. It began with the 1974 Lausanne Congress, when a group who were later termed "radical evangelicals," especially in the Majority World, raised a serious theological and practical question regarding the relationship between evangelization and social justice.[7] This voice was later encapsulated in the formation of the International Fellowship of Mission Theologians in the Two-Thirds World (INFEMIT), which also established a training and research institution (the Oxford Centre for Mission Studies in 1983) and a publishing operation (both *Transformation* journal and Regnum Books International).

With their regional partners, they have successfully advanced holistic mission as the essential component of evangelical mission.[8] The 2010 Lausanne Congress in Cape Town demonstrated this accomplishment as plenary speakers regularly presented many contextual cases which combined evangelism and

---

5. For a recent study, see Julie C. Ma, "Touching Lives of People through the Holistic Mission Work of the Buntains in Calcutta, India," *International Bulletin of Mission Research* 40, no. 1 (Jan. 2016): 72–83. Also see Sarah Breed, "Mercy in Calcutta," *Charisma* magazine, 13 March 2014, https://www.charismamag.com/life/social-justice/19990-mercy-in-calcutta.

6. Ivan Satyavrata, *Pentecostals and the Poor: Reflections from the Indian Context* (Baguio City: APTS Press, 2017).

7. For the full historical development of radical evangelicalism, see Al Tizon, *Transformation after Lausanne: Radical Evangelical Mission in Global-Local Perspective* (Oxford: Regnum, 2008).

8. Ian E. Woolnoug and Wonsuk Ma, eds., *Holistic Mission: God's Plan for God's People*, Regnum Edinburgh Centenary Series 5 (Oxford: Regnum, 2010). This book showcases the institution's leading role in the development of holistic mission studies.

social engagement as two sides of one coin. Doug Birdsall, the international director of the movement at the gathering, was completing his PhD study at the Oxford Centre on the movement's development as it engaged with three partners, one of which was INFEMIT.[9]

About a generation later Pentecostals followed the evangelical path in theorizing their version of holistic mission. The publication of *Called and Empowered* (1991) signaled the turning point in holistic mission thinking. Organized by Murray Dempster, Byron Klaus, and Doug Petersen of the Vanguard University of Southern California, the volume provides a biblical and theological foundation, challenging Pentecostals to expand their mission thinking beyond evangelism, church planting, and ministerial training. Petersen, one of the "Vanguard Three," completed his PhD work through the Oxford Centre for Mission Studies in 1995 by successfully defending his dissertation, "A Pentecostal Theology of Social Concern in Central America." As a missionary to Latin America who led Latin America Childcare (now renamed "ChildHope"), his research was based on this vast educational program as an example of Pentecostal holistic mission.

In 1996, the three organized an international conference in Costa Rica that involved Pentecostal mission scholars and practitioners, Latin American evangelical scholars, and leaders of the Oxford Centre for Mission Studies.[10] In 1998, the Brussels Consultation of the Division of Foreign Missions of the (US) Assemblies of God took place. Although the consultation document gives the impression that the missions arm of the US Assemblies of God organized this, the main impetus may have come from the Oxford Centre for Mission Studies and the Vanguard Three, as the document was published a year later in the Centre's journal, *Transformation*.[11] The series of initiatives by the "radical" Pentecostal mission leaders clearly implied a close connection with the "radical evangelical" mission thinking from the Oxford Centre. Their persistent pursuit of Pentecostal holistic mission finally resulted in the revision of the constitution and bylaws of the US Assemblies of God by adding "showing love" and "serving

---

9. S. Douglas Birdsall, "Conflict and Collaboration: A Narrative History and Analysis of the Interface between the Lausanne Committee for World Evangelization and the World Evangelical Fellowship, the International Fellowship of Evangelical Mission Theologians, and the AD 2000 Movement" (PhD diss., Oxford Centre for Mission Studies/Middlesex University, 2012).

10. The conference presentations were later published in a book: Murray Dempster, Byron D. Klaus, and Douglas Petersen, eds., *The Globalization of Pentecostalism: A Religion Made to Travel* (Oxford: Regnum, 1999).

11. Brussels Consultation of the Division of Foreign Missions of the Assemblies of God, "Brussels Statement on Evangelization and Social Concern," *Transformation* 16, no. 2 (1999): 41–43.

(the poor and suffering)" to the strategies for mission.[12] This overview is an internal perspective positioning care of holistic ministry in the development of Pentecostal mission practice and thinking.

Intentional Operations

In recent decades, we have witnessed more systematic Pentecostal social services programs throughout the world. One example is PENTSOS (Pentecost Social Services), a social service and development arm of the Church of Pentecost, Ghana. Established in 1979 under a different name, its website lists four major areas of service: development and relief, health service, education, and a cooperative society for mutual support and social services.[13] It also works with Lead Afrique International to run its character-building program "Mandate and Focus," which contributes to the overall well-being of members of The Church of Pentecost and the citizenry of the nation at large, and extends "to the mission fields" of the denomination outside Ghana. PENTSOS is led by lay leaders and has contributed to the establishment of ninety Pentecostal schools, one vocational training school, two senior high schools, two skills learning and development centers, and eight health care facilities, including three hospitals. It serves the vision and mission of its denomination, the Church of Pentecost. It does not disclose its financial data.

A second example is found in North America. The most representative diakonic operation in the US Assemblies of God is Convoy of Hope, based in Springfield, Missouri, the same city where the denomination's headquarters is located. Established in 1994 by Hal Donaldson, the organization serves "real needs in communities" with love and compassion. Its website lists six specific areas of service: women's empowerment, disaster services, community events, agriculture, rural initiatives, and children's feeding. It reports more than 193 million people served since its founding, over 550 disaster responses both in the US and worldwide, and almost half a million children fed. It now operates in 127 countries with $368.8 million in revenue.[14]

A third example is in Asia. Yoido Full Gospel Church of Seoul, Korea, was founded by David Yonggi Cho and established in 1999 as a nongovernment

---

12. General Council of the Assemblies of God, *Minutes of the 53rd Session of the General Council of the Assemblies of God* (Springfield: General Council of the Assemblies of God, 2009).

13. PENTSOS, https://pentsos.org/.

14. Convoy of Hope, "Initiatives & Campaigns," https://convoyofhope.org/initiatives/.

organization called Good People International. As an international humanitarian relief and development organization, it is

> dedicated to raising voice about the situation of the vulnerable people around the world who are exposed to the extreme danger of poverty, diseases, disaster and providing systematic and professional aid regardless of ethnicity and nationality. We implement various programs for the people in need in many countries around the world, including child protection, education, water, sanitation and hygiene, disease prevention and treatment, community development, emergency relief, etc.[15]

Local programs include more than 1.1 million medical services and partnerships with 130 group homes and thirteen community centers. Its international operations include health and medical service, education, water/sanitation, income generation projects, and others through twenty-four field offices in sixteen countries, all in Africa, Asia, and the Caribbean. It also conducts emergency relief operations in disaster areas. Its financial report is not included in its publicity.

Each of these three full-scale "care and serve" operations has been shaped by its social circumstances and needs. Their beginnings are also different: by an individual (for Convoy of Hope), a megachurch (The Good People), and a denomination (PENTSOS), perhaps reflecting their cultural contexts. While these high-profile programs have been formed and developed, we need to remember that hundreds or even thousands of small-scale Pentecostal initiatives are also in operation all over the world. For instance, in Malaysia, large and small Pentecostal churches run addiction programs, orphanages, homes for the elderly, and even dialysis centers. Also, more studies on Pentecostal holistic mission are appearing, indicating the maturity of its practices and theories.[16]

"Progressive" or "Holistic"? External Discussions
David Martin

While Pentecostals were pushing the boundaries of mission from "soul-saving" to "caring," outsiders, particularly social scientists, published their findings. Starting with the spread of Pentecostalism in Latin America from the 1960s,

---

15. Good People International, "Good People Make the Good World," https://www.goodpeople.or.kr/assets/GOOD_PEOPLE_PR_BROCHURE_ENG.pdf.

16. For the latest publication, see Wonsuk Ma, Opoku Onyinah, and Rebekah Bled, eds., *Good News to the Poor: Spirit-Empowered Responses to Poverty* (Tulsa, OK: ORU Press, 2022).

David Martin analyzed the development of this sector of Christianity in the predominantly Catholic religious landscape, and probed the reasons for its success. One of his observations was the strong appeal of the Pentecostal faith to the poor and deprived. As this faith brought transformation to their attitude to life, their personal life, and their work habits, their economic level rose and their family life improved. This force, nourishing a "new sense of individuality and individual worth," brought transformation to all Pentecostal believers, especially as we consider the area of economics.[17] However, Martin also observed trends among those who achieved a new socioeconomic status that would hinder the movement's continuing cycle of transformative effect. We will revisit this later.

"Progressive Pentecostalism"

Miller and Yamamori's *Global Pentecostalism* fits squarely with the ongoing development of Pentecostal holistic mission, both in practice and in reflection, and the growing attention it has received from non-Pentecostal academia. This research's contribution to the study of Pentecostal mission is significant.

First, the authors, who were not Pentecostal members, did not start the project with Pentecostals in mind. As presented in the book, they had established the following selection criteria: the Christian communities should (1) be fast-growing, (2) be in the Majority World, (3) have active social programs addressing needs in their communities, and (4) be indigenous movements that were self-supporting and not dependent on outside contributions. When they analyzed the churches and organizations which met the requirements, they discovered that nearly 85 percent were Pentecostal or charismatic.[18] The book affirmed the long-held assumption that caring for the suffering was inherent in the Pentecostal mission tradition.

Second, the book indirectly points to the unique spiritual source which gave birth to Pentecostal social programs, and which sustained them toward greater success. That said, Miller and Yamamori insisted on their journalistic stance with the sociology of religion in their scholarly toolbox.[19] They freely quote statements made by the community members and leaders as their unique Pentecostal spiritual experiences; these included hearing from the Lord as

---

17. David Martin, *Tongues of Fire: The Explosion of Protestantism in Latin America* (Oxford: Blackwell, 1993), 232.
18. Miller and Yamamori, *Global Pentecostalism*, 8.
19. Miller and Yamamori, 7.

the primary motivation for their social programs. The interview with Mama Maggie of Cairo, Egypt, is a good example and full of her theological beliefs and experiences.[20] It is hard to imagine that the selected Pentecostal church was the only Christian church in the given area that was facing the same challenges every day. The question is: What made this particular Pentecostal church respond to the common challenges while others did not?

At least two points may be considered. Pentecostals from the beginning have been known to be the "poor." The assumption is that the poor understand the plight of their fellow poor. Now convinced that they have gained a special status in God's kingdom (and in society), their next action is to share this "good news" with the other poor. The other source of their action could be their unique Pentecostal experiential spirituality: empowerment through baptism in the Holy Spirit. These two factors, and others, may give birth to a certain theological understanding of their identity facing the problems.

Third, in each of the Pentecostal churches or organizations, the role of leadership features prominently. Although the Pentecostal belief in the empowerment of the Holy Spirit for every believer has a democratizing effect for ministry, the role of visionaries and leaders is the hallmark of the countless religious enterprises initiated by Pentecostals. Examples include Oral Roberts, who pioneered preaching through TV, and David Yonggi Cho, who founded Yoido Full Gospel Church, the largest single congregation in the world.[21] Their leadership in ministry is often against many odds, demanding their enduring persistence and tenacity that can come only from an outside source – in this case, the Holy Spirit. Applying the same logic that we used above, one may argue that not all Pentecostal or charismatic churches and communities automatically initiate and maintain the same enterprising care ministries. There may be other Pentecostal or charismatic congregations in the same area or areas facing similar challenges. Elsewhere I have highlighted the significance of leadership in the shaping of Asian Pentecostal-charismatic ecclesiology.[22]

Miller and Yamamori's book confirmed these points by singling out three major contributing factors to the innovative social services of the Pentecostal communities: the size of the congregation, the theological view of the pastor

---

20. Miller and Yamamori, 57–58.

21. See, for example, Dean Miller, *50 Pentecostal and Charismatic Leaders Every Christian Should Know* (Minneapolis: Chosen Books, 2021).

22. Wonsuk Ma, "Two Tales of Emerging Ecclesiology in Asia: An Inquiry into Theological Shaping," in *The Church from Every Tribe and Tongue: Ecclesiology in the Majority World*, eds. Gene L. Green, Stephen T. Pardue, and K. K. Yeo, Majority World Theology Series 5 (Carlisle: Langham Global Library, 2018), 53–73.

and people, and the social and political context of the country.[23] The book has served Pentecostal mission by affirming its ethos and theological assumptions by presenting many global Pentecostal communities. It also challenges Pentecostal mission thinkers and practitioners to bring clarity to the locus of holistic social engagement within the broader mission discussion. We now turn to them.

Closing the Loop

What is the "remaining task" for Pentecostal holistic mission? I like to place it in the model of three concentric circles of Pentecostal mission to identify several areas needing further reflection. Figure 10.1 identifies the inner core representing both the motivation and the goal of Pentecostal mission, the first layer as evangelism (saving souls), the second as holistic *diakonia* (caring for the suffering), and the third being justice (righting wrongs).[24] Holistic

Figure 10.1

---

23. Miller and Yamamori, *Global Pentecostalism*, 53.

24. For more discussion, see Julie C. Ma and Wonsuk Ma, *Mission in the Spirit: Towards a Pentecostal/Charismatic Missiology*, Regnum Studies in Mission (Oxford: Regnum, 2010); Wonsuk Ma and Julie C. Ma, "Missiology: Evangelization, Holistic Ministry, and Social Justice," in *Routledge Handbook of Pentecostal Theology*, ed. Wolfgang Vondey (London: Routledge, 2020), 279–89.

mission occupies the middle of this three-tier structure of Pentecostal mission. It serves a crucial role in developing the third circle – justice mission – and in maintaining the integrity of Pentecostal mission. Borrowing the analogy of the Trinity, these three form the one reality, Pentecostal mission, while each serves a distinct function. This section will highlight three areas for further development: challenges of holistic mission, its goal, and the source of motivation and sustainability.

Challenges of Holistic Mission

The challenges of Pentecostal holistic mission stem from a discussion which can be summarized in two questions: whether a focus on care will take attention and resources away from evangelism, the priority of Pentecostal mission, and whether it will expand to become what is called the "social gospel." This debate again parallels the process that evangelical mission discussions have undergone in the past. The very word "(w)holistic" has served as a corrective to the exclusive focus on evangelism by insisting on social service as another "pillar of mission."[25]

After the monumental declaration by the Lausanne Movement, an intense debate followed that boiled down to a hegemony war between the evangelism camp (predominantly from North America) and the holistic camp (mainly from the Global South) in the 1970s and 1980s. The genesis of the Lausanne Movement was to establish an alternative and more evangelical mission movement away from the social gospel of ecumenical missiology that was developed by the International Missionary Council and later the Commission of World Mission and Evangelism of the World Council of Churches.[26] Thus, the concern about another form of the social gospel is completely understandable. On the other hand, the holistic mission camp adamantly insisted that the reality and voice of what was traditionally viewed as the "mission field" should be an integral part of evangelical mission. The matter was settled through a gradual process, as witnessed in the 2010 Cape Town gathering, and the growth of Christianity in the Global South was the main contributor.

---

25. Lausanne Movement, "The Lausanne Covenant," https://lausanne.org/content/covenant/lausanne-covenant#cov.

26. For a collection on the development of and reflections on ecumenical missiology, see Kenneth R. Ross, Jooseop Keum, Kyriaki Avtzi, and Roderick R. Hewitt, eds., *Ecumenical Missiology: Changing Landscapes and New Conceptions of Mission*, Regnum Edinburgh Centenary Series 35 (Oxford: Regnum, 2016).

In the Pentecostal mission circle, I heard one US career missionary to Asia raise a concern that the unusual appeal for compassion operations would divide the sole attention of the churches given to evangelism, church planting, and training. This has to do with the relationship between the two inner circles – evangelism and holistic mission. The discussion below will explore a conceptual solution to this challenge. In the meantime, at least two areas may also provide some direction toward the solution. One is the experience of Pentecostal mission where "intuitive holism" has contributed to evangelism and growth.[27] This experience is analogous to how Jesus's compassion ministry, although through supernatural means, provided an occasion to proclaim God's kingdom. The other is the social reality where open evangelism is simply impossible, leaving only two options: witnessing through compassionate action and living out the gospel.

The second issue is a legitimate concern: whether care ministry will lead Pentecostal mission toward the social gospel. This matters to the relationship between the two outer circles – holistic mission and justice mission. Over the years, the church has witnessed the emergence of radical mission movements such as liberation theology, which has accommodated violent means to achieve a just society. While this issue-focused mission gave birth to the social gospel movement, the church also shared responsibility, as the dominant and conservative churches failed to address the plight of the poor and the oppression of the powerful. The "engine room" discussion below attempts to address this.

The Lordship of Christ: The Goal

What is the difference between Christian holistic mission and the work of secular nongovernmental organizations (NGO)? This question concerns the motivation, resources, and outcomes of the mission process. Pentecostal mission shares with its evangelical counterpart the conviction that the kingdom of God is the governing principle.[28] Bringing the reign of God into individual and community life through the redeeming work of Christ is the final purpose and goal of Christianity; hence Pentecostal mission. Pentecostalism has been

---

27. For example, Joel A. Tejedo, "Pentecostal Civic Engagement in the Squatter Area," in *Good News to the Poor: Spirit-Empowered Responses to Poverty*, eds. Wonsuk Ma, Opoku Onyinah, and Rebekah Bled (Tulsa: ORU Press, 2022), 321–44.

28. For example, *Called and Empowered* includes three chapters on the kingdom of God and mission. Murray Dempster, Byron Klaus, and Douglas Petersen, *Called and Empowered: Global Mission in Pentecostal Perspective* (Ada: Baker Academic, 1991).

unapologetically christological in its doctrinal expression. An example is the Wesleyan stream of Pentecostalism: Christ as the Savior, (Spirit) Baptizer, Healer, Sanctifier, and the Coming King.[29]

Accordingly, all three layers of Pentecostal mission should point to the centrality of Christ's lordship as the redeemer of lost humanity. Our focus, thus, should go beyond the relationship between evangelism and holistic mission, as both (and all three) should ultimately bring people to Christ's lordship. This allows each layer to function as a unique expression of mission, while enriching others.

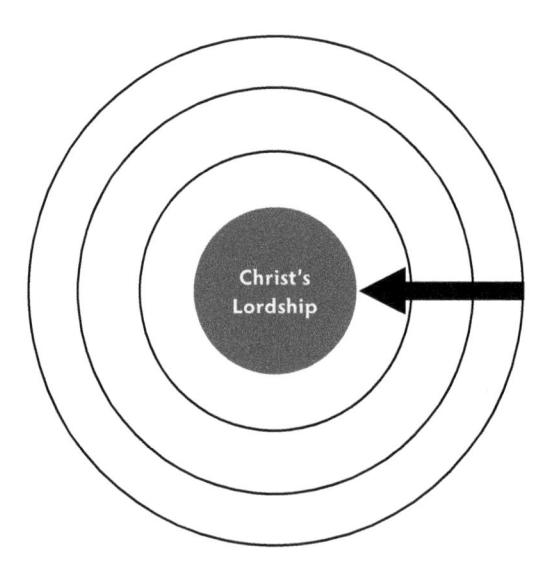

Figure 10.2

Regarding the relationship between evangelism and holistic mission, *Global Pentecostalism* indirectly affirmed the connection as one of the criteria that the churches were growing (in number), even though Miller and Yamamori excluded communities that used social services explicitly for evangelism purposes.[30] We can admit that growth can be due to various reasons, but one cannot help but assume that their social outreaches had a strong witnessing component, resulting in the numerical growth of the faith communities. The recently reported "breakthrough" among the Bhojpuri people in India is a

---

29. Non-Wesleyan traditions drop the "Sanctifier," while some further modify (e.g. Korean Assemblies of God substitute "Sanctifier" with "Blesser"). See Wonsuk Ma, "David Yonggi Cho's Theology of Blessing: Basis, Legitimacy, and Limitations," *Evangelical Review of Theology* 35, no. 2 (2011): 140–43.

30. Miller and Yamamori, *Global Pentecostalism*, 2.

good case where evangelism and social service work seamlessly strengthen each other and bring Christ's lordship to millions.[31] This is particularly true as Miller and Yamamori reviewed churches in the Global South, some of which were in areas where open evangelism was not permitted.

This connection is also attested to by non-Christian authorities because Christian relief operations often face restrictions. For instance, Christian organizations involved in the relief operation after the Banda Aceh tsunami were specifically required by the Indonesian government not to include any religious activities. This Muslim nation understood that Christians had used social service as an evangelistic tool. In a different way, the limitations may be self-imposed. During the Syrian refugee crisis in Europe, the German church went through a heated debate about whether it was "ethical" to take advantage of the vulnerability of the refugees to seek to convert them to Christianity.[32]

To Pentecostals, however, compassionate work that is disconnected from evangelistic intent violates the ultimate purpose of their mission. All three layers should point to and contribute to submission to Christ's lordship. If Christ's love and his command (e.g. Matt 22:39) motivate or even compel believers to care for others, the same should also urge believers to share the good news of his redemption. This sets Christian care ministry apart from secular NGOs.

The Empowerment of the Holy Spirit: The "Engine Room" of Pentecostal Mission

As discussed above, the work of the Holy Spirit sets Pentecostal social engagement apart from its evangelical counterpart, although the two share many commonalities. This pneumato-centric motivation, however, does not replace the traditional Christocentric focus of all the Christian traditions.

For all three layers of Pentecostalism, the empowering presence of the Holy Spirit should be a common motivation. Here, "empowerment" is used as a shorthand to include the breadth of religious experience. It assumes the sense of election that the Lord has called an individual or community for a specific purpose. Then, through the unique Pentecostal experience of baptism

---

31. Victor John and Dave Coles, *Bhojpuri Breakthrough: A Movement That Keeps Multiplying* (Monument: WIGTake Resources, 2019).

32. See Tom Heneghan, "German Christians Disagree about Evangelizing to Muslim Refugees," Sojourners, 30 October 2015, https://sojo.net/articles/german-christians-disagree-about-evangelizing-muslim-refugees.

in the Holy Spirit, the believers receive "power" to be effective in witnessing to Christ's lordship. They are then sent to the ends of the earth to carry out this mission (Acts 1:8). This affirms the absolute place of believers in God's mission.

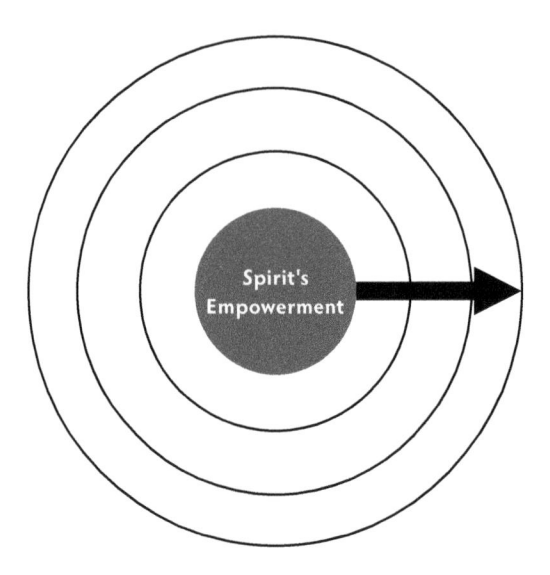

Figure 10.3

In many settings, the very presence of a Christian whose life has been radically transformed through the empowering presence of the Holy Spirit serves a missional purpose. To those who search for the meaning of life, there is no better demonstration of God's good news than a changed life. The sense of God's calling motivates believers to serve those who are in need. The messianic declaration of Jesus often serves as the motivation:

> The Spirit of the Lord is on me,
> because he has anointed me
> to proclaim good news to the poor.
> He has sent me to proclaim freedom for the prisoners
> and recovery of sight for the blind,
> to set the oppressed free,
> to proclaim the year of the Lord's favor. (Luke 4:18–19)

The Spirit's anointing is the primary driving motivation for Jesus to proclaim good news to those who are suffering and marginalized. Similarly, the prophet is called, empowered by God's Spirit, and sent to establish justice in the nations (Isa 42:1–4). This passage also depicts the outcome of the Spirit's presence:

commitment to the task, resilience in the face of adversity, and sensitivity to the powerless.³³

Perhaps the most important characteristic may be the continuing cycle of empowerment. Once a "nobody," but transformed by the Spirit and reaching out to others, the Christian now reproduces Spirit-empowered believers to continue this cycle of empowerment. This is the genius of Pentecostal mission. A recent study of Aimara indigenous people in Bolivia illustrates this. Many migrant Aimaras in urban centers such as La Paz found neo-Pentecostal churches a conducive environment to shape their new identity. Using the Power of God Church as a case, Marcelo Vargas concludes that the ethos of its community life, worship, and mission helps urban Aimaras to adapt to the new Christian faith without abandoning their Aimara worldview.³⁴ These "empowered" Aimara believers, in turn, assist others in successfully adapting to the new lifestyle.

This pneumatological missiology may help Pentecostals to negotiate the challenge that David Martin observed among Latin American Pentecostals. When Pentecostals are no longer poor but instead are powerful, how can they still identify with the poor? This, in other words, is an issue of power, calling for a healthy balance between Pentecostalism's ability to expand among the masses by remaining of the masses, and its ability to advance their condition. Martin rightly pointed out that this balancing act is easier said than done: "If the former [the 'no longer poor'] remains powerful, the latter [the 'poor'] must operate at the margin."³⁵ Prosperity teaching breeds the unending appetite for more gains for "me." The Spirit's empowerment as the overall motivation for mission would allow believers to interpret their socioeconomic improvement as part of the Spirit's empowerment for witnessing.

The two preceding discussions bring strength and clarity to Pentecostal holistic mission. The christological focus guides all three layers to point to the same goal, thus fostering the interlayer resourcing and differentiating it from NGOs. The pneumatological focus adds distinctives to the motivation, ethos, and goal of Pentecostal holistic mission. This completes the full picture of the *missio Dei*, God's mission. God the Father wills and plans the restoration of fallen humanity and his creation by sending his Son as the redeeming sacrifice. God

---

33. See Wonsuk Ma, "Prophetic Servant: Ideology of Spirit-Empowered Leaders," *Spiritus: ORU Journal of Theology* 5, no. 2 (Fall 2020): 225, 228.

34. Marcelo Vargas, "The Aimara Identity of Poor Neo-Pentecostals in Urban La Paz, Bolivia," in Ma et al., *Good News to the Poor*, 157–75.

35. Martin, *Tongues of Fire*, 232.

the Son fulfilled the requirement of redemption by giving his own life and sending his people to the world with good news. God the Holy Spirit glorifies and fulfills the work of Christ by empowering his people to live victoriously and to go where they are sent to witness to Christ's salvation.

Conclusion

To conclude I want to mention questions raised by *Global Pentecostalism* and touch on the third layer of Pentecostal mission.

Lingering Questions

There are two questions I will discuss. The first is the thorny issue of the prosperity gospel in some sectors of Pentecostal-charismatic Christianity. In a significant way, the studies of Martin and Miller and Yamamori contrast with each other. The former's concern represents empowered or blessed Pentecostals continually seeking more for themselves to the point that they forget how to deal with the poor. The extreme expression of this self-centered desire for material blessing is the prosperity gospel.

However, the latter study presents those who have been empowered/blessed as now reaching out to those who suffer. What would it take for the church to help believers be good stewards of blessing? This certainly touches on the issue of discipleship. On the practical side, learning from positive examples around us will always help. One example may be a group of Pentecostal businesspeople who have overcome the lure of capitalism and submitted their lives and riches to the lordship of Christ. Demos Shakarian, an Armenian refugee to Southern California, became a successful dairy farmer. He later organized the Full Gospel Businessmen's Fellowship International to empower businesspeople to experience the Holy Spirit and learn to steward their assets for God's mission. The organization played an important role in the growth of the charismatic movement in the States.[36]

The second question is the continuity issue. Miller and Yamamori presented the prominent position that the leaders occupied in each case-study church. When the founding visionary leader has moved on, what happens to the holistic mission operation? Among Pentecostal care programs, often the program itself disappears once the champion or missionary is gone. One way to address this

---

36. Demos Shakarian, John L. Sherrill, and Elizabeth Sherrill, *The Happiest People on the Earth: The Long-Awaited Personal Story of Demos Shakarian* (Old Tappan: Chosen Books, 1975).

issue is institutionalization, as seen in The Good People by Yoido Full Gospel Church and PENTSOS of the Church of Pentecost, Ghana. It would make an interesting study to follow up the same churches after two decades to check their sustainability. In a different way, Mercy of Calcutta successfully continues its massive operation after the era of the American founding couple, and the Buntain Foundation still raises needed funds from the States.

The Third Layer

The outer circle of Pentecostal mission may be called "justice mission." This may be described as "righting wrongs." If holistic mission is caring for the suffering, justice mission is tracing the roots of the system that continually yields victims, and addressing it. Pentecostals have not yet openly discussed this dimension as part of their mission thinking and practice. As in holistic mission, however, Pentecostals have intuitively engaged with various issues. Providing education to those who would not otherwise have the opportunity is one example. Ramabai of a high caste confronted the social system by pioneering girls' education, especially of lower castes or untouchables, against the social norm. Sometimes, justice mission can be an outgrowth of holistic mission. But it will require a robust discussion as it includes very difficult issues such as oppressive regimes, systematic corruption, unjust economic systems, gender inequality, and many more.

Such engagements will take Pentecostal mission into the public space, and it is doubtful if Pentecostals are ready. Scholarly debates on public theology among Pentecostals are, therefore, encouraging.[37] However we move forward, Christ's lordship is the goal and the Spirit's empowerment is the primary motivation. How both equally guide to justice mission is to be seen.

References

Anderson, Allan. *An Introduction to Pentecostalism: Global Charismatic Christianity*. Cambridge: Cambridge University Press, 2004.
———. "Pandita Ramabai, the Mukti Revival and Global Pentecostalism." *Transformation: An International Journal of Holistic Mission Studies* 23, no. 1 (Jan. 2006): 37–48.

---

37. For example, Amos Yong, *In the Days of Caesar: Pentecostalism and Political Theology* (Grand Rapids: Eerdmans, 2010).

Birdsall, S. Douglas. "Conflict and Collaboration: A Narrative History and Analysis of the Interface between the Lausanne Committee for World Evangelization and the World Evangelical Fellowship, the International Fellowship of Evangelical Mission Theologians, and the AD 2000 Movement. PhD diss., Oxford Centre for Mission Studies/Middlesex University, 2012.

Breed, Sarah. "Mercy in Calcutta." *Charisma* magazine, 13 March 2014. https://www.charismamag.com/life/social-justice/19990-mercy-in-calcutta.

Brussels Consultation of the Division of Foreign Missions of the Assemblies of God. "Brussels Statement on Evangelization and Social Concern." *Transformation* 16, no. 2 (1999): 41–43.

Dempster, Murray, Byron D. Klaus, and Douglas Petersen, eds. *Called and Empowered: Global Mission in Pentecostal Perspective*. Ada: Baker Academic, 1991.

———. *The Globalization of Pentecostalism: A Religion Made to Travel*. Oxford: Regnum, 1999.

General Council of the Assemblies of God. *Minutes of the 53rd Session of the General Council of the Assemblies of God*. Springfield: General Council of the Assemblies of God, 2009.

Good People International. "Good People Make the Good World." https://www.goodpeople.or.kr/assets/GOOD_PEOPLE_PR_BROCHURE_ENG.pdf.

Heneghan, Tom. "German Christians Disagree about Evangelizing to Muslim Refugees." Sojourners, 30 October 2015. https://sojo.net/articles/german-christians-disagree-about-evangelizing-muslim-refugees.

John, Victor, and Dave Coles. *Bhojpuri Breakthrough: A Movement That Keeps Multiplying*. Monument: WIGTake Resources, 2019.

Ma, Julie C. "Touching Lives of People through the Holistic Mission Work of the Buntains in Calcutta, India." *International Bulletin of Mission Research* 40, no. 1 (Jan. 2016): 72–83.

Ma, Julie C., and Wonsuk Ma. *Mission in the Spirit: Towards a Pentecostal/Charismatic Missiology*. Regnum Studies in Mission. Oxford: Regnum, 2010.

Ma, Wonsuk. "David Yonggi Cho's Theology of Blessing: Basis, Legitimacy, and Limitations." *Evangelical Review of Theology* 35, no. 2 (2011): 140–43.

———. "Prophetic Servant: Ideology of Spirit-Empowered Leaders." *Spiritus: ORU Journal of Theology* 5, no. 2 (Fall 2020): 217–34.

———. "Two Tales of Emerging Ecclesiology in Asia: An Inquiry into Theological Shaping." In *The Church from Every Tribe and Tongue: Ecclesiology in the Majority World*, edited by Gene L. Green, Stephen T. Pardue, and K. K. Yeo, 53–73. Majority World Theology Series 5. Carlisle: Langham Global Library, 2018.

Ma, Wonsuk, and Julie C. Ma. "Missiology: Evangelization, Holistic Ministry, and Social Justice." In *Routledge Handbook of Pentecostal Theology*, edited by Wolfgang Vondey, 279–89. London: Routledge, 2020.

Ma, Wonsuk, Opoku Onyinah, and Rebekah Bled, eds. *Good News to the Poor: Spirit-Empowered Responses to Poverty*. Tulsa: ORU Press, 2022.

Martin, David. *Tongues of Fire: The Explosion of Protestantism in Latin America.* Oxford: Blackwell, 1993.

McGee, Gary. "Missions, Overseas (North American Pentecostal)." In *The New International Dictionary of Pentecostal and Charismatic Movements*, edited by Stanley M. Burgess and Eduard M. van der Maas, 885–900. Grand Rapids: Zondervan, 2002.

Miller, Dean. *50 Pentecostal and Charismatic Leaders Every Christian Should Know.* Minneapolis: Chosen Books, 2021.

Miller, Donald E., and Tetsunao Yamamori. *Global Pentecostalism: The New Face of Christian Social Engagement.* Berkeley: University of California Press, 2007.

Ross, Kenneth R., Jooseop Keum, Kyriaki Avtzi, and Roderick R. Hewitt, eds. *Ecumenical Missiology: Changing Landscapes and New Conceptions of Mission.* Regnum Edinburgh Centenary Series 35. Oxford: Regnum, 2016.

Satyavrata, Ivan. *Pentecostals and the Poor: Reflections from the Indian Context.* Baguio City: APTS Press, 2017.

Shakarian, Demos, John L. Sherrill, and Elizabeth Sherrill. *The Happiest People on the Earth: The Long-Awaited Personal Story of Demos Shakarian.* Old Tappan : Chosen Books, 1975.

Tejedo, Joel A. "Pentecostal Civic Engagement in the Squatter Area." In *Good News to the Poor: Spirit-Empowered Responses to Poverty*, edited by Wonsuk Ma, Opoku Onyinah, and Rebekah Bled, 321–44. Tulsa: ORU Press, 2022.

Tizon, Al. *Transformation after Lausanne: Radical Evangelical Mission in Global-Local Perspective.* Oxford: Regnum, 2008.

Vargas, Marcelo. "The Aimara Identity of Poor Neo-Pentecostals in Urban La Paz, Bolivia." In *Good News to the Poor: Spirit-Empowered Responses to Poverty*, edited by Wonsuk Ma, Opoku Onyinah, and Rebekah Bled, 157–75. Tulsa: ORU Press, 2022.

Woolnoug, Ian E., and Wonsuk Ma, eds. *Holistic Mission: God's Plan for God's People.* Regnum Edinburgh Centenary Series 5. Oxford: Regnum, 2010.

Yong, Amos. *In the Days of Caesar: Pentecostalism and Political Theology.* Grand Rapids: Eerdmans, 2010.

11

The Impact of the Pandemic on Theological Education: A Hybrid Assessment

By Steven Ybarrola and Juliet Lee Uytanlet

I (Juliet) read *Global Pentecostalism* by Dr. Ted Yamamori and Donald Miller back in 2011 as part of the class readings of Dr. Steven Ybarrola on the "Indigenous Church in the Age of Globalization." The book opened my eyes to the impact of Pentecostalism on a global scale and its social engagement. I was very happy to meet Dr. Yamamori himself when he attended the Lausanne Diaspora Conference "Hybridity, Diaspora, and *Missio Dei*" held in the Biblical Seminary of the Philippines in 2018. I got to listen to and observe him up close as I joined the Global Diaspora Network meetings together with other Lausanne catalysts on Diaspora. I am deeply humbled to witness the kindness, graciousness, wisdom, and humility of Dr. Yamamori.

I (Steve) knew of Dr. Yamamori long before I ever met him. I was at Asbury Seminary when he eventually began teaching regularly on Holistic Mission at the school; it was then that I met him. Dr. Yamamori has a strong commitment to higher education, as witnessed by his own academic work at Texas Christian University (BA) and Duke University (PhD), as well as his teaching at several Christian schools of higher education. Because of his commitment to academia, Dr. Uytanlet and I are coauthoring this chapter on the impact of COVID-19 on seminary education at two institutions in very different parts of the world.

Biblical Seminary of the Philippines Online Program: A Brief History

The Biblical Seminary of the Philippines (BSOP, located in Valenzuela City, Metro Manila, and established in 1957) conceived the idea of introducing the online platform as an innovation in 2013 to minimize students printing their papers. That same year, some faculty attended the Overseas Council's seminar on Online Education, which led to a vision to provide online education not only for seminary students, but also for Christian leaders serving in churches, in the Philippines and beyond.

The seminar served as an important communication channel to persuade the social system of the institution, particularly the faculty, to adopt the innovation. Dennis Yam, the online program director, reminisces in his article "The Journey to Online Education"[1] on how this program developed and grew. The first task was to find the most suitable online classroom platform that would be cost-efficient and user-friendly. The seminary learned about Google Suite (now Google Workspace) after visiting Faith Academy of Antipolo City in 2015. This led to Yam applying for BSOP's free use of the Google products as an educational institution; this was granted that same year.

Yam provided information and conducted training for faculty to learn how to use the Google Classroom. There was even a trial live broadcast on 30 September 2015 using Google Hangouts with a limited online audience for a class on Hermeneutics. In May 2016, Yam prepared a proposal to then-president Joseph Shao. BSOP Online Classes officially started in August 2016 with three course offerings and instructors: Apologetics with Dennis Yam, Pastoral Ministry with Samson Uytanlet, and Global Missions with Juliet Uytanlet. There were eleven students enrolled for these classes.

The Impact of the COVID-19 Pandemic on the BSOP Online Program

The whole world was groping in the dark at the beginning of the COVID-19 pandemic in 2020. The Philippines confirmed its first case on 30 January 2020, with a Chinese national from Wuhan who arrived in the country on 21 January via Hong Kong. She had mild symptoms and later recovered. Another case was reported the following day. The companion of the first case had also tested positive but had more symptoms. The patient eventually died of cardiac arrest on 1 February, which became the first COVID-19 death outside China.

---

1. Dennis Yam, "The Journey to Online Education," ed. Rebecca Williams, *BSOP in Focus* 114 (Jan.–Mar. 2022), 1 and 3; see also Juliet Lee Uytanlet, ed., "News and Events," *BSOP in Focus* 94 (Jul.–Sep. 2016), 3.

The Philippines had yet to discover how this virus could wreak havoc on the Filipinos, affecting their livelihoods and threatening their lives.[2]

On 12 March President Rodrigo Duterte declared total lockdown for Metro Manila from 15 March to 14 April to contain the spread of the virus to other parts of the country. Schools were asked to close during this period.[3] In BSOP, the pandemic resulted in a campus lockdown and the closing of dormitories. The seminary required all students to return to their own homes or countries immediately. However, the lockdown also limited all forms of public transportation. One student was forced to walk six miles with all his books and luggage as he returned to his home. Some students who could not find flights were forced to rent apartments within Metro Manila. Other students who had booked their flights were stranded in the dormitory as their flights were canceled. Students and some faculty faced an unprecedented challenge of finding their way back home as they were leaving the campus.

The academic office decided to continue classes using Google Classroom. Much of the faculty had experienced teaching online classes already, and for those who had not, there was renewed interest. And although many of the faculty had undergone past trainings provided by Yam, stored knowledge is different from applied knowledge. A refresher class was offered in the summer of 2020 to update faculty on the new features of Google Classroom and a three-session training was provided for those who had not attended past trainings. During the following academic year (2020–21), some faculty preferred Zoom over Google Classroom, and the academic office allowed all faculty to use whichever platform they deemed most effective for them.

The four elements of diffusion of innovation are innovation, communication channels, time, and the social system. Everett Rogers writes, "An innovation is an idea, practice, or object that is perceived as new by an individual or other unit of adoption."[4] The innovation may not necessarily be new, but it is a known idea not yet adopted. The reasons for not adopting could be how effective the communication channels employed in diffusing the innovation

---

2. Department of Health, "DOH Confirms First 2019-NCOV Case in the Country; Assures Public of Intensified Containment Measures," Press Release, 30 January 2020, https://doh.gov.ph/doh-press-release/doh-confirms-first-2019-nCoV-case-in-the-country. E. M. Edrada et al., "First COVID-19 Infections in the Philippines: A Case Report," *Tropical Medical Health* 48 (2020), article no. 21, https://doi.org/10.1186/s41182-020-00203-0.

3. CNN Philippines Staff, "Metro Manila to Be Placed on 'Lockdown' Due to COVID-19," CNN, 12 March 2020, https://cnnphilippines.com/news/2020/3/12/COVID-19-Metro-Manila-restrictions-Philippines.html.

4. Everett Rogers, *Diffusion of Innovations*, 5th ed. (New York: Free Press, 2003), 12.

were or how prepared the social system was to accept the new idea. In this case, the social system was the seminary board, executive leaders, faculty, and students. To measure the rate of adoption, five qualities of an innovation need to be considered: relative advantage, compatibility, complexity, trialability, and observability. Resources such as expertise, finances, technology, machines, or skill can become hindrances for accepting the new idea. Time then becomes an important element to prepare or convince the social system to adopt the innovation.

From the data provided by Suzanne Li, the registrar, out of the twenty full-time faculty of the 2016–17 academic year, only five were readily involved in online teaching. The following academic year, two more faculty were added to the list. By the 2019–2020 academic year, there were nine faculty (including one adjunct faculty) who were teaching online. When the pandemic occurred, all full-time faculty had to use the online platform.[5] The table provides a breakdown of the numbers.

Before Pandemic	AY 2016–17	AY 2017–18	AY 2018–19	AY 2019–20
Total No. of Faculty	20	18	22	16
No. of Online Faculty	5	7 (2 new)	7	9 (2 new)
No. of Online Courses	11	9	15	14
Platform	Google Classroom	Google Classroom	Google Classroom	Google Classroom

During Pandemic	AY 2020–21	AY 2021–22
Total No. of Faculty	13	14
No. of Online Faculty	13+5 adjunct	14+9 adjunct/visiting
No. of Online Courses	29	39
Platform	Google Classroom/Zoom	Google Classroom/Zoom

It took almost a decade from its inception to the present for most faculty to adopt this innovation. The rate of adoption was relatively slow given that the idea was conceived in 2013. Yam provided various trainings to inform and equip the faculty for this new platform. It was not easy to motivate and encourage all faculty to teach online, for several reasons: (1) in-classroom was popularly perceived to be the best mode for instruction; (2) there were those

---

5. This data is provided by the BSOP Registrar Suzanne Li. The data is limited to the MA and MDiv programs. The total number of faculty includes only full-time faculty. The number did not include adjunct, visiting, and nonteaching faculty members.

who were not adept at using the new technology; and (3) security issues were raised. If the faculty refused to adopt this innovation, then the students would not be able to adopt it, either.

In hindsight, Yam sees this pandemic as the natural force that led to most faculty adopting an online platform and teaching online.[6] Online education became a serendipity for the sake of continuous theological training for the students.[7] As I write in 2022, all classes are held online using Google Classroom or Zoom. The online platform enabled us to have students not only in the Philippines, but also in other Asian countries, in the Middle East, and in North America.

There are advantages and disadvantages to online education. Among the advantages, faculty and students can avoid the traffic of Metro Manila. They no longer need to commute. They save money, gas, and hours of being in transit. Students can stay in their homes and turn on their computers to attend classes. They can change their backgrounds, mute, or turn off their videos. They can even multitask as they listen to the lectures.

But there are also disadvantages. The Internet connection can be poor. This is a big challenge with the Philippines ranking sixty-fifth out of 180 countries for fixed broadband and seventy-seventh out of 137 countries for mobile data.[8] It is also tempting for students to hop onto social media or multitask while they are supposed to be in class. The lack of real-life interaction can hamper friendship development among students. Additionally, the lack of online resources in our library can be a hurdle in student performance and excellence.

Online Theological Education as The New Normal

The Asia Graduate School of Theology is in partnership with the BSOP in providing postgraduate programs such as Biblical Studies, Christian Clinical Counseling, and Intercultural Studies. The pandemic affected the travel plans of international students and even local students living in the Visayas and

---

6. Yam, "Journey to Online Education," 1, 3.

7. According to the Philippine's Commission on Higher Education (CHED), flexible learning which included an online platform was encouraged and implemented during the pandemic to avoid infection or spread of the virus. See CHED Memorandum Order 4, series of 2020, https://ched.gov.ph/wp-content/uploads/CMO-No.-4-s.-2020-Guidelines-on-the-Implementation-of-Flexible-Learning.pdf.

8. Republic of the Philippines Department of Information and Communication Technology, "PH Internet Speed Rankings Continue to Climb Upward in May 2021," https://dict.gov.ph/ph-internet-speed-rankings-continue-to-climb-upward-in-may-2021/.

Mindanao areas. Early in the pandemic, restrictions on travel led to many problems such as the closing of borders to noncitizens, canceled or delayed flights, high prices of airfares and swab tests, and the additional costs of having to be quarantined for days on end. The choice to continue offering these postgraduate programs through an online platform became a challenge and a blessing.

The pandemic prevented international students from coming to the country. Some students who preferred on-campus learning were disappointed. One student decided to defer his studies to wait for the on-campus format. As the program director of the intercultural studies program, I talked to the students, encouraging them that the present setup was a blessing in a number of ways: (1) they saved money since they did not need to purchase tickets; (2) they did not need to pay for board and lodging; (3) they did not need to face the concerns of traveling and adjusting to a new country and culture; and (4) they could remain in their present ministries and with their families.

After year one, students saw the advantage of online theological education. They performed well and continued their studies and ministries. Some even realized that they preferred this and were hoping the online format would continue even after the pandemic ended.

In the post-pandemic world and with the continuous advancement of technology, it is inevitable that the online platform is here to stay even as it becomes more robust and easier to use. Perhaps online theological education will bring training to more Christian leaders locally and globally. There are many exciting possibilities with this online platform, but the question is whether the social system is ready to adopt it, or if the people need more time.

Overview of Asbury Seminary's Response to COVID-19

It was early spring of 2020 when we began hearing of this new virus that was spreading around the United States and the world. I had been in China in 2003 with a sociology colleague when the SARS virus broke out in that country, but being foreigners who did not speak the local language (we were there to give a series of lectures using translators), it was left to broadcast media to inform us about the outbreak of that virus.

At that time, we were told that it was limited to Southern China, though we now know that it was much more widespread in the country, including Beijing where we were spending our last few days. I recall my fourteen-and-a-half-hour flight back to Chicago, during which a woman behind me was coughing and sneezing the whole way. As we left the plane, she commented to the flight attendant, "I sure hope I didn't get the virus they're talking about." I thought to myself, "Boy, I sure hope you didn't, either!"

But in the spring of 2020, something else was happening: COVID-19 was spreading quickly, with deadly force. I was teaching a PhD seminar face-to-face, but Asbury Seminary decided (and rightly so) to have classes meet via Zoom. So, the twelve students I had in the class met with me via Zoom. I could see all the students, and they could jump into the conversation with little direction from me (my students are much more technologically savvy than I am). At least for my courses, that semester went off without any problems.

Many universities, colleges, and especially seminaries suffered because of COVID-19, and many in the United States couldn't weather the financial downturn caused by the virus and were forced to close. I believe Asbury Seminary's quick response to the threat of this virus and its quick institution of a plan of action to mitigate its effects are what largely kept us from the same fate. Asbury developed a team of knowledgeable scholars, called the Covid Response Team (CRT), to direct the seminary in its policies and actions. As a result, Asbury did not experience widespread illnesses due to COVID-19, and those who did get sick were well directed in what they should do.

Asbury Seminary's Approach to Online Teaching

Like many higher education institutions in the United States, Asbury Seminary began offering courses online well before COVID-19. When I came to Asbury in 2006, it was in my contract that I was expected to teach at least one course online per year. Those who had come to teach at the seminary earlier were only encouraged to teach online. This was a new experience for me as I had previously taught at a liberal arts college that had not started online teaching during my fifteen years there. Although I taught my classes face-to-face at this college, I did use the online platform Blackboard to have my students interact in discussion groups before class and turn in their assignments. I also posted additional readings and course-related materials for my students to access. Thus, while I had not taught online prior to coming to Asbury, I was acquainted with using these platforms.

As a result of its commitment to online as well as face-to-face learning, Asbury invested in the technology and personnel necessary to train and equip us to be successful at teaching online. We used the online platform Moodle and had a team of IT experts at our disposal. But we realized that there needed to be other options for our students, so we developed a hybrid system of teaching/learning. This was born out of the Church Planting Initiative at Asbury which aims to "equip church leaders for planting new churches and ReMissioning existing congregations so they can become reproducing, disciple-making movements."[9]

Not wanting to pull those already involved in ministry or church planting from their contexts while they received their training, nor simply have them as individuals connecting through an online format, Asbury developed a cohort model where the students would take courses online but would also come together periodically for intensive residencies (a few days to a week). In this way, they could connect with others involved in church planting as well as get to know their professors better. In recent years, we have expanded this hybrid model and developed Asbury Global, where students take courses partly online and then gather at various sites around the US for a two-and-a-half-day intensive residency.

Prior to the pandemic, Asbury Seminary, like many higher education institutions in the United States, had already developed various online and hybrid delivery methods and was being innovative when it came to meeting the needs of our students through them. These also allowed us to better serve the global church as students living in other parts of the world could take courses without necessarily having to come to a campus in the United States. The one exception to this, however, was students in our PhD programs in Intercultural Studies and Biblical Studies. Many believed that for students studying at this level, it was important that they were part of a learning community with easy access to their professors and resources available on campus.

Changes in Asbury's Teaching Approach as a Result of the Pandemic

Looking back to the spring of 2020, it is amazing to me how quickly (though not without problems) Asbury was able to adjust to the radical change in circumstances. By the fall of 2020 it seemed that COVID-19 was more under control, so Asbury allowed courses to go back to face-to-face (though it would probably be more accurate to say mask-to-mask since masks and social distancing were required). The CRT was keeping a close watch on national and local health guidelines to make sure that we were following the best-known science at the time.

However, I, like several of my colleagues, suffer from an immune deficiency illness, which meant that even with the precautions taken, I could not go back into the classroom. So, in the fall of 2020 I taught a course where students were

---

9. See: https://asburyseminary.edu/church-planting/.

in the classroom, but I was joining them via Zoom. I had a teaching assistant in the classroom, but I had to be a part of the class virtually. The problem was that I believe learning is more than just imparting and acquiring knowledge. Instead, I believe it happens best when people in a class have a sense of being a learning community. Unfortunately, it was very difficult to develop this sense of community from a distance.[10] I wanted to learn from my students as well as they shared their understanding and experiences.

But since I wasn't in the classroom, I depended on my teaching assistant to listen in and evaluate the discussions. Overall, this went well. Unfortunately, I did have one student go up to the microphone[11] after my lecture on culture and ethnocentrism and proceed to go on a rant. My assistant and I kept trying to interrupt him so we could address his comments, but he wouldn't allow us to do so. Finally, from my Zoom input, I did something that I had never had to do in thirty years of teaching: I told the student he would have to stop talking and sit down. Had I been in the classroom, I could have handled the situation quite differently.

There were many good stories as well. I was teaching a course for our incoming PhD Intercultural Studies students, and I was Zooming into the classroom. However, we had several international students, three from India and one from Myanmar, who were unable to get their visas to come to the States before the semester started, so had to Zoom into the class as well. They were joining us using synchronous Zoom – that is, they were joining us live. I had other colleagues who also had these students in their courses and had them use synchronous Zoom to participate. One of these colleagues is the dean of our Advanced Research Programs, which oversees our PhD and ThM programs. As we talked about our experiences of having these students join the class in this way, we wondered if this was something we might want to try on a test basis in the future for our international students. I doubt that this innovation would have been imagined if it were not for the limitations on travel due to COVID-19.

---

10. See Parker Palmer, *To Know as We Are Known: A Spirituality of Education* (San Francisco: HarperOne, 1993).

11. This was another aspect of the class that was quite awkward: students had to come to a microphone so that I could hear what they were saying.

Conclusion

In her analysis of BSOP's response to the pandemic, Dr. Uytanlet discusses the various aspects of innovations that Everett Rogers lays out in some detail in his book *Diffusion of Innovations*. In normal circumstances, there are often several reactions to proposed innovations ranging from early adopters to laggards (i.e. those who are late to adopt, if they adopt at all). As Rogers states, "The point of reference for the laggard is the past. Decisions are often made in terms of what has been done previously."[12]

At other times, such as during a pandemic, innovations are thrust upon us; there is not time to mull over or debate whether an innovation should be adopted. Time is of the essence. As we look at the rapid changes in teaching methods and the use of technology that both BSOP and Asbury Seminary experienced at the onset of the pandemic, we believe that the innovations that the schools had previously adopted in teaching and the use of technology for online and hybrid teaching served them well when other technologies were called for – another aspect of innovation adoption that Rogers discusses.

I (Steve) am getting to the end of my teaching career, and I much prefer teaching in the classroom to online classes (maybe I'm a laggard, looking to the past!), but going through this experience has helped both Dr. Uytanlet and me to appreciate the benefits (and the drawbacks) of how we can use technology to better serve the *missio Dei* as we help prepare the next generation of church leaders and scholars.

References

CNN Philippines Staff. "Metro Manila to Be Placed on 'Lockdown' Due to COVID-19." CNN, 12 March 2020. https://cnnphilippines.com/news/2020/3/12/COVID-19-Metro-Manila-restrictions-Philippines.html.

Department of Health. "DOH Confirms First 2019-NCOV Case in the Country; Assures Public of Intensified Containment Measures." Press Release, 30 January 2020. https://doh.gov.ph/doh-press-release/doh-confirms-first-2019-nCoV-case-in-the-country.

Edrada, E. M., et al. "First COVID-19 Infections in the Philippines: A Case Report." *Tropical Medical Health* 48 (2020), article no. 21. https://doi.org/10.1186/s41182-020-00203-0.

Palmer, Parker. *To Know as We Are Known: A Spirituality of Education*. San Francisco: HarperOne, 1993.

---

12. Rogers, *Diffusion of Innovations*, 284.

Republic of the Philippines Department of Information and Communication Technology. "PH Internet Speed Rankings Continue to Climb Upward in May 2021." https://dict.gov.ph/ph-internet-speed-rankings-continue-to-climb-upward-in-may-2021/.

Rogers, Everett. *Diffusion of Innovations*. 5th ed. New York: Free Press, 2003.

Uytanlet, Juliet Lee, ed. "News and Events." *BSOP in Focus* 94 (Jul.–Sep. 2016).

Yam, Dennis. "The Journey to Online Education." Edited by Rebecca Williams. *BSOP in Focus* 114 (Jan.–Mar. 2022).

12

Reframing Leadership to the Digital Native: Making Discipleship an Immersive Experience

By Philip Yan

> We will not hide them from their descendants;
> we will tell the next generation
> the praiseworthy deeds of the LORD,
> his power, and the wonders he has done.
> He decreed statutes for Jacob
> and established the law in Israel,
> which he commanded our ancestors
> to teach their children,
> so the next generation would know them,
> even the children yet to be born,
> and they in turn would tell their children.
> Then they would put their trust in God
> and would not forget his deeds
> but would keep his commands (Ps 78:4–7)

Clearly, we have an unshakeable responsibility to teach, guide, and nurture our next generation in their faith journey. But we are confronted with a crisis: young adults are the biggest group missing in the church; indeed, many of them find church or faith (or both) irrelevant. We need to reframe our leadership mindset.

The Perpetual Crisis the Church Can No Longer Afford to Normalize

Young adults (ages 22–35) are the biggest group of church dropouts. Recent research has shown that young adult church dropouts rose to 64 percent in 2019 from 59 percent in 2011.[1] Additionally, "two out of three Canadian young adults who attended church weekly as a child or youth in the 1980s, 1990s, and early 2000s no longer do so today" and "despite being raised in a Trinitarian confessing church, one in two of these young adults would now self-identify as 'spiritual but not religious,' 'no religion,' 'atheist,' or 'agnostic.'"[2]

While some may view the young people who are leaving church as "lost sheep," these "church dropouts" are instead a formidable force with great potential. Unfortunately, one report showed that only a quarter of young adults in post-secondary studies said someone from their home church tried to make a connection for them. On the other hand, fewer than 3 in 10 ministry youth workers said they had a ministry plan for making these connections.[3]

Many young adults may leave the organized church, but not all are leaving their faith. They leave because they don't find their place in church, they don't see the relevancy of church or faith or church activities, they don't have guidance in struggling with life and faith, and they don't have a community. Furthermore, they are expected to make donations and serve, but they are not intentionally nurtured and equipped according to their potential.[4] Simply put, they don't feel understood and connected in church. The corollary is expected: The generation after them, the teens, are growing up in church with few young adults as role models they can look up to. What future is there for them?

This is a crisis we must tackle as a high priority. The prevalent opportunity loss will continue if we do not have a radical perspective shift in what it means to be the church. Collectively, we need to do some soul searching. What kind of leadership, for instance, is being exemplified for the benefit of our younger generation, the future of church, and its influence in the public space? We need to strategically invest in our young people and build them up as resilient disciples.

---

1. David Kinsman and Mark Matlock, *Faith for Exiles: 5 Ways for a New Generation to Follow Jesus in Digital Babylon*. Grand Rapids: Baker Books, 2019), 15.

2. Barna Research, 2019.

3. Rick Hiemstra, Lorianne Dueck, and Matthew Blackaby, *Renegotiating Faith: The Delay in Young Adult Identity Formation and What It Means for the Church in Canada* (Toronto: Faith Today, 2018), www.renegotiatingfaith.ca.

4. Sam Eaton, "59 Percent of Millennials Raised in a Church Have Dropped Out – And They're Trying to Tell Us Why," Faithit, 4 April 2018, https://faithit.com/12-reasons-millennials-over-church-sam-eaton/4/.

My wife and I have been serving in young adult ministry for over twenty years. We learned that young adulthood today is no longer defined by traditional age boundaries. Navigating life for many young adults presents more challenges than it did for previous generations. This is because young adults today have a prolonged maturing from age eighteen to thirty-five. There is a new life stage called *emerging adulthood*, as young adult identity formation and its accompanying shift into adulthood has been delayed by five to seven years since the 1980s.[5]

In this phase of life, they are maneuvering into transitions and making critical decisions. In this journey of adulting, young adults desire three things: inspiration (lived faith and challenges), guidance (mentoring by mature adults in faith), and community (people with whom they flourish together). Yet the eighteen- to thirty-five-year-olds are still not intentionally invested in in these areas.

How Relatable Is Church?

My focus here is on making good use of digital technology to connect with digital natives, many of whom are young adults. I want to understand how digital technology can open new doors to making discipleship an immersive experience. For discipleship ministry to be effective, it must be personal and authentic, and have real-time interaction. Therefore, I'm advocating for the integrated use of digital technology as a relatable engagement medium. It fosters community building, but it can never replace genuine human interaction. We need a new mindset to focus on helping the digital natives to flourish with inspiration, guidance, and community, reaching them even beyond the church walls.

According to John Palfrey, "digital natives (those born after 1980 and who grew up with the Internet) are more likely to 'see relationships differently' as well as access information in new ways from previous generations."[6] They are Millennials, Generation Z, and Generation Alpha. Digital natives are the most connected generation in human history. Not only are they digitally connected, but they are also globally connected. Their connectivity through digital channels is a key source of influence in their growing network of friends and relationships, the information they receive, the formation of their worldview

---

5. Hiemstra, Dueck, and Blackaby, *Renegotiating Faith*.
6. "John Palfrey," Wikipedia, last updated 23 August 2022, https://en.wikipedia.org/wiki/John_Palfrey.

and culture, their options of dreams and lifestyles, their questions about belief and identity, their finding love partners, and their struggles with faith matters and conflicting opinions.

In short, they live in a complex space/culture which church leaders do not understand. They are a digital generation, but also a generation with quite a bit of anxiety. Unfortunately, the church is often not in their space – there is a chasm between us.

We who care about the next generation should cultivate connections that make our intergenerational relationship stick. To serve digital natives effectively, we need to connect with them in their space. Our objective must be to empower them to be resilient disciples. We need to intentionally build bridges to reach their world.

We can learn here from the apostle Paul:

> To the Jews I became like a Jew, to win the Jews. To those under the law I became like one under the law (though I myself am not under the law), so as to win those under the law. To those not having the law I became like one not having the law (though I am not free from God's law but am under Christ's law), so as to win those not having the law. To the weak I became weak, to win the weak. I have become all things to all people so that by all possible means I might save some. (1 Cor 9:20–22)

The same principle applies to equipping a digital generation who will carry the gospel impact wherever they go.

Making Discipleship an Immersive Experience
From Physical Proximity to "Phygital"

For healthy church growth and far-reaching impact, making resilient disciples should be a high priority. A lot is at stake if we keep losing the next generations to worldly influences. The Barna Group's research shows that connectivity for young adults is a key factor in their optimism about the world, in their feeling cared for and supported, and in believing that church is relevant. The "Connected Generation" Report shows that young adults desire the following:

1. Connection and community
2. Prayer and emotional support
3. Opportunities to serve and help others

4. A Bible-centered message of hope and encouragement.[7]

Traditionally, we plan our activities in person. Proximity used to be a convenient factor in attending church. With the new digital culture even more ubiquitous after the COVID-19 pandemic, we need to reframe our leadership mindset in engaging young adults to ensure that their physical and digital presence – *phygital* – matters to their spiritual development. There are activities they can attend in person; there can also be online engagements they participate in with a support and feedback system. There should be growth materials, share and serve opportunities, and as-needed mentoring in person and online. The key is thoroughly planned organization and execution for a seamless user experience. The digital natives would appreciate having a young adult ministry tailored to their needs in a connected community.

Artificial Intelligence (AI) technology has been acting as an evangelist for our worldly values round the clock. We can use the same technology to ensure that God's message is there, that church is there, that support is there, and that the faith community is there any time people need it. Fundamental to a successful phygital ministry approach is data collection from all the engagements: analytics from websites, Facebook, YouTube videos, segmented digital content, user feedback, news, frequency of engagement, and so on. All of these are measurable, and the analytics indicate areas of improvement in ministry plans.

For the experience to be immersive and effective, digital communications need to be appropriately integrated instead of making sporadic appearances.

A Community of Phygital Orbit

The "phygital orbit" framework empowers growth with a rich community experience. It encompasses the following three success factors:

- Identifying segments of the young adults in their contexts, growth pathways, life transitions, and potential and spiritual gifts;
- Knowing where the young adults are in their faith journey pathways and desires, and offering appropriate direction to ensure growth is taking place;
- Having a measurable feedback system in place to gauge the gravity of their engagement.

---

7. Barna Group, "Key Findings," The Connected Generation, 2020, https://theconnectedgeneration.com/key-findings/.

The following example illustrates the benefits of forming a phygital orbit.

A new ministry at a multigeneration church starts a new digitally connected ministry that aims to support young adults 24/7. The ministry team establishes many small groups with training for leaders in place, plus regular large-group gatherings and social projects.

Multiple Touchpoints Based on Life Transitions

This plan requires some unique digital actions. First, the young adult pastor sets up a content creation/digital community leadership team to cultivate a connected culture that fosters supportive touchpoints based on their life transitions. The following are some examples:

- An online prayer group for graduating students
- A Christian network for job searching
- A career-change supporting cohort
- A habit-building on-demand microlearning module supported by scheduled online group mentorship
- Learning programs, such as premarriage, financial literacy, and discipleship sessions.

All programs are connected to an online success storytelling platform and private regular online counselling "rooms."

The phygital framework is encompassed in the orbit model shown in figure 12.1.

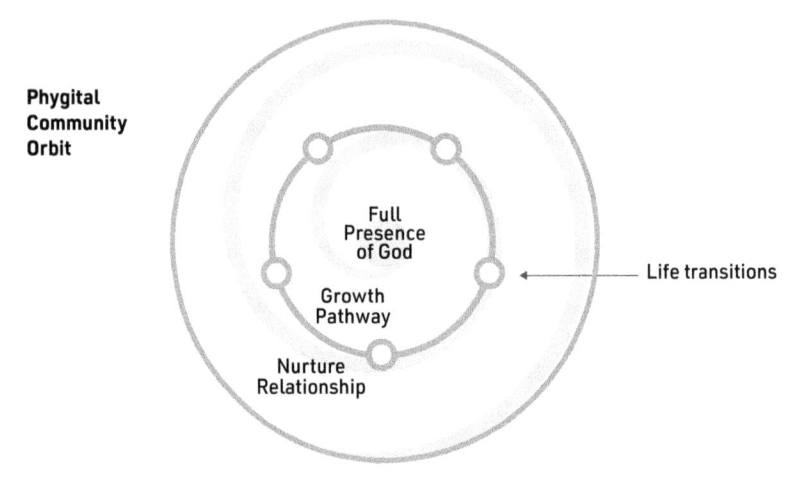

Figure 12.1

One Main Door to All Touchpoints

Most churches have their digital engagement scattered across different social media platforms such as Facebook, Instagram, YouTube, WhatsApp, and Slack. The true seamless connection is having all user engagements on a mobile app as one main door to all digital connections.

Feedback Often – Integrated Experience Design

All connected touchpoints from physical gatherings, online learning, mentorship, micro-social sharing, and engagement are "tracked" through quick ten-second feedback before or after the engagement. Building a feedback system is a part of the digital community culture. This is possible with a user-focused experience design approach, functional applications, and a scalable customer relationship management (CRM database).

All engagement data will be entered into a centralized CRM system, and the patterns of data will show clusters of stronger "gravity," or lack of it. They will inform the ministry leaders to review the strength of the community orbit and make appropriate adjustment.

A Meaningful Dashboard

All engagements – such as a "like" on post comments, testimonial contributions, and sharing of fun times or social projects – will be represented by points and entered as they connect all things tracked. The system will generate a report on these data. Customized reporting will go to different pastors, leaders, and mentors for information updates, recommendations, and names for personal follow-up. In addition, the automation process will save the administration time.

All data collected will allow for the church to perceive the spiritual discernment pattern. For example:

- Where are the young adults on their spiritual journey?
- What else should church do to help them flourish in faith?
- Do we need better clarity on a particular spiritual pathway to help young adults move forward?
- Can they see their own growth patterns and embrace opportunities?

Reflection for leaders:

- Can we create a ministry without a defined growth path?
- Can ministry plans be effective with longevity without a data feedback system and a dashboard of the community orbit?

- If digital ministry is focused on pushing content, search engine optimization, and the program's popularity, will all these activities truly benefit the emerging adults in their growth journey?
- What are our measurement and success indicators in our phygital young adult ministry?

Engage in Young Adults' Spiritual Growth Pathway

Young adults' growth pathway is dynamic, often marked with uncertainties, a need to search for options, and a desire to discern God's guidance. They need mentors and/or spiritual guides to be present when they are at a crossroad or in a transition. In general, we engage young adults in deep conversation in the following aspects of their growth pathway:

1. Knowledge – to know what is happening around them
2. Understanding – to relate the above knowledge to their life journey and faith
3. Discernment – to make sense of the understanding to arrive at God-honoring decisions
4. Wisdom – to take bold steps in implementing their desires.[8]

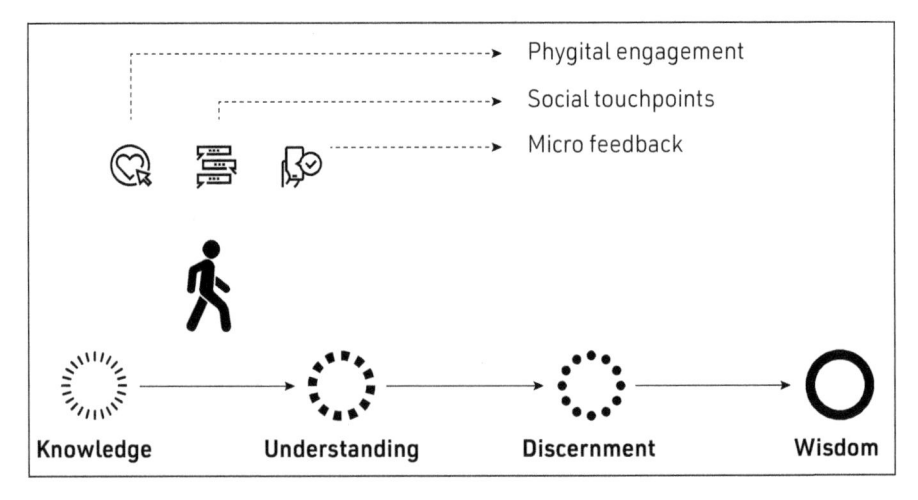

Figure 12.2

---

8. The spiritual growth pathway is adapted from the principles of Strategic Discernment taught in Bakke Graduate University's Metrics of Innovation Course, 2020, by Dr. Willy Kotiuga.

From Knowledge to Understanding
Jen has just graduated with an engineering degree. She went to engineering school partly because 80 percent of her immediate and extended family members are engineers. After graduation, she looked back at her footprint and saw what truly made her happy. After a period of struggling and soul-searching, Jen saw a different person in herself and decided that engineering was not for her.

From Understanding to Discernment
Kevin studied graphic design and had been a designer for several years. To his friends, he had a high-profile corporate dream job. Kevin, however, was not happy. He started to turn off the notifications from his church app and the prayer app he used to engage with regularly. He found it getting harder to get up for work every day. Finally, Kevin reached out to his mentor because of a challenge at work. In helping Kevin handle the challenge, his mentor also guided him to play back his journey to the design profession. Kevin remembered he had once wished to have a part in telling stories about caring for the community and living healthy. Through further support from his spiritual mentor, Kevin made a radical decision in his career and is now working as a digital community mobilizer for affordable housing.

From Discernment to Wisdom
Michelle is a social media content creator. She has been working with several professional schools at different universities. She leads a team to create media strategies and provide visual and written content to promote their offerings and mobilize continuing learning. She recognizes that God has given her the character of a curious learner. She is well-read and can connect the logic of knowledge, the pattern of human learning, and how people respond to the surrounding culture. One day, when Michelle was exploring new African drum music introduced by a fellow small-group member on Slack, she felt that God was pointing her to the African countries from where she has been sponsoring children. She felt a desire to create a free digital learning platform for children in the Global South to access foundational schooling. Michelle has no idea how to approach this big task, but she plans to research and connect to all related projects and learn from their successes and failures. She is actively expanding her network and connecting with like-minded Christians for the purpose of building a global teaching network. A new phase is about to unfold.

What Led Me to Ministry with Digital Engagement

As former young adult ministry practitioners, my wife and I have gone through phases of change that have pushed us to extend our comfort zones in doing people-focused ministry. Here is my story.

Watching a Movie Twenty Minutes Late

Back in 2005, my wife and I engaged in young adult ministry for university students with a different approach from what we used to do. Our focus was on starting with a much smaller group size and paying more personal attention to everyone. Then, we would extend our care to their peers outside our small group. After a while, we realized that our conversations with these young people were incomplete. Every time we met, we learned that certain things in their lives had moved on. It felt like watching a movie twenty minutes late – something was amiss in our connection. It dawned on us that not only were we not current in their culture, but the mode of communication among young people had also moved to the digital space.

Exploring What Works for a Deeper Connection

We started to puzzle out what was missing. The students were talking on MSN Messenger at night, and after 11 p.m. was the best time to dialogue. Signing up for a new platform is simple today. Back then, I had to look up a technical manual to get the connection. We would log on and say hi to our young friends. They were surprised to see us there, but eventually they got used to our presence when we consistently showed up at 11 p.m. (Note that this was six years before texting became common.)

The Versatility of Multichannel Conversation

Later, I saw the number of people using MSN drastically decrease. When I asked our young friends about it, they surprised me with this question: "Have you heard of Facebook?" *What?* These young people would swing from one platform to another just because of a newer and cooler option. I was shut out because Facebook was restricted to university student access only. One student offered me a Facebook account from his two accounts at his university and the business school he was at. That was my first taste of engaging in multichannel conversations with multiple parties simultaneously. Young people would pop in from one channel to another, and there was no need to complete any exchange as we do in person.

The Calling for Omnichannel Spiritual Engagement and Community Building

I learned that we older folks needed to be in step with digital communication as the world kept advancing and the culture around us kept evolving. If we want to serve the next generations, then we need to show up at different touchpoints and meet them where they are via the website, Facebook, private groups, Instagram, or private message. Here are some of the learnings I have gathered in my young adult ministry journey:

1. *The scatter coffee moment works just as fine online.* Remember how you built relationships with your colleagues – the impromptu conversation with a coffee in your hand by the water cooler or in the hallway? Similarly, our conversations at church could be around the coffee station or in the foyer before or after Sunday service. By the same token, the at-the-moment terse exchange on social media is a way of showing interest in people. Such virtual "coffee moments" are micro-engagements that may eventually lead to something meaningful when we interact with people on their digital platforms.

2. *People want to know that somebody cares.* Private messages, comments on their posts, and sharing helpful information are some of the best ways to show our care today. In real life, people are selective in opening themselves up to their pastors. In the digital realm, the connection makes it easy to see what the person cares about. It helps build a bridge to engage in further conversation.

3. *The pitfalls of one-way communication.* A church website, sermon broadcast, and social media announcement have their place as well as their limitations. For our 2005 young adult group, I created a photo-rich website so that our young friends could share our gatherings with others (there was a members-only section). When Facebook became public use, we closed the website because the communication via a website was one-way and passive. Broadcasting and announcing are useful for informing, but lacking in direct engagement, two-way exchange, and analytics to review the reach and adjust the manner of messaging.

4. *Micro-engagements enrich the spiritual pathway.* Authentic sharing helps build trust. When people share their faith journey and follow each other's life paths, they may gain a glimpse of different facets of a person's life. Engagement in small bites is conducive to connecting the community with encouragement. Accumulated meaningful micro-engagements become a fertile base in touching lives just as water is needed to nurture crops. Digital tools open windows to

all kinds of micro-engagement opportunities in enriching growth in a faith community. They prepare a starter to engaging further conversations face-to-face.

5. *There's power in showing up.* There is indisputable value in the traditional ministry approach that focuses on creating invitations to participate. In many biblical accounts, we notice that God not only calls and invites his people, but ministers to them as well. One time, we drove out of town to visit a student who was studying away from home. He insisted on paying for our dinner because we were in "his hood." Our visit turned out to be a wonderful bonding time. Similarly, in the digital space, we can show up for meaningful relationship-building and work on earning trust. Showing up and being present means we care.

Reflections
God Works Out of the Box

My digital transformation journey is not about upgrading digital technology. It is a deliberate walk to follow my ministry calling by utilizing the tools that work for the purpose. In the Old Testament, God has unusual ways to reveal himself beyond signs and wonders. For example, he designs a giant ark and has it built to accommodate a family and all kinds of animals. He carves out a portable tablet in the early Stone Age to declare his Ten Commandments. He designs the tabernacle as the temple on-the-go. He teaches a health care guide for best health practices in the wilderness.

All these show that being innovative is one of God's attributes. He uses cutting-edge technologies that suit the time in delivering his work.

Ministry Is to Touch the Heart First

There are three things that we rarely address in Christian ministry but that we must address if we are to continue to be relevant in providing the gospel to the world.

First, we must use innovation. You read my above-mentioned references to God's employing unusual ways to fulfill his plans. In human history, those were indeed innovative advancements at the time. God never hesitates to "rock the boat."

Second, we must use experience. God does not restrict our experiences only in form. His design thinking allows us to cultivate an intimate connection in worship, function, and creative cultural expressions. In today's language, it is the contemporary practice of experience design.

Finally, we must minister to the heart. In church, we talk a lot about teaching, learning, knowledge, and serving. Before a change takes its form, the heart is first moved. In the Bible, we learn that when God shows up, it is never about knowledge first. He would use a small voice, an unexpected appearance, a speaking animal, a ladder to heaven, and food delivery by birds to touch hearts through an intimate experience.

References

Barna Group. "Key Findings." The Connected Generation, 2020. https://theconnectedgeneration.com/key-findings/.

Eaton, Sam. "59 Percent of Millennials Raised in a Church Have Dropped Out – And They're Trying to Tell Us Why." Faithit, 4 April 2018. https://faithit.com/12-reasons-millennials-over-church-sam-eaton/4/.

Hiemstra, Rick, Lorianne Dueck, and Matthew Blackaby. *Renegotiating Faith: The Delay in Young Adult Identity Formation and What It Means for the Church in Canada.* Toronto: Faith Today, 2018. www.renegotiatingfaith.ca.

Wikipedia. "John Palfrey." Last modified 23 August 2022. https://en.wikipedia.org/wiki/John_Palfrey.

13

Diaspora Mission[1] and Bible Translation[2]

By S. Hun Kim

The Phenomenon of Change with Diaspora[3]

Due to the explosive growth of the global church at the end of the twentieth century and its leading role in twenty-first-century mission, the prospects for world mission are being changed. In particular, the acceleration of diaspora following the end of the postcolonial era in the 1960s will challenge the future of mission. Diaspora mission is one of the most important changes. South American mission theologian Samuel Escobar agreed that diaspora mission is a significant issue in terms of direction and a challenge for traditional forms

---

1. This chapter was first featured in a volume of the Regnum Edinburgh Centenary series: Chandler Im and Amos Yong, eds., *Global Diasporas and Mission* (Oxford: Regnum, 2014). "Diaspora mission" in this chapter is intended to distinguish it from overseas mission, thus avoiding unnecessary confusion between two concepts. Here it is a mission effort to mobilize potential human resources on the move for mission and to reach out to unreached people through evangelism in a diasporic context. This chapter is edited and updated.

2. "Bible translation" is defined here as a translation work for vernacular languages that have no Bible. Recent statistics show that only 724 languages of 5.9 billion people have the full Bible and 3,589 languages have portions of Scripture only. Refer to http://www.wycliffe.net/resources/2022 Global scripture Access, excerpted on 3 Nov 2022 on the website.

3. Here, "diaspora" is used with the same meaning as "migration," which encompasses all sorts of people on the move. For Tereso Casiño, "diaspora" refers to the overarching structure under which all forms of mobility take place, while "migration" serves as a tool to account for a diasporic process or condition. However, Enoch Wan and Sadiri Joy Tira separate "diaspora" from "migration" as it implies a biblical concept, particularly in terms of diaspora missiology.

of mission engagement.⁴ It can be said that mission is not about "going there" but is "from everywhere to everywhere" and indeed is "at our doorstep."

For more than half a century, Bible translation was initiated and done by missionaries with linguistic skills at the location of the language group in need of Bible translation. Bible translation was regarded as a part of frontier mission, and most Bible translation works have been completed for unreached people groups and unwritten language groups on mission fields.

However, at the turn of the twenty-first century, the number of diasporas from non-Western countries who were now in Western countries (e.g. migrant workers, asylum seekers, refugees, international students, trafficked people, and permanent immigrants) increased. The Cambridge Survey of World Migration attempted to classify six patterns of migration based on push and pull factors of people: (1) internal versus intercontinental/international migration; (2) forced versus free migration; (3) settler versus labor migration; (4) temporary versus permanent migration; (5) illegal versus legal migration; and (6) planned versus flight/refugee migration.⁵

Among these people, asylum seekers (or refugees) are identified as strategically significant for frontier mission because of their unique situations. Most are of or from ethnic groups coming from regions that are hard to access by outside Christian workers. Because of persecution, civil war, force majeure, and political instability, many are forcibly pushed out of their homelands and moved to refugee camps nearby or end up in the cities of receiving countries in Europe and North America.

Since I was on assignment with Wycliffe Global Alliance (formerly Wycliffe Bible Translators) in Europe, the landscape surrounding demographics has changed considerably. For example, today, almost half of London's population consists of those of foreign origin and more than three hundred languages are spoken in that city. Europe, in particular, is a unique place for Bible translation since a huge influx of diasporas from Africa and other parts of the world began in the 1960s after postcolonialism. In fact, on the European continent there were several Bible translation projects for ethnic language groups before and after the collapse of the former Soviet Union. My project (hereafter called the Sura language project in Iran)⁶ was one of the projects that has been implemented

---

4. Samuel Escobar, *A Time for Mission* (Leicester: Inter-Varsity, 2003), 66.
5. Robin Cohen, ed., *The Cambridge Dictionary of World Migration* (Cambridge: Cambridge University Press, 1995), 5–6.
6. For security reasons, I use a pseudonym for my language project. The "Sura" language is one of the major language groups in Iran.

in Europe. In 1990, several clusters of the Sura language group were scattered all over the continent and were found in London, Oslo, and Copenhagen. It turned out that some of the members were in fact sincere Christians.

Here, I illustrate two similar cases of Bible translation in diaspora contexts: the Korean project in East Asia more than a century ago, and the Sura project in Iran in which I was involved. Through this brief study on missionally significant cases, I draw some relevant conclusions of missional implications for diaspora mission and Bible translation.

Korean Bible Translation with the Korean Diaspora in China/Manchuria and Japan in the Early Stages of Protestant History in Korea[7]

There are three things we must understand about the history of Korean Bible translation. First, publications in Korean include the four gospels and Acts, which were printed in Yokohama in 1884, a New Testament that was printed in 1897 in Fengtian, and a complete Bible that was printed in Yokohama in 1911. It is assumed that this last translation was done intentionally for the ethnic Korean diaspora in China as we can also find evidence of translations[8] for Manchurian, Mongolian, Xinjing, Kazakhstan Turkish, and Tibetan languages at that time.

Second, in addition to the above, another Korean Bible was translated by Scottish missionary Rev. Dr. John Ross, John McIntyre, and their Korean diaspora team in Manchuria. At the start of the translation work, John Ross, as a cultural historian and linguist in Manchuria, made contact with some Korean diaspora merchants who traded herbal medicines across the border between China and Korea to learn the Korean language. Ross met Lee Ungchan, who agreed to collaborate with him on a variety of translation works. Ross, with the help of Lee, published the Korean Primer (1877), The Korean Language (1878), Yesu sunggyo mundap (Bible Catechism; 1881), and Yesu sunggyo yoryung (Outline of the New Testament; 1881). In 1877, Ross and Lee began translating the New Testament, later aided by McIntyre and several other Koreans, including Seo Sangyun and Paek Hongjun. In 1882, Ross published the Gospels of Luke and John, the first gospels to be translated into Hangul.

---

7. This section is drawn from two sources: Wang Weifan, "The Bible in Chinese," *Nanjing Theological Review* (1993): 85; and Keith Pratt and Richard Rutt, *Korea: A Historical and Cultural Dictionary* (Richmond: Curzon Press, 1999).

8. Weifan, "Bible in Chinese," 85.

Then, in 1887 under the initiative of Ross, the first complete translation of the New Testament was finally published in Korean. Once published, these translated materials were smuggled to Korea and used by a wide indigenous audience. It is reported that Seo Sangyun, a member of the translation team, risked his life to carry over fifteen thousand copies of the Korean Bible in his backpack in three years.[9]

One of the unique contributions of the Korean Bible translation was to help many people become Christians through reading the distributed Bible even before foreign missionaries came for ministry. According to Min-Young Jung,[10] this laid the foundation for the early missionary movement in Korea, and the Korean Bible enabled the Korean church to grow as a healthy and rapidly multiplying indigenous church.

Third, the Gospel of Mark was independently translated by Lee Sujung, a Korean sojourning in Japan, and published in Japan. Copies of this translation were later taken to Korea by Horace Grant Underwood and Henry Appenzeller, North American missionaries. Underwood once reported to his mission board at home: "Instead of sowing seed, we are already harvesting what has been already sown."[11]

Bible Translation with Diaspora: The Case of the Sura Language in Iran
Displaced Translation as a Strategic Mission in Europe with Iranian Refugees

The Sura project was initiated by diaspora Christians from Iran in 1990. A cluster in the UK gathered with Wycliffe Bible translators in Cyprus and discussed the possibility of translation work for the Sura language. One dedicated Sura Christian volunteered to commit himself to the project. This was what we call "displaced translation," which is a kind of translation that must be done in the context of diaspora due to a hostile environment toward Bible translation, particularly for ethnic language groups in creative access countries. The UK became a base because a Sura diaspora community existed near London who could help check and review the translated materials. Further, the Iranian Christian community was ready to support the project.

---

9. Min-Young Jung, "Diaspora and Timely Hit: Towards a Diaspora Missiology," in *Korean Diaspora and Christian Mission*, eds. Hun Kim and Wonsuk Ma (Oxford: Regnum, 2011), 64.

10. Jung, "Diaspora and Timely Hit," 64.

11. Jung, 64.

Today, more than five hundred unreached people groups[12] are estimated to live in Europe alone. It is believed that displaced translation strategy could be one of the most effective alternatives in Bible translation mission as we work with people groups who resettle in free societies. We believe that this diaspora phenomenon is a "divine conspiracy" in which God plans to redeem every nation through the scattered people.

Holistic Approach[13] through the Sura Translation Process

I joined the project in 1994 when I was waiting for a new language assignment in the UK with my family after finishing linguistic training with SIL[14] in Singapore. After several trips and a long stay in the Republic of Azerbaijan and Istanbul, Turkey, for the acquisition of the language (which is a dialect of the Sura language), in 1997 I moved to the place where a native speaker began translation work in the southwestern part of London.

"F" (pseudonym), who was a key native translator and Muslim background believer in Iran, had already produced the Gospel of John in audio format for testing among the Sura people in 1994. We soon began making drafts of the entire New Testament by working with Sura people in London, Oslo, and Copenhagen. Finally, we completed the first draft in 2003, and in 2009 it was published in book format. Meanwhile, we developed online media to enhance the accessibility of the translated books on a website. This included other books such as the Four Gospels in audio format that would benefit not only Sura people in Iran but also diaspora Sura around the world.

I served as a project coordinator and exegetical checker for the accuracy of the translated materials based on the original text. Besides these routine processes, one of the issues that surprised me was my relationships with native translators and helpers. The situation of Sura diaspora people in Europe was

---

12. An "unreached people group" refers to an ethnic group without an indigenous, self-propagating Christian church movement. Any ethnic or ethnolinguistic nation without enough Christians to evangelize the rest of the nation is an unreached people group. It is a missiological term used by evangelical Christians. The term is sometimes applied to ethnic groups in which fewer than 2 percent of the population are evangelical Christians.

13. Originally, a "holistic approach" in mission meant that the church's mission is intrinsically holistic or "integral." Word and deed must work together to complement one another (see C. R. Padilla, "Holistic mission," in *Dictionary of Mission Theology*, eds. John Corrie et al. [Nottingham: Inter-Varsity Press, 2007], 157–62). However, in this context, a "holistic approach" is a kind of practice for focusing both on work and on human need in the diasporic context of mission.

14. SIL is an independent organization from Wycliffe Global Alliance that supports technical skills needed for Bible translation. This includes linguistics.

vulnerable, unstable, and financially difficult. While building friendships with them, I also felt concern for their jobs, their Christian communities, their family issues, their legal status in the UK, and more. In one case, I hired a language helper to paint houses and put up wallpaper so that he was financially stable and could also focus on translation work.

Mission is a holistic process not for achieving our own immediate goals, but for experiencing an incarnational lifestyle for all who are involved.

Ultimate Partnership for the Kingdom of God

Bible translation in diasporic contexts allows us to reflect ourselves in many aspects of mission activities. One of the overriding concerns for the Sura project was the matter of partnership among stakeholders. In the early stages of the translation, I was involved in the northern dialect team in the Republic of Azerbaijan to get cooperation between two similar dialect projects. A partnership was formed with the United Bible Society, the Institute of Bible Translation, Kitab Sirketi (Azerbaijan Bible Society), Wycliffe, local churches in Baku, Azerbaijan, and an Iranian mission organization in the UK. Despite several disagreements on policies and processes in translation, the whole Bible in the northern dialect of the Sura language was published in 2010.

In a similar way, the project also faced partnership issues among several organizations involved in the early 1990s in the UK. However, every partner and person learned to share burdens according to their specific expertise because they were on a common mission. For example, the indigenous mission organization for Iran focused on securing copyright for the Bible while Wycliffe provided technical support and financial aid. In the actual translation process, there were mother-tongue translators, local testers, reviewers, and IT supporters. Some diaspora in London committed themselves to support through prayer and finance. One local Baptist church in New Malden, Surrey, adopted the project as a part of their church's mission. Through the synergized and voluntary efforts of each kingdom partner, at last the Sura New Testament was published in 2009, and in 2012 the whole Bible was published.

Mission is not the property of one institutional organization or megachurch. Mission happens by the power of the Holy Spirit and the cooperation of the whole body of Christ.

Missional Implications for Bible Translation and Diaspora Mission in the Future

In recent years, a theology of diaspora that has been coined "diaspora missiology" has been developed. The Third Lausanne Congress in Cape Town, South Africa, in 2010 was an encouraging occasion for the global diaspora mission movement. The issue of diaspora and its missiology was included as one of the predominant features of the congress program and acclaimed as a new paradigm for world evangelization for the coming era.

As Tereso Casiño conclusively summarized in his article "Why People Move: A Prolegomenon to Diaspora Missiology," "missionary efforts among people on the move are biblically valid, theologically consistent, and historically grounded. Under the redemptive plan of God, people move because the migratory or diasporic flows and transitions provide them with opportunities to encounter more of God's redemptive acts."[15]

To fulfill God's redemptive plan for people on the move, Bible translation could be more effectively and strategically utilized if the displaced project is mobilized in the diasporic context for the unreached people groups and unwritten language groups. We must, however, keep in mind the following missional implications:

First, ethnic Bible translation in the diasporic context may be an effective mission strategy for the people who are not yet evangelized but who are in limited-access areas. As seen in the case of the Korean Bible translations, those in limited-access contexts could access the Word of God through the Bible translated in China and Japan with Korean diaspora. They could then grow by reading it, initially with the help of outsiders.

Second, ethnic Bible translation can be mobilized more in diasporic contexts. Traditionally, Bible translation has happened in the place of ethnic language groups, and in many cases these were hard to access, particularly the least-reached people groups in the frontier areas. However, because of the large scale of geographical and demographical mobility of people in this century, there are more possibilities for implementing ethnic Bible translation in the diasporic context, as seen in the Sura project executed in Europe.

Third, ethnic Bible translation in the diasporic context may be a good example of the holistic approach of Christian mission. The goal of Bible translation is not only to produce a vernacular Bible in a certain language, but also to reproduce disciples of Jesus during translation work. Ultimately, everyone

---

15. In S. Hun Kim and Wonsuk Ma, *Korean Diaspora and Christian Mission* (Oxford: Regnum, 2011), 57.

who is involved in the translation must grow together as a body of Christ. In the context of diaspora, ethnic people are often easily exposed to the natural human propensity to depend on others because they face isolation, fear, insecurity, bereavement, and trauma. This vulnerable situation provides more opportunities for others to provide practical and spiritual help. In this sense, Bible translation is not only a long-term process in translation, but also a life-changing journey *through* the translation process for a language community.

Fourth, ethnic Bible translation in the diasporic context will provide a symbiotic partnership for the kingdom of God among participants. Bible translation is not a project that one person finishes by him- or herself. Bible translation is the product of many people under the supervision of the Holy Spirit. Therefore, translation projects must include a number of participants, including local and other ethnic churches and Christian individuals.

Finally, ethnic and "cluster" Bible translation is key for the diaspora mission and multiethnic societies. For example, in Europe, there are an increasing number of clusters in society, and these clusters tend to reflect their own subcultures and communities. A street kids' Bible in Amsterdam was recently published because many were not able to understand the contemporary Bible in Dutch. Other examples of cluster Bible translations are the Bike Bible and the Metal Bible.[16] It is essential to provide relevant materials for the people or cluster group to be evangelized in the diasporic mission environment.

Conclusion

There is no era like the current one: a human tidal wave is flowing unprecedentedly from everywhere to everywhere in the world. For those of us who have been in mission for a while, this phenomenon requires a response.

In Bible translation for vernacular language groups, we must reconsider the conventional approaches and methodologies employed for more than half a century. Displaced translation (i.e. ethnic Bible translation) is a strategic approach for the unreached and unwritten vernacular language groups in the diasporic context. This approach carries significant issues for the mission context: holistic mission, discipleship through the translation process,

---

16. The Bike Bible contains the whole New Testament and life stories of bikers. It is published by a group at the Christian Motorcyclists Association and Bible for the Nations. The Metal Bible is a Bible for those who love hard rock/metal music and is published by Johannes Jonsson and Roul Akesson through Bible for the Nations.

symbiotic kingdom partnership, and Scripture use for ethnic and social clusters in the diasporic context.

References

Im, Chandler, and Amos Yong, eds. *Global Diasporas and Mission*. Regnum Edinburgh Centenary. Oxford: Regnum, 2014.

Jung, Min-Young. "Diaspora and Timely Hit: Towards a Diaspora Missiology." In *Korean Diaspora and Christian Mission*, edited by S. Hun Kim and Wonsuk Ma, 59–71. Oxford: Regnum, 2011.

Kim, S. Hun, and Wonsuk Ma. *Korean Diaspora and Christian Mission*. Oxford: Regnum, 2011.

Padilla, C. R. "Holistic Mission." In *Dictionary of Mission Theology*, edited by John Corrie et al., 157–62. Nottingham: Inter-Varsity Press, 2007.

Pratt, Keith, and Richard Rutt. *Korea: A Historical and Cultural Dictionary*. Richmond: Curzon Press, 1999.

Weifan, Wang. "The Bible in Chinese." *Nanjing Theological Review* 14.15, 1991: 75–90.

14

People, Places, and Partnership in Transnational Missions

By Stanley John

I first met Dr. Ted Yamamori at a Lausanne Global Diaspora meeting in Toronto in 2009. That was the first of many gatherings; over the next decade we traveled together to Qatar, Kuwait, Korea, and the Philippines, and I hosted him in Wilmore, Kentucky, during his lectures at Asbury Theological Seminary. Ted listened well and spoke with precision, offering thoughtful guidance and wisdom to those of us who had the privilege to serve with him. He embodies the very principles of transnational missions discussed in this chapter, having crisscrossed the world to mentor leaders and develop networks and partnerships through his work at Food for the Hungry International and the Lausanne Movement.

Introduction

> Now those who had been scattered by the persecution that broke out when Stephen was killed traveled as far as Phoenicia, Cyprus and Antioch, spreading the word only among Jews. Some of them, however, men from Cyprus and Cyrene, went to Antioch and began to speak to Greeks also, telling them the good news about the Lord Jesus. The Lord's hand was with them, and a great number of people believed and turned to the Lord. (Acts 11:19–21)

The book of Acts offers a vibrant glimpse into the early days of the birth and growth of the Christian movement. The biblical narrative is rich in its description of the early leaders, the geographic expansion of the burgeoning community, and the dynamics of interregional and doctrinal developments taking place as the gospel crossed from a primarily Jewish starting point to being at home among the Gentiles. An analysis of the church's interconnections and exchanges, an examination of the ethnic and cultural identity of its early leaders, and attention to their travel between the various locations offer insight into the organization and organic structure of transnational religion at work. Taking Acts 11:19–21 as our starting point of reflection, I want to trace three key themes of transnational missions in the book of Acts – namely, people, places, and partnerships.

The story of the unnamed men bringing the gospel to the Greeks in Antioch is a missiological breakthrough in Acts.[1] This is the moment when the gospel decisively crosses to the Gentiles. We begin to feel the full force of the pivotal role of these unnamed men when we consider that no one else was engaged in gentile mission yet. Consider that the disciples had received the Great Commission of Jesus (Matt 28:18–20) and his final words laying out the visionary direction for the disciples to be witnesses in Jerusalem, all Judea, Samaria, and to the ends of the world (Acts 1:8). Furthermore, the global diaspora of Jews and residents of the global cities of the world were present in Jerusalem on the day of Pentecost when they heard the praises of God in their native languages. They were witnesses to the hospitality of the Holy Spirit to use the few disciples to speak the languages of the many. In a reversal of Babel (Gen 11), God did not necessitate that the nations learn Hebrew to encounter the living God; rather, through the baptism of the Holy Spirit, God empowered them for linguistic translatability of the gospel. The multilingual, multinational seeds of the global family of God spread into the nations.

Yet, none of the apostles ventured to Samaria. After the destruction of the Northern Kingdom in 722 BC the Assyrian Empire dispersed its people and resettled the land with foreigners intermixing with the residents. Hence, Jews avoided Samaria, seeing the Samaritans as an impure and corrupted people.

Despite the final words of Jesus (Acts 1:8), the example of Jesus going to Samaria and speaking with the woman at the well (John 4), and the teachings of Jesus in which he spoke of "the good Samaritan," we do not see a concerted mission effort to this region until we read of a deacon named Philip (Acts 8). Propelled by the persecution that broke out with Stephen's martyrdom, Philip must have reasoned, "Surely, the Samaritans too must hear the good news of

---

1. Timothy C. Tennent, *Invitation to World Missions: A Trinitarian Missiology for the Twenty-First Century* (Grand Rapids: Kregel, 2010), 152.

the gospel!" After his successful mission there, he finds himself sharing the gospel with the African official who is baptized and goes on his way rejoicing.

In Acts 10, we read of the transformation of Peter in overcoming his prejudices and ethical and dietary restrictions to share the gospel with Cornelius, the Roman official. The narrative repeatedly emphasizes the divine initiative in bringing the good news to the Gentiles (10:3, 19, 34, 44, 47; 11:18). God's initiative in mission is reiterated during the Jerusalem Council (Acts 15) as the apostles debate the ethical and spiritual ramifications of the Gentiles coming to faith (Acts 15:7–10). The apostle James offers the concluding remarks at the Council highlighting the divine primacy in mission: "Simon has described to us how God first intervened to choose a people for his name from the Gentiles" (Acts 15:14).

Theme One: People in Transnational Mission

By the time we reach Acts 11, we have read about the outbreak of persecution that led to the scattering of the disciples from Jerusalem (Acts 8:1; 11:19). The English word "diaspora" comes from the Greek word *diaspeiro* that is used to describe the scattered believers. That word is made up of two Greek words: *dia*, meaning through, and *speir*, meaning seed. The idea is that the people movements are the seeds that are being scattered into the nations.

Because of the scattering some people made their way north to Antioch (in modern-day Turkey), which was the third-largest city in the Roman Empire. Here, the writer of Acts specifies that they were sharing the gospel only with the Jews. It was hard for the early believers to think of the gospel's implications beyond their own tribe. Acts 11:20, however, introduces us to some unnamed men from Cyprus and Cyrene who began to speak to the Greeks also. The writer offers this summary statement: "The Lord's hand was with them, and a great number of people believed and turned to the Lord."

We do not know anything about the identity or names of the men who evangelized the Gentiles – we know only the place from which they originate. They are from Cyrene, a city located in modern-day Libya in North Africa. The city was in an area earlier settled by Phoenicians, with indigenous North African inhabitants and many Greek and Jewish settlers (sometimes estimated at one-third each). The culture included a mix of these various elements.

These men were perhaps ethnically Jewish diaspora people who had settled in these cities but had joined this Jesus movement in Jerusalem. And they are now making their way to the city of Antioch. While others were sharing the good news about the Lord Jesus only with Jews, these unnamed men thought of the inclusion of the Gentiles in the family of God.

What was it that allowed them to think of the inclusion of the Gentiles in the family of God? Could it be that their diasporic identity uniquely shaped them to think of their inclusion? Could it be that their exposure to multiple peoples in their migrant experience and their growing up in schools and communities where they were minorities alongside other nationalities shaped their psyche? Because of these things, could they hear the words of Jesus and grasp the full implications for a global gospel that envisions people from every nation, tribe, and tongue?

The multiplicity of cultures and locations is a common feature of the early missionaries and gospel workers of the New Testament. Consider the apostle Paul. In terms of his ethnic identity, Paul was Jewish; his tribal identity was as a Benjaminite. He belonged to the religious sect of Pharisees and was a radicalized religious extremist who was ordering the killing of Christians, but who, when he had an encounter with the risen Lord, had a dramatic altering of religious beliefs.

We know Paul was born in Tarsus (Acts 22:3), which is in modern-day Turkey. He was most likely raised in Jerusalem and was trained under Gamaliel. He was a tentmaker by trade (Acts 18:3) and a Roman citizen (Acts 16:37). He was probably one of the Cilicians who belonged to the Synagogue of the Freed Persons (Acts 6:9; 21:39) – meaning people who were previously slaves but who were freed. It is likely that Paul was a Roman citizen because several generations earlier his ancestors were slaves in Rome. Linguistically, we know that Paul was at least bilingual, speaking and writing fluently in Greek but also strong in Hebrew when he made his defense to the Jews in Acts 21. He has two names: Saul, his Hebrew name, and Paul, his Greek name. Also consider Timothy, who was born to an intercultural couple of Greek and Jewish heritage. Or Barnabas, who was originally from Cyprus (Acts 4:36), and who probably had ties with some of the Cypriots who helped evangelize Antioch initially (Acts 11:20).

Could it be that Paul's multicultural identity uniquely shaped him for missional effectiveness? Paul is what we might call a "transnational migrant." He embodies the multiple places of belonging in his self-identify and self-description. Linda Basch, Nina Glick Schiller, and Cristina Blanc-Szanton define transnationalism as the "process by which immigrants forge and sustain multi-stranded social relations that link together their societies or origin and settlement. We call these processes transnationalism to emphasize that many immigrants today build social fields that cross geographical, cultural, and political borders."[2] "Transnational" emphasizes Paul's multiple regular cross-border engagements that characterized and shaped his life.

The ministry and encounter with the "ethnic other" and the "religious other" took place within a migrant context. The persecution of the church in Jerusalem scattered the peoples all over the world. In this story, believers came to Antioch, a foreign city in modern-day Turkey that borders Syria. This was a booming and thriving city located by the river Orontes and along the Silk Road known for its trade with the world. People flocked to the urban cities. It is in this place that the gospel encounters people. Migration presents the opportunity for exposure and immersion which can uniquely prepare people for global mission. The new place of residence gives rise to the complexities of identity and intercultural, intergenerational creations of new identities which are brought together for transnational mission.

What is interesting about the story of the unnamed men from Cyprus and Cyrene is that the migrants were the missionaries. Often, the rhetoric of mission with diaspora highlights migrants as people needing to be served or reached with the gospel. While in many places and in many cases migrants who are refugees are fleeing violence or war and are in dire need of shelter, food, and the hope of the gospel, there is another reality to which we must be attentive.

Nearly half of the world's migrants are Christians. This presents unique opportunities to reflect not only on reaching migrants but also sharing Christian fellowship and partnership in mission. Migration challenges the modernistic, dualistic, binary framework of reached and unreached, us and them, from here to there, homeland missions and foreign missions, citizen and alien. It requires the shedding of our penchant for a simplistic framing of the world in favor of building a fresh framework that accounts for the complexity and innovation taking place sociologically to which missiology must respond. Reports of African missionaries in Europe and North America, Latin American missionaries in the Arab world, Filipino missionaries in the Middle East, and Indian missionaries in the United States highlight the global movement of missionary force from "everywhere to everywhere." These stories capture the complexity and remind us that what God is doing and how God is at work does not fit into neat modernistic categories.

---

2. Linda Basch, Nina Glick Schiller, and Cristina Blanc-Szanton, *Nations Unbound: Transnational Projects, Postcolonial Predicaments, and Deterritorialized Nation-States* (Abingdon: Taylor & Francis, 1994), 7.

Theme Two: Places in Transnational Missions

Urban migration provides opportunities for the peoples of the world to intersect and cross paths and in the process opens possibilities for interreligious encounter. In a previous era, a Christendom context assumed that most if not all peoples in the same locale shared the same faith. Hence, the assumption was that people must travel overseas to encounter the religious "other" in missionary service. The thinking was that people must engage in cross-cultural travel to qualify as doing missionary work because the paradigm assumed that the same culture meant the same faith.

Ralph Winter reminds us that we "simply have not caught up with recognizing that the world's peoples can no longer be defined in geographic terms."[3] The question then arises: How do we think about people in nonspatial terms? Paul and the early apostles seemed to be able to crisscross the then-known world with relative ease for the sake of the gospel as though travel and global networking came as second nature to them.

The diaspora shaping of Paul is evident upon a closer look at his life. As stated earlier, we know he was born in Tarsus, grew up in Jerusalem, and traveled throughout the empire persecuting Christians. But upon his conversion, he went with Ananias to Damascus, Syria, where he began his preaching ministry. When opposition arose the believers got him out of the city (Acts 9:23–25). In Galatians, Paul tells us that he went to Arabia for some time before he went to Jerusalem (Gal 1:17). When he went to Jerusalem (Acts 9:26) to join the disciples, they were unaccepting of him because they were afraid. So, Barnabas took him and brought him to the apostles. And when the Hellenistic Jews tried to kill him, they sent him to Tarsus, his birthplace, where he spent the next decade of his life. We then learn that Barnabas goes to Tarsus in search of Saul and brings him to Antioch, where he is mentored at the Antioch church. Barnabas and Saul are sent to Jerusalem to bring remittances from the Antioch church for the Jerusalem church. Sometime later, the Holy Spirit prompts the Antioch church to "set apart Barnabas and Saul" to launch the first missionary journey. Their first stop is Cyprus! Why? Cyprus was the hometown of Barnabas. The locations of their immediate start and their return are part of their identity; they are not haphazard choices made by the twirling of the globe, but strategic, intentional, organic, and developmental in their journey.

In his first missionary journey, Paul, Barnabas, and John Mark set out from Antioch in Syria's seaport of Seleucia (in southern Turkey), headed to

---

3. Quoted in Luis Pantoja Jr., Sadiri Tira, and Enoch Wan, *Scattered: The Filipino Global Presence* (Manila: LifeChange, 2004), back cover.

the island of Cyprus, continued through modern-day Turkey (Pamphylia, and Antioch in Pisidia, Lycaonia, Iconium, Lystra, and Derbe; on their return route, they passed through Pamphylia and Pisidia, Perga, and Attalia), and caught a ship back to Antioch.

For the second missionary journey, Paul and Silas set out from Antioch, taking the land route through the southern Turkish cities of Derbe, Lystra, and Iconium, where Timothy joined the team. Timothy was bicultural, his father being Greek and his mother Jewish. They continued from there through Phrygia, Galatia, and on to Troas on the northwestern coast of Turkey on the Aegean Sea. From there, they embarked on a ship to set sail for the region of Macedonia, thus crossing into Europe for the very first time. From their starting point in Philippi, they traveled throughout the cities of northern Greece (Amphipolis, Apollonia, and Thessalonica), and then sailed down to Achaia and Athens and then Corinth in southern Greece, where they met Aquila and Priscilla. On their return journey they stopped at Ephesus in western Turkey, before returning to Caesarea, Jerusalem, and then back to home base in Antioch in Syria.

In his third missionary journey, Paul visited churches again in southern Turkey (Galatia and Phrygia), returned to Ephesus in western Turkey, and then went to Macedonia and Greece, back to western Turkey (Troas and Miletus), back to Caesarea, and then to Jerusalem. By the end of the book of Acts, we know Paul's travels encompassed all of Turkey, into Europe, and all the way to Rome.

Each of the three journeys and the final journey to Rome highlights the significant travel by both ship and boat, the new ventures, and the recurring visits of Paul and his coworkers. There were coworkers who traveled with Paul from Antioch – some dropped off the trip, others were added on to the team, new workers joined the group, and still others were emissaries from Paul to the churches and vice versa.

How did Paul hold all these places and people together? Was there a structure? Was there a mode of management of church planting, member care, and support for workers? Paul's native genius followed the trails of the Jewish diaspora as the strategy for church planting using indigenous and transnational leaders reaching out across the diasporas for whom travel, cross-border exchange, and movement came as second nature, eventually going far beyond their ethnic exclusivity and reaching out to the nations around. To follow the trails of the diaspora, reaching back to places of origin, places of sojourn, and diverse locales, provides a natural pathway for mission.

Theme Three: Partnerships in Transnational Missions

How did the disciples, the early church, and Paul in particular, launch a church-planting movement that became a global movement? Paul was creating a transnational network of relationships and partnerships that became the blueprint that held the incipient gospel movement together. The networks exist because of relationships between people. Paul calls them coworkers (Gk: *synergoi*), his partners in ministry, whom we might call "transnational agents." "Transnational" captures the cross-border travel and "agents" identifies the agency, volition, and individuality of the persons. These networks and agents are maintained through transnational exchanges. The constant, steady travel back and forth and movement of parchments, writings, and blankets become the natural avenue through which connections are forged, maintained, and employed for kingdom purposes.

Paul's letters served the purpose of knitting together this vast network of churches and personnel. He found ways to connect them to each other by requesting that the letters be shared among the churches. The finances raised in one place and sent to another captured Paul's vision of an interconnected church. These financial, cultural, and social remittances solidified relationships and became the capital that was exchanged on these networks. While I appreciate the heart of the three-self principle (self-supporting, self-governing, and self-propagating), Paul's view of the church was never so independent. He envisioned and practiced a thoroughly cross-border exchange for the substance and support of churches.

Early church leaders exemplify the innovation and resilience of interconnectivity and religious engagement across borders. Today, we see fellow passengers on international flights with religious symbols and amulets prominently displayed on their arms and neck. Devout Hindus will stop by the temple on their way to the airport to get a *prasad* and a marking on their forehead before their travels. The Indian church where I grew up in Kuwait would request church members to bring back song books, Bibles, books, calendars, and even drums and tambourines when fellow migrants visited their families in India. People innovate to remain connected. If one communication application is blocked by a government, people will turn to another. Some countries block the use of Facebook Messenger, and when people turn to WhatsApp and that is blocked, they then turn to WeChat, Kakao Talk, Viber, and a host of other applications signaling the ways people forge pathways to remain connected across borders.

In our church-planting and church-management efforts, we have yet to let the genius of Paul infuse our thinking. Along with teaching homiletics and hermeneutics, seminary and leadership training curricula must include training in how to form partnerships, how to create a movement and a network built on relationships, how to raise up leaders who will raise up other leaders, and how to keep them connected through regular discipleship and leadership reviews.

Paul shows us that his letters became the model through which he connected the entire network. He offered greetings from coworkers, addressed letters to specific people, and encouraged exchange to create interdependence. In so doing, he created a vibrant network of ministries that would lay the foundation for the growth of the church. Cross-border connections and regular exchanges become the tools that allow people to remain connected. God's kingdom work moves forward through kingdom networks and partnership.

Conclusion

God's kingdom advances through persons knit together with sacred worth whose multiple identities and belongings are brought together for unique missional significance. The migration of peoples challenges our notions of places to reflect on a borderless world where God's kingdom people crisscross effortlessly and naturally because these places and locations are parts of their identity.

Finally, the great task for kingdom effectiveness lies in the spiritual art of networks and partnerships – people who can weave together multiple cultures and places and find ways to facilitate the flow of the gospel to every nation, tribe, and tongue. Ministry in our new context presents tremendous opportunities for witness. Our old models and assumptions will not work; however, the call of the Lord of the harvest is for the eternal values of the kingdom to guide us forward. We must forge new pathways, partnerships, and avenues to fulfill our Master's calling to make disciples of all nations because we now live in a borderless world.

References

Basch, Linda, Nina Glick Schiller, and Cristina Blanc-Szanton. *Nations Unbound: Transnational Projects, Postcolonial Predicaments, and Deterritorialized Nation-States*. Abingdon: Taylor & Francis, 1994.

Pantoja, Luis, Jr., Sadiri Tira, and Enoch Wan. *Scattered: The Filipino Global Presence*. Manila: LifeChange, 2004.

Tennent, Timothy C. *Invitation to World Missions: A Trinitarian Missiology for the Twenty-First Century*. Grand Rapids: Kregel, 2010.

15

Home: Reflections on Next-Generation Diaspora[1]

By Lorajoy Tira-Dimangondayao

I am a third-generation Christian and fully indoctrinated in evangelical missions. But, at some point, I began to ask, "What is the point of what we do? Why are we so committed to the Great Commission?" I have heard my thoughts in the words of friends who, like me, have been raised with the privilege of Jesus-devoted families.

After some reflection, I believe that the reason we do what we do as Christians is to make a *home*. Anglican theologian Miroslav Volf describes "home" this way: "In the Jewish and Christian traditions, the object of hope expressed in the image of home is inextricably bound with transcendence: it is either God's gift, or God's very being, or, as we will argue, both God's gift and God."[2] He goes on:

> At their best, homes are places where love, peace, and joy come together. In such homes, each rejoices over and each rejoices with all others, and all rejoice in their common social and material space; each loves others and is loved by them, and all tend to their common space; each individually and all together are at

---

1. This piece was adapted from a presentation at the Diaspora and Mission workshop of the Christian & Missionary Alliance's denominational gathering, the Alliance World Fellowship (AWF) Quadrennial 2021 in Guayaquil, Ecuador, on 21 October 2021.

2. Miroslav Volf, "The World as God's Home: Lecture 1, Modern Homelessness," Edward Cadbury Lectures, University of Birmingham, Birmingham, 28 May 2019, https://www.birmingham.ac.uk/schools/ptr/departments/theologyandreligion/events/cadburylectures/2019/index.aspx.

peace, enjoying and working to enhance the material and social circumstances that are their home.³

In the household codes of the New Testament, we see a further development of the image of home: home for the Roman family is the domicile of the family, where the paterfamilias directs his household, and in which his wife and children are actively involved in the family enterprise. The household is synonymous with family business.⁴ (We also see this in some collective cultures, such as those in the Philippines.)

So, tied to the concept of "home is family," Professor David Goa, a Canadian public theologian in the Orthodox tradition, writes that the Christian family "is concerned for growth into union with God and nurturing each family member's capacity to love the life of the world. The spiritual life of the family is precisely to cultivate and nurture this capacity in the children, in each other and in the stranger."⁵

Yet today, many people are experiencing a sense of spiritual, emotional, and physical homelessness. Certainly, this is the case for people on the move who have been uprooted or dislocated from their homelands.⁶ The answer to this homelessness is the indwelling of God.

My memories begin in the late 1970s aboard the "world's largest floating bookstore," the MV *Logos*. On the ocean, far away from my birth country of the Philippines, I learned to walk and talk. I learned English even before my mother's home language. My mom was a nursing instructor from the northern islands and my dad was an industrial engineer from the deep south. They had met in Metro Manila as university students and had joined the Christian movement of Operation Mobilization, committing to actively participate in "motivating and mobilising others to live out [God's] purposes."⁷

The multigenerational and multi-accented residents of the MV *Logos* came from very different economic and sociocultural backgrounds. My nursery

---

3. Volf, "World as God's Home."

4. Margaret Y. MacDonald, "Kinship and Family in the New Testament World," in *Understanding the Social World of the New Testament*, eds. Dietmar Neufeld and Richard E. DeMaris (London: Routledge, 2010).

5. David J. Goa, "Reflections on the Spiritual Vocation of Family," paper for the Summer Institute on the Spiritual Life, Monastery of All Saints of North America, Dewdney, British Colombia, Davidgoa.ca, 14, https://static1.squarespace.com/static/5a7691c96957da992caf9f6e/t/5e44cea6907146602d6ccddc/1581567655939/Reflections+on+the+Spritual+Vocation+of+the+Family.pdf.

6. See Volf, "World as God's Home"; and Hartmut Rosa, *The Uncontrollability of the World* (Medford: Polity Press).

7. OM Ships International, "About OM Ships," https://www.om.org/ships/about.

school teacher was a princess of Tonga and my best friend's father was a doctor from the Netherlands. My parents' best friend joined as well. He operated a watch shop in Manila. The ship picked up more residents from ports scattered across the oceans. The residents would live together on a dollar a day, sharing what they had with each other and with the guests who visited the bookstore onboard. My father has joked that of all the Christian organizations, "MV *Logos*, the commune-on-a-ship, was the hippiest of them all."

These early memories of belonging to a family comprising diverse individuals, eating communal dinners at galley tables, and sharing the tasks of running the boiler room, cleaning toilets, and preparing meals for many, marked my mind and my heart. The *belonging* in that floating home demanded to be replicated in my understanding and practice of my faith in the years to come. It defined my faith journey. Everything spiritual about me features the realities and metaphors of family.

After two years of living on the ship (ages one to three) and collecting over sixty stamps of entry in my Philippine passport, I moved with my parents to Regina, Saskatchewan. My father had been admitted into a divinity program at Canadian Theological Seminary as a foreign student, and my mother and I went along. At our port of entry in Calgary, Alberta, our two suitcases were stolen, along with my father's briefcase, which contained "all the cash we had in the world." Hearing of our airport disaster, we were welcomed to Regina by the dean of students who ushered us into a charity-furnished apartment. My parents quickly became involved in the seminary community on Fourth Avenue and the church we joined in Hillsdale. I spent the next two years playing with Canadian-born and similarly transplanted children on the school campus and in the church facility. In kindergarten, I learned to sing "God Save the Queen." If we were "foreigners" in Canada's Queen city, I did not notice. *Belonging* was a mark of *my home*.

Later in my childhood, I would witness and partake in family in yet another Canadian city – Edmonton. Following my father's studies, my parents were called to intern with, then join, the permanent staff at Millbourne Alliance Church (MAC), a primarily European-background congregation in south Edmonton. Their assignment was to provide spiritual direction for a growing community of international students and foreign-born New Canadians from the Philippines. At MAC, I met "white" men and women renamed Tita, Tito, Lolo, and Lola by the Filipinos they embraced, and for whom they provided adoptive homes. Also at MAC, I witnessed my father and other Filipinos invited into leadership capacities, fully integrated into the spiritual and community life of the church. If it was novel in Canada's initially Euro-descent congregations for members to intentionally go beyond "Canadian hospitality" to give New Canadians a place of genuine belonging, I was not aware of it.

My parents were devoted followers of Jesus, and the faith communities they collaborated with recognized that some people were alone and displaced, and that the antidote for that displacement was *belonging* and "communitas." The latter was a term developed by cultural anthropologist Victor W. Turner, referring to "an experience of oneness or unity felt by those sharing a rite-of-passage experience." Turner's wife, anthropologist Elizabeth Turner, extends his description: "*Communitas* is thus a gift from liminality, the state of being betwixt and between. During this time, people find each other to be just ordinary people after all, not the anxious prestige-seeking holders of jobs and positions they often seem to be. People see each other face to face."[8]

The model I have embraced is that of my parents' unconditional embrace of the other. While some communities define themselves by lines of inclusion and exclusion, my parents welcomed in a way that said, "Join us at our table. Come as you are." It did not matter who they were.

I have heard it said that the surest way to recognize authenticity is to first familiarize oneself with the genuine article. With the deep sense of *belonging* found in some communities, I can say that I have encountered true fellowship; I saw it in my parents' lives and in the Jesus-followers around me. Our investment was in relationships, not numbers.

In the process of articulating my spiritual journey, I have noted how many of my memories are marked by the cultural liminality of my childhood – I was raised in Canada but never felt Canadian enough. I looked Filipino but was not accepted as a Filipino who knew the realities of Filipino life. Outside my home and away from my faith community, I was acutely aware of being an outsider at school and, to varying degrees, in my Edmonton communities.

As an adult, I recognize the security that was afforded me by the privileges of my upbringing, and I realize how this contrast of displacement and belonging has contributed to my own desire to call the "outsider" into "family." Shaped by the family who raised me, I recognize that the church of Jesus Christ is called to call in the outsiders, inviting them past a proverbial "welcome mat" into the collaborative life of family.

I am a member of one of Edmonton's oldest Christian churches, Beulah Alliance Church (BAC), a hundred-year-old congregation that has expanded to include a sizeable multicultural membership, Arabic and Spanish congregations,

---

8. Edith Turner, *Communitas: The Anthropology of Collective Joy* (New York: Palgrave Macmillan, 2011), 4.

and a satellite congregation that is led by a pastor who arrived in Canada from Vietnam as an asylum-seeking child. In May 2021, BAC installed a second-generation Canadian of Korean descent, born in Vancouver, in the position of lead pastor. One of our executive pastors was born in Guatemala. The other is French Canadian.

Still, in many of the Canadian congregations I see, the board of elders is Euro-centric and the lay leadership remains predominantly of the dominant or majority culture. Further still, many Canadian congregations continue to grapple with the realities of generational and demographic shift. While some churches, including BAC, are attempting to employ a culturally hybrid model over a homogeneous model – inviting people from diverse backgrounds to positions of leadership and responsibility – other congregations maintain a solidly monocultural leadership (even when New Canadians or "older" Canadians sit in the pews). This even as we have seen that 90 percent of the AWF inclusive membership is found in Africa, Asia, and Latin America[9] – and Jesus-followers from those continents sit in our pews.

Furthermore, as immigration levels in Canada continue to rise, mono-ethnic churches continue to propagate. Canadian Christians are representing more varied ethnocultural backgrounds, yet many remain isolated and the Canadian church fragmented. This development in the church is reflected across Canadian society. Outside local congregations, community demographics are changing, but are Canadian communities moving beyond basic hospitality and answering the human need for belonging? We must, in the image of home and family, intentionally work on our pathways of discipleship toward leadership. What this means is intentional and strategic discipleship. The image that can help is of the children of a household being trained to actively participate in the family business.

According to Statistics Canada, international migration accounted for 82.8 percent of all population growth in Canada during the first three months of 2019.[10]

---

9. AWF Executive Committee, "Inclusive Membership (2019)," Global Assembly, AWF Quadrennial Convocation, 20 October 2021, Guayaquil, Ecuador.

10. *The Daily*, "Canada's Population Estimates, First Quarter 2019," 19 June 2019, https://www150.statcan.gc.ca/n1/en/daily-quotidien/190619/dq190619c-eng.pdf?st=_SF3Vdvp. COVID-19 pandemic restrictions greatly reduced immigration numbers. See *The Daily*, "Canada's Population Estimates, Fourth Quarter 2020," 18 March 2021, https://www150.statcan.gc.ca/n1/en/daily-quotidien/210318/dq210318c-eng.pdf?st=GBVYuHEV. The federal government has announced plans to drastically increase immigration numbers to revive the Canadian economy post–COVID-19. See Government of Canada News Release, "Government of Canada Announces Plan to Support Economic Recovery through Immigration," 30 October

At what point, if ever, do these individuals find true *belonging*?[11] Is the mere presence of international students, foreign workers, or New Canadians at events indicative of mutuality and belonging? What have we done to bring them to a place of belonging? Have we listened to their stories? Have we understood how they understand and navigate the world? Have we invited them into family discussion and planning, using the wisdom and gifts they bring?

Immigrant-background children are a growing segment of Canada's population. The most recent numbers we have in Canada on immigrant children come from the 2016 Census, which reported that 37.5 percent of children aged fifteen and under were first-generation immigrants or had at least one parent who was foreign-born.[12] Further, Census projections suggested that by 2036, between 39.3 percent and 49.1 percent of those aged fifteen and under living in Canada would be foreign-born or have at least one first-generation parent.[13]

I share my own migrant story to illustrate the identity-forming process for an immigrant-background child in a diverse society. While my journey is uniquely mine, its complexity reflects the journeys of millions of people who are resettling in new places. We are all in search of belonging and home. This is both a journey and a desire. It has the potential to play an integral role in bringing people, particularly migrants, home.

A Challenge in the Diaspora Community

"Christianity is a white religion, Mom." My son was eleven and was eager to report his new knowledge. He was reading about the early European explorers, settlers, and missionaries in his social studies course. My first thought was to protest loudly, but a few moments of thought and prayer allowed me to recognize his context. First, there was his Alberta social studies curriculum. To address the Canadian colonial past, students are encouraged to examine the effects of European settlement. Second, there was the inescapable truth that my child was born into and was being raised and educated in a proudly diverse

---

2020, https://www.canada.ca/en/immigration-refugees-citizenship/news/2020/10/government-of-canada-announces-plan-to-support-economic-recovery-through-immigration.html.

11. Canada is the first country in the world to introduce a points-based immigration system and to formalize and implement an official multiculturalism policy.

12. Statistics Canada, "Census in Brief: Children with an Immigrant Background: Bridging Cultures," 25 October 2017, https://www12.statcan.gc.ca/census-recensement/2016/as-sa/98-200-x/2016015/98-200-x2016015-eng.cfm.

13. Statistics Canada, "Census in Brief."

and pluralistic society. Every day, he interacted with people from around the world who held different beliefs.

It is tragic that many people conflate Christianity, colonialism, nationality, and race. As the dominance of Western Christendom wanes, Christians are called to answer for power differentials found in history. Furthermore, representations of Jesus framed by dominant Western traditions are also being challenged.

Being from an immigrant background, I find it interesting that New Canadians from non-Christian backgrounds tend to conflate the four, while our public institutions boast of our cultural, racial, and religious diversity. To combat this, the church must actively educate congregants on wider church history, balanced local history, and the global church. Moreover, with the demise of Western Christendom, Christians must rediscover and emulate the kingdom values found in the first-century church.

Canadian congregations must also recognize that, according to current immigration trends and forecasts, most immigrants to Canada are coming from countries that have recent colonial histories. This has many implications. For example, when local congregations minister to Filipinos, they are advised to study modern Filipino traits as an outcome of Spanish and American influences, and of the continuing subjugation we see in the global economy. These cultures (and their occupations of the Philippines) have shaped the Filipino's sense of self, community, and God. A foreign-born, Canadian-raised person may very well be the child of not just the French and English empires, but also of the Spanish, of the American, and maybe even of the globalized economy all rolled into one. This same Filipino, in the impressionable years of adolescence, may, if alienated and not supported in family, form reactive allegiances in response to perceived prejudice and discrimination.[14]

At a time when racial division and historical injustice seem to be coming to the forefront, it is imperative that the church reject images of superiority and subjugation. We must instead seek to embody the family and the home, where people are loved into being and given a platform from which to add their voice to our song. We must perpetuate the image of a home where gifts are drawn out and put into service for the family enterprise and the flourishing of our communities and the world.

---

14. Lorajoy Tira-Dimangondayao, "From Hospice to Home," in *Beyond Hospitality: Migration, Multiculturalism, and the Church*, eds. Charles A. Cook, Lauren Goldbeck, and Lorajoy Tira-Dimangondayao (Toronto: Tyndale Academic Press, 2020), 121–31.

The Jesus Way

Indeed, a vision of family provides both the centripetal and the centrifugal force to reinforce our identity and send us out – it holds us in and pushes us out. Along this line, if we believe that Jesus is the Christ – the healer for everyone everywhere – then local congregations must represent this in tangible ways. Foreign-born children, particularly visible minority children, need to see co-ethnics represented in church leadership and actively participating in church life. This necessitates immigrant-background adults becoming more involved. The truth of the home and family must supersede the reality of the earthly.

As I look back, I see how my childhood cultural confusion was curtailed by the strength of my parents' Christian conviction. When faced with a perceived cultural discrepancy, I would turn to my parents for an explanation of the contrasting values I witnessed. "Daddy, why do we not do *this* the way other Filipinos [or Canadians] do?" My father would respond with, "We must be guided by *the Jesus way*." I may have been confused, but my parents were not, and their preference for a Jesus-modeled culture over our culture of national origin or our adopted Canadian culture provided me with a framework for working through future cultural conflicts.

No earthly culture is perfect; all have values and norms that need to be redeemed. When fielding cultural concerns, I remember how my parents provided stability for me by pointing to the Jesus way. While they taught me to be sensitive to a spectrum of cultural expectations, for them, desirable behavior boiled down to following the Jesus way. This Jesus way prioritized working together in the spirit of humility and peace over establishing a "right way" solely based on cultural expectations.

The 2016 Census showed that "the majority of children [with an immigrant background] under the age of 15 (74.0 percent) were from an Asian country [including the Middle East] of ancestry, an American country of ancestry (excluding the United States) or an African country of ancestry."[15] This contrasts with previous migration trends, with "almost half (46.1 percent) of the population between the ages of 35 and 64 and almost 70 percent of the population aged 65 and older [originating] from a European country of ancestry and the United States." With continued migration, it comes as no surprise that cultures will collide.

In *Legacies: The Story of the Immigrant Second Generation*, Alejandro Portes and Rubén G. Rumbaut study second-generation youths of immigrant background. One proposed contextual factor for adaption is "the host society

---

15. Statistics Canada, "Census in Brief."

and its reception of newcomers." They echo the "well-established sociological principle . . . that the more similar new minorities are in terms of physical appearance, class background, language, and religion to society's mainstream, the more favorable their reception and the more rapid their integration."[16]

Christian unity, manifested in a shared family-centered and Christ-centered culture, transcends cultural differences. A healthy church family can adequately assist foreign-born children and their families in adjusting to local life. Local churches can uphold a culture that models Jesus over what is perceived to be local culture. Likewise, instead of aligning with ethnocentric norms dictated by the culture of origin, parents can be discipled to guide their children in the ways of Jesus.

We must also teach parents about kingdom goals and investments over the preoccupying pursuit of the "immigrant dream" that is frequently driven by material aspirations. Further, instruction in Christ's family culture from a young age instills an appreciation for family values that will hopefully guide the foreign-born to become bridge-builders between cultures and communities.

My parents, always hoping to return to their home country, did not apply for Canadian citizenship until I was a teenager. So, at the age of fifteen, after a childhood of singing allegiance to the Queen, I became a citizen of Canada. I started voting when I was eighteen. The diaspora child is on the road to naturalization and fullness of citizenship; however, legal citizenship is not enough. Internalization of the new country's values, full participation in national life, and the externalization of national identity is the goal.

Likewise, full partnership in the faith community is the goal. Naturally equipped with a knowledge of both the culture of national origin and the culture of the new country, diaspora children may be mentored in the ways of Jesus's family for partnership in God's home-making in the world.

The intentional discipleship of immigrant families in the context of genuine relationship is essential. Beyond providing immigrant integration services such as adopted language classes, community kitchens, clothing drives, and income tax assistance, churches must provide foreign-born congregants with equal avenues for service, as responsibilities demonstrate trust and acceptance and cultivate a sense of investment and belonging in the family enterprise.[17]

---

16. Alejandro Portes and Rubén G. Rumbaut, *Legacies: The Story of the Immigrant Second Generation* (Berkeley: University of California Press, 2001), 47.

17. Tira-Dimangondayao, "From Hospice to Home."

To reiterate, Census Canada predicted that by 2036, "between 39.3 percent and 49.1 percent of the entire population of children aged 15 and under [living in Canada] will be foreign-born or have one first-generation parent."

Local congregations must prioritize the discipleship of families, particularly the children of immigrant backgrounds, for ongoing partnership with God in the family business of making human homes in which God desires to dwell.

Foreign-born children have the potential of being valuable partners in the family business and they should be motivated, equipped, and mobilized. The journey to belonging may start long before responsibility is fully realized, but when the foreign-born are accepted, mentored, and trusted with family goals and responsibilities, they move past the welcome mat to a permanent seat at the family table. When congregations move "outsiders" and "visitors" from the foyer to the kitchen, fewer lines will be drawn based on responses to "Where are you from?" Instead, allegiances will be formed by the answers to the question "Where are you serving?"[18]

Conclusion

We do what we do because we want to invite others into family and into the family business of home-making. We want to show them – through our lives – that God is making a life in us, with us, and that he wants to make his home with us. This idea of home is the imagery of eternal life. This reality transforms communities – and the world.

Revelation 21:3 in the NRSV says:

> And I heard a loud voice from the throne saying,
>
> "See, the home of God is among mortals.
> He will dwell with them;
> they will be his peoples,
> and God himself will be with them."

The New Century Version reads: "And I heard a loud voice from the throne, saying, 'Now God's presence is with people, and he will live with them, and they will be his people. God himself will be with them and will be their God.'"

The New Life Version reads: "I heard a loud voice coming from heaven. It said, 'See! God's home is with men. He will live with them. They will be His people. God Himself will be with them. He will be their God.'"

---

18. Tira-Dimangondayao.

It's all about this: Christ in us – at home in us – is the hope of glory. That is good news, the gospel, for a homeless world. There is a metaphor of the indwelling of God. It looks like metal held to the high temperatures of fire. In the fire, the metal is transformed and glows with the flame. So long as it stays one with the fire, the metal appears like the fire.[19] God himself is at home in us so that we and others may exclaim, as Arie Verduyn describes, "I see in you the face of God!"[20]

References

AWF Executive Committee. "Inclusive Membership (2019)." Global Assembly, AWF Quadrennial Convocation, 20 October 2021, Guayaquil, Ecuador.

The Daily. "Canada's Population Estimates, First Quarter 2019." 19 June 2019. https://www150.statcan.gc.ca/n1/en/daily-quotidien/190619/dq190619c-eng.pdf?st=_SF3Vdvp.

———. "Canada's Population Estimates, Fourth Quarter 2020." 18 March 2021. https://www150.statcan.gc.ca/n1/en/daily-quotidien/210318/dq210318c-eng.pdf?st=GBVYuHEV.

Goa, David J. "Reflections on the Spiritual Vocation of Family." Paper for the Summer Institute on the Spiritual Life, Monastery of All Saints of North America, Dewdney, British Colombia. Davidgoa.ca. https://static1.squarespace.com/static/5a7691c96957da992caf9f6e/t/5e44cea6907146602d6ccddc/1581567655939/Reflections+on+the+Spritual+Vocation+of+the+Family.pdf.

Government of Canada News Release. "Government of Canada Announces Plan to Support Economic Recovery through Immigration." 30 October 2020. https://www.canada.ca/en/immigration-refugees-citizenship/news/2020/10/government-of-canada-announces-plan-to-support-economic-recovery-through-immigration.html.

MacDonald, Margaret Y. "Kinship and Family in the New Testament World." In *Understanding the Social World of the New Testament*, edited by Dietmar Neufeld and Richard E. DeMaris, 29–43. London: Routledge, 2010.

OM Ships International. "About OM Ships." https://www.om.org/ships/about.

Portes, Alejandro, and Rubén G. Rumbaut. *Legacies: The Story of the Immigrant Second Generation.* Berkeley: University of California Press, 2001.

Rosa, Hartmut. *The Uncontrollability of the World.* Medford: Polity Press.

---

19. Miroslav Volf, "TH5/734: The Home of God," class lecture, Vancouver School of Theology, Vancouver, BC, 9 July 2021.

20. See Arie Verduyn, "Deeper Life and the Missional Mind: Morning October 21 – AWF Quadriennal Convocation 2021," Guayaquil, Ecuador, YouTube, https://youtu.be/0AcdBQogOyE.

Statistics Canada. "Census in Brief: Children with an Immigrant Background: Bridging Cultures." 25 October 2017. https://www12.statcan.gc.ca/census-recensement/2016/as-sa/98-200-x/2016015/98-200-x2016015-eng.cfm.

Tira-Dimangondayao, Lorajoy. "From Hospice to Home." In *Beyond Hospitality: Migration, Multiculturalism, and the Church*, edited by Charles A. Cook, Lauren Goldbeck, and Lorajoy Tira-Dimangondayao, 121–31. Toronto: Tyndale Academic Press, 2020.

Turner, Edith. *Communitas: The Anthropology of Collective Joy*. New York: Palgrave Macmillan, 2011.

Verduyn, Arie. "Deeper Life and the Missional Mind: Morning October 21 – AWF Quadriennal Convocation 2021." Guayaquil, Ecuador. YouTube. https://youtu.be/0AcdBQogOyE.

Volf, Miroslav. "TH5/734: The Home of God." Class lecture, Vancouver School of Theology, Vancouver, BC, 9 July 2021.

———. "The World as God's Home: Lecture 1, Modern Homelessness." Edward Cadbury Lectures, University of Birmingham, Birmingham, 28 May 2019. https://www.birmingham.ac.uk/schools/ptr/departments/theologyandreligion/events/cadburylectures/2019/index.aspx.

16

Training Leaders for Diaspora Missions in South Korea: The Yamamori Strategy Models

By Tereso C. Casiño

Tetsunao Yamamori's connection to South Korea has a long history. It is both diverse and complex. As a Japanese immigrant to the US, first as an international student, and later as a naturalized citizen, Ted surprises many in Korea with his love for the people in the peninsula. Many Koreans still feel uneasy dealing with the Japanese because of Japan's occupation of the country from 1910 to 1945 and the many conflicts in the history that straddles the two nations. There is also the issue that has been euphemistically called "comfort women" (women and girls forced into sexual slavery in occupied countries and territories) and other atrocities that the Japanese military committed on the Korean peninsula during World War II. Fast-forward to the late twentieth century and the dawn of the millennium and Ted's name became better known in Christian circles, especially among leaders across the nation.

To many Korean leaders who have known him personally, Ted is a man with a mission and vision for the invigoration of higher education in the Korean peninsula, and they specifically note his involvement in a university in the capital of the North that specializes in science and technology and its counterpart in Yanbian, China. However, there is one side to Ted that many Korean church leaders do not know, and that is his advocacy and support for the training of leaders for diaspora missions in South Korea and beyond. Ted reflects,

In my travels, I have come across Korean people everywhere. What is gratifying to me is that many of these Koreans are firm believers in the Lord Jesus Christ and are passionate about proclaiming the gospel. Wherever they are, they begin prayer gathering among themselves. They not only try to reach out to their own people living in diaspora, but also the people of the host nations.[1]

Below I seek to enlighten readers of Ted's connection to South Korea through the lens of leadership training among those involved in diaspora missions and intercultural ministries. To understand the significance of his involvement in and contributions to the training of leaders for diaspora missions, I will highlight two major strategies: short-term training through missions agencies, and campus-based training.

Setting the Stage for Training Leaders for Diaspora Missions in South Korea

The twentieth and twenty-first centuries in the Korean peninsula have witnessed the heavy traffic of migration flow into the Land of the Morning Calm. For years, people from all walks of life have moved to Korea to live, work, study, or marry. They are diplomats, skilled and unskilled workers, students, musicians, military personnel, scholars, professionals, refugees, or intercultural individuals and families, among others. But Koreans themselves have had their own share of migration away from their homeland.[2] In this, missionary work among Koreans in diaspora is traceable to the 1900s when the Korean church began reaching out to Koreans scattered in Japan, northeast Asia, and Siberia.[3] At home, efforts to minister to the international migrants on Korean soil had a slow start, although they gained traction after the 1988 Seoul Summer Olympics. To understand how this evolved over time, it is important to follow the trails of migration in Korea in five stages.[4]

---

1. Tetsunao Yamamori, "Foreword," in *Korean Diaspora and Christian Mission*, eds. S. Hun Kim and Wonsuk Ma (Oxford: Regnum, 2011), xi.

2. For an insightful discussion, see Doug K. Oh, "History of the Korean Diaspora Movement," in Kim and Ma, *Korean Diaspora and Christian Mission*, 181–96.

3. David J. Cho, "Asian Mission: Historical Perspective," in *Asian Mission: Yesterday, Today and Tomorrow*, ed. Timothy Park (Pasadena: Institute for Asian Mission, 2008), 40.

4. For a similar discussion, see Tereso C. Casiño, *WITHEE Mission International: A Strategic Model for Diaspora Missions in the Twenty-First Century* (Anyang, South Korea: WiThee Mission International, 2015), 6–10.

The *first* period of migration occurred between 1950 and 1953 during the Korean War. During this period, military personnel under the United Nations command from seventeen countries arrived in the Korean peninsula. This multinational force brought people to fight alongside South Korean soldiers to fend off attacks from the North and ultimately to stop the spread of Communism to the South.

The *second* period commenced the reconstruction efforts and industrialization of South Korea between 1954 and 1988. After the retreat of North Korean soldiers and the ending of the Korean War, noncombatant foreigners arrived to take part in the reconstruction endeavors in a war-torn nation. The first half of this reconstruction effort was spent rebuilding the country, while the second opened doors for modernization, industrialization, and economic prosperity. As the economy grew, so did the Korean *chaebols* (conglomerates) and the small businesses that attracted foreign talent, including musicians and entertainers working in establishments near military bases, hotels, and clubs. Highly skilled workers and technology experts also arrived as South Korea succeeded in bidding for and hosting the Summer Olympics in 1988. This period witnessed Korea's "economic miracle."

The *third* stage spans 1989 and 1992 and is known as the post-Olympic period. The economic boom in the aftermath of the Summer Olympics made South Korea a destination for expats. The immigration flow grew heavy as foreigners began arriving in the country to work in small businesses, factories, and agricultural sectors. Many would come as tourists, and some would stay beyond their visa status to work. The majority of those who came during this period belonged to the Korean Chinese community from China. The presence of these expats affected the monocultural and monolinguistic dynamic of Korean society, considering that up until the Summer Olympics Korean society had remained basically monolithic in its nature and structure.

The *fourth* period saw an increase in migration flow mainly through the Industrial Trainee Program (ITP) between 1992 and 2006. With the increasing influx of foreigners entering the nation for work in what are euphemistically called "the 3-D Jobs" (Dirty, Dangerous, and Difficult), the South Korean government initiated the ITP in 1992. This program paved the way for new batches of foreigners to enter the country for work. These workers landed in various sectors of employment, namely, industry, agriculture, fishing, and small businesses. Changing the tide of the economic rise in Korea was the economic recession that hit the nation in 1997. This resulted in the mass layoff of migrant workers. However, the economic crisis unified many Christian communities and religious organizations to look after the social welfare of foreigners who lost their jobs. The strain of the recession also resulted in the departure of thousands of migrant workers in 2004. But this did not stop the migration flow altogether, as foreigners sought new avenues to enter the country through visas other than those which the ITP originally afforded: religious visa-holders, international students, and native English teachers from seven nations, namely the US, Canada, the UK, Ireland, South Africa, New Zealand, and Australia.

The *fifth* period ushered in the Employment Permit System (EPS), which was introduced by the national government in 2006 and continues today. The EPS aimed to replace the ITP and extends additional rights and job protection benefits for migrant workers. This period also witnessed the increasing number of Koreans (mostly males) marrying foreign brides. As the nation's low birth rate continued in the face of an aging population, some male Koreans married migrant women working in South Korea; others used agencies that would connect them with women abroad for a potential match for marriage.[5]

Throughout these major waves of migration into South Korea, churches and Christian believers became increasingly aware of the need to reach out to foreigners for both evangelism and discipleship.[6] For example, during the third wave of migration, missions among the Chinese community began to develop throughout the nation's capital, Seoul, and other major port cities like Busan and Incheon.

Even among the US Forces stationed in the country, worship celebrations, fellowships, and religious-oriented events began to blossom. However, intentional missions among the diaspora communities in the country had a slow start and gained traction only during the fourth and fifth migration waves.[7] Ted Yamamori understood the kind of approach that the Korean church needed to take to meet the needs of the diasporas and migrants across the country. He would adopt a *two-pronged strategy* that would pave the way to

---

5. Jasmine Bacurnay Lee stands out among the list of international brides as she became the first naturalized Korean of Filipino descent to be elected as a proportional member of the National Assembly of the Republic of Korea in 2012.

6. Wee Hian Chua asserts that "mission work must not be thought to require crossing oceans and seas. When national Christians preach the Gospel to people from another social stratum, they can be classified as missionaries" ("Encouraging Missionary Movement in Asian Churches," cited in Marlin L. Nelson, *Asian Missions Handbook: Practical Policies and Principles* [Seoul: Voice, 1996], 60).

7. "Target 2030" is a twenty-five-year plan by the Korean church to enlist, train, and commission 100,000 missionaries from 2006 to 2030. For analysis of the first five-year stage of the plan, see Paul Han, "The Initial Purpose and Real Intention of Target 2030," Korea Missions Quarterly (2012): 13–17.

train leaders for missions and ministries among people on the move, including Korean nationals and internationals.

Strategy 1: Training Leaders through Missions Agencies

When Ted published *Penetrating Missions' Final Frontier*, the nomenclature of diaspora missions, or "diaspora missiology," was not yet part of the vocabulary in the missions literature. He used a descriptor that was appropriate and accepted in the 1980s and 1990s (i.e. "cross-cultural ministry at home").[8] Little did he know that this concept would evolve into a movement using a different nomenclature. As former CEO/president of Food for the Hungry International and having served in numerous faith-based and nongovernmental organizations, Ted understood the significant role of missions agencies in networking and partnership.

A Shared Vision for Training Leaders for Diaspora Missions

As far as training leaders for missions among the migrants in South Korea was concerned, Ted connected with South Korean pastor Rev. Chang-Sun Moon. The two leaders first met in Cape Town, South Africa, during the Third Lausanne Congress on World Evangelization. This acquaintance appeared providential as the two leaders would soon bond together as like-minded brothers in world missions, including ministries among people on the move. As their friendship and ministry partnership blossomed – and thanks to Moon's visionary and strategic missions services among the migrants in his country – Ted would find an inroad into training leaders for diaspora missions in South Korea through a missions agency.

Moon and his wife, Jin-Suk Im, began ministering to the migrants and diaspora groups in their homeland in October 1992. This was the year when the Korean government opened the country to industrial workers following the success of hosting the Summer Olympics in 1988. At this time, there was no coherent approach to ministering to expats in the country, although a handful of church-related organizations had begun serving the migrants.[9] A

---

8. Tetsunao Yamamori, *Penetrating Missions' Final Frontier: A New Strategy for Unreached Peoples* (Downers Grove: InterVarsity Press, 1993), 154.

9. This was the time when most Korean congregations focused on sending missionaries overseas, leaving out the spiritual needs of the internationals living in the country. Marlin Nelson, a long-term missionary to South Korea, wrote, "We also need to think about other people of

few pastors launched outreaches here and there among the industrial workers, mostly either as lone rangers or with a local church partner.

The Missions Networking Effect

In the early 1990s, close collaboration among denominations and missions organizations in ministering to the expatriates in South Korea still felt far away. However, this changed in 1994 when Moon joined the Evangelical Ministers' Fellowship in Korea (EMFK), an organization launched by a select group of faith leaders (Filipinos and Koreans) with Rodolfo Dumapias as its founding chairman and me serving as vice chairman. Dumapias was a seasoned Filipino diplomat serving as chargé d'affaires, consul general, and later as the ambassador to South Korea.[10] The EMFK vision and mission was succinct: "EMFK stands for Evangelical Ministers' Fellowship in Korea. It is an association of Korean and Filipino evangelical pastors, missionaries, and church workers from various fellowships and denominations who are engaged in ministering to foreigners in Korea, primarily the migrant workers."[11] It held festivals, fellowships, retreats, and worship celebrations for the migrant workers. As a catalyst for EMFK, Moon served as administrator and editor-in-chief of the network's periodical, *Vision*, which was first published in 1996.

For over three years as EMFK's main administrator, Moon labored tirelessly across denominational lines, contacting and connecting with like-minded individuals, denominational leaders, churches, and organizations, including government and nongovernmental agencies, for the sake of the migrant workers. EMFK united various groups for a unified approach to ministering to the migrants. As Ambassador Dumapias put it,

> The EMFK served as a catalyst in the evangelism process not only to Filipinos but also to other foreigners such as the Nigerians, Nepalese, and the Chinese. EMFK became the central network among the evangelical pastors for mutual support, coordination

---

other nationalities and begin to do cross-cultural mission work too" (Nelson, *Asian Missions Handbook*, 26).

10. Ambassador Rodolfo Dumapias has all the characteristics and features of what Yamamori calls "God's special envoy" (Yamamori, *Missions' Final Frontier*, 51–67). For a personal account of his active role in missions while serving in the diplomatic corps, see Rodolfo Ignacio Dumapias, *Kingdom beyond Diplomacy: Journey to the End of the Age*, Foreword by Sadiri Joy Tira (Manila: Global Diaspora Network, 2015).

11. Chang-Sun Moon, "From the Editor's Desk," *Vision* 3 (Sep. 1996): 16.

of their activities, and mapping out their respective strategies in their outreach program.[12]

Moon was in the middle of all these growing networks, putting together the ministries and services of the fledgling organization. These administrative roles afforded him the experience and know-how to develop and execute plans and actions for a more coherent and cohesive approach to migrant missions.

The Emergence of an Innovative Missions Agency

In 1997, after almost four years of administering the EMFK networks, Moon and his wife founded WITHEE Mission International (WMI). He relinquished his administrative and editorial roles at EMFK to focus on developing and expanding the fledgling missions organization. Looking back, Moon reflects,

> When my wife and I first launched a ministry among foreigners in South Korea in 1992, not everyone thought we were doing legitimate mission work. In those days, missionary work was viewed basically as something done overseas. Ministering to migrants in our own backyard did not seem to qualify as "mission." In 1997, God allowed us to establish WITHEE Mission International. We did not anticipate that the small organization would eventually create an impact on many lives, especially foreigners who came to South Korea either for employment or studies.[13]

WITHEE is an acronym for "We Illuminate Thy Holy Eternal Entity," which Moon discerned as what God wanted him to develop as a missions organization. WITHEE's strategy is straightforward: to raise and send migrants to the 10/40 Window areas and the rest of the world. While it follows the general intent of the mission of the body of Christ, WITHEE is focused on migrant people as inclusive in the Great Commission (Matt 28:19-20). The arena for WITHEE is the 10/40 Window with special attention to unreached people groups. The primary objective is fourfold:

(1) To create a cooperative missionary effort in reaching out to the whole world; (2) To pioneer and build the church in the 10/40

---

12. Rodolfo I. Dumapias, "My Journey as a Christian Ambassador," in *Scattered: The Filipino Global Experience*, eds. Luis Pantoja, Jr., Sadiri Joy Tira, and Enoch Wan (Manila: LifeChange, 2004), 319-20.

13. Cited in Casiño, *WITHEE Mission International*, 2.

Window area; (3) To have stronger unity in working together as one Body of Christ in proclaiming the good news of salvation in Jesus Christ to nationalities regardless of denominational affiliations and backgrounds; and (4) To rebuild the ancient ruins and raise up the age-old foundations (Isa 58:12).[14]

Today, WMI has 102 affiliated missionaries serving in twenty-three nations on four continents.[15] A closer analysis of WITHEE's vision and mission statement will show a shift from a territory or *geographic-centered* mission to a *people-centered* mission. Moon realized that Korea was also a "mission field," similar to places to which Korean missionaries were sent out.[16]

The Role of the Migrant Mission Training School

In March 1997, WITHEE launched a training arm known as the Migrant Mission Training School (MMTS). The program was designed to equip those who are currently involved with, or leaders who aspire to minister among, the diaspora groups in South Korea. From its humble beginnings, MMTS has developed into a short-term sustainable program with a customized curriculum designed particularly for the needs of diaspora leaders in the nation and those who are reaching out to migrants across the peninsula.[17] It is run by experts and experienced lecturers from a variety of disciplines, including seasoned practitioners. MMTS is intentionally interdenominational and has a strong multiethnic and intercultural component and composition.

The MMTS curriculum typically runs for sixteen weeks. Trainees include church leaders and Christian migrants who invest time, energy, and resources so they can engage in meaningful and productive missional activities among the diasporas living, working, or studying in South Korea. The curriculum consists

---

14. Message sent through Viber social media platform by Chang-Sun Moon on 28 February 2022.

15. The international scope of WITHEE's mission echoed that of the former EMFK acting chairman Samuel Natividad, whom Moon served alongside: "This is EMFK's vision not only among foreign migrant workers but for all people" ("Reach for Victory and for Holiness," *Vision* 3 [Sep. 1996]: 2).

16. For an excellent treatment of this paradigm shift in missions, see Jeon Ou Nam, "The Paradigm Shift of the Missionary Concept: From Territory-Centric to Person-Centric," *Korea Missions Quarterly* (2012): 184–200.

17. For a study on training leaders in diaspora across Asia, see Tereso C. Casiño, "Theological Education of Diaspora Leaders in the Asian Region," *Torch Trinity Journal* 11, no. 1 (Nov. 2008): 45–62.

of class lectures, projects, group interactions and presentations, ministry exposure, and immersion practicum through fieldwork and internship.

Participants at MMTS come from a diverse group; they are pastors, missionaries, seminary students, deacons and deaconesses, government workers, individuals from academia, and church leaders who do actual fieldwork after completing their studies in diaspora missiology. Sixty percent of the trainees are male; 40 percent are female. After finishing the sixteen-week study, participants receive a certificate of completion. The curriculum is divided into three major categories: Understanding, Targets and Methods, and Achievements. Resource people at MMTS go through a vetting process to ensure they fit in the program and possess appropriate qualifications in their area of discipline. Each class is designed to address specific issues in diaspora ministry. Topics include "Global Mission and Its Flow," "History and Status of Migrant Mission in Korea," "Policy and Law of the Government," "Mission on Migrant Workers," "International Students Mission," "Intentional Transition in Missions," "Establishing Migrants Mission," and "Quality and Leadership of Migrant Mission Ministers," to name just a few.

Since 2011, Ted has been serving as senior advisor to both WMI and MMTS. During his numerous visits to South Korea, he has participated in MMTS events, including graduation and the commissioning of missionaries. When the COVID-19 pandemic made it difficult for him to travel to Korea, Ted would send video clips to MMTS trainees and graduates. In the spring of 2022, MMTS held its twenty-third training. Out of 510 graduates since the inception of MMTS, 371 commissioned alumni are actively serving in the country; the rest are engaged in missionary work in their respective homelands.[18] Echoing the approaches set forth by the Lausanne Diaspora Leadership Team during the Third Lausanne Congress in Cape Town, MMTS operates with the following slogan: "*For* the Migrants, *Through* the Migrants, *Beyond* the Migrants."[19]

---

18. For WMI and MMTS's commitment to commission migrants to serve in their homelands after their training in South Korea, see Chang-Sun Moon, "The Reverse Send-off of Non-permanent International Residents," in *21C New Nomad Era and Migrant Mission: The Theory and Practice for Migrant Mission*, eds. Chan-Sik Park and Noah Jung (Seoul: Christianity and Industrial Society Research Institute, 2010), 293–99.

19. The original rendering was "missions *to* the diasporas, missions *through* the diasporas, and missions *beyond* the diasporas." See Lausanne Diaspora Leadership Team, *Scattered to Gather: Embracing the Global Trend of Diaspora*, updated ed. (Manila: LifeChange, 2014), 24–27.

Strategy 2: Campus-Based Training through Institutions of Higher Education

Although Ted is strongly committed to partnering with agencies like WMI and MMTS to train leaders for migrant ministries and diaspora missions in South Korea, he has also been focused on another mode of delivering the training program. For this, he looked to institutions of higher learning. To reiterate, he was already familiar with the MMTS program operated by WMI. He had presented lectures at its sessions, spoke at special events, and attended graduation ceremonies as either a guest speaker or someone giving the charge to the graduates. Ted knew that this grassroots approach was important considering the growing need to train leaders for migrant ministry across South Korea.

However, he also realized that it is one thing to train local leaders, but another to train those attending seminaries and theological institutions offering formal studies that culminate in a degree or diploma. For years, MMTS and WMI successfully offered programs that handed out a certificate of completion to participants who completed their training. Ted understood that there was another way to deliver this model. His years of experience as a former educator at schools in the US proved useful as he turned his sights on the educational institutions that would augment the already established MMTS platform in South Korea.[20]

Designing a Second Strategy for Training Leaders for Diaspora Missions

The backdrop of the vision to establish campus-based training for leaders ministering to migrants and diaspora communities stemmed from Ted's leadership of and participation in the Lausanne Diaspora Educators Consultation held on 11–14 November 2009 in Seoul. The host of the conference was Torch Trinity Graduate University, a premier theological

---

20. It is important to note how Korean society was impacted by pioneering missionaries who introduced the Western educational system across the peninsula. Notable among these educational institutions that endure today are Yonsei University, Ehwa Womans University, Pai Chai High School, Pai Chai University, and Soong-Sil University, among others. YongJo Ha insightfully asserts, "Education by missionaries did not just happen in Seoul but in other parts of Korea as well. . . . Those missionaries came and established a firm foundation for education in Korea. . . . These seeds grew and became the Korean Church, and they allowed us to embrace a large vision, take what we have seen and heard, and eventually reach out to the nations of the world" (YongJo Ha, "The Vision and Mission of the Korean Church," in *The Global Legacy and Mission of the Korean Church*, eds. Steven S. H. Chang and Julius J. Kim [Seoul: Torch Center for World Missions/Torch Trinity Graduate School of Theology, 2011], 54).

institution that provides graduate and doctoral degree programs to leaders from six continents, including Korean diaspora students.[21] The proceedings of the consultation were published as a monograph in preparation for the Third Lausanne Congress that took place the following year in Cape Town.[22] Educators at the consultation also produced a charter of diaspora missiology. In his postconsultation remarks, Ted stressed, "I feel that the recent Lausanne Diaspora Educators Consultation has clenched diaspora as a legitimate and exciting field of missiology."[23]

Expressing his appreciation to the experienced scholars and conveners – Sadiri Joy Tira and Enoch Wan – Ted noted how they succeeded "to crystallize the various aspects of what should constitute as missiology."[24] This pivotal consultation paved the way for succeeding conferences on diaspora missions held on Torch Trinity campus. Ted saw this coming and acknowledged the strategic role an academic institution can play in preparing leaders for diaspora missions, asserting, "The academic discourse on diaspora has emerged as a biblical and strategic field of missiology."[25] Six months later, Torch Trinity hosted another diaspora event dubbed "Global Legacy and Mission: Korean-North American Diaspora Consultation."[26]

Communicating the Second Strategy for Training Leaders for Diaspora Missions

Preliminary talks about offering a training program through higher education began as early as summer 2016, when Ted made a series of visits to South Korea for speaking engagements and networking activities. He first shared his vision with Chang-Sun Moon, and the two began processing the concept.

---

21. Sang Bok David Kim, the school's first president, aptly notes, "Torch Trinity Graduate University is in the strategic city of Seoul. International students, particularly Korean-diaspora students, are coming to Torch Trinity from English-speaking nations: the United States, United Kingdom, Canada, Australia, New Zealand, and other countries. No better school is found more suitable for second or third generation diaspora students. They will discover their motherland and learn their mother tongue and culture while studying at Torch Trinity" ("Torch Trinity for Korean Diaspora Students," *Torch Trinity* [Summer 2013]: 6).

22. Lausanne Diaspora Leadership Team, *Scattered to Gather* (2010).

23. "'Seoul Declaration on Diaspora Missiology' at Torch Trinity!," *Torch Trinity* (Winter 2009): 46.

24. "Seoul Declaration on Diaspora Missiology."

25. Lausanne Diaspora Leadership Team, *Scattered to Gather*, 2.

26. For the proceedings, see Steven S. H. Chang and Julius J. Kim, eds., *The Global Legacy and Mission of the Korean Church* (Seoul: Torch Center for World Missions/Torch Trinity Graduate School of Theology, 2011).

When I joined the two leaders in November of that year, the concept was already past its incubation stage. As expected, the idea gained traction and the three of us crystallized a pathway to mobilize universities and theological schools for missions training among migrants. We spent five days discussing the vision and its potential implementation. Our daily meetings coincided with the 2016 annual conference of the Korea World Missions Association (KWMA), of which Ted and I were guest presenters. Our daily conversations and debriefings became easier because we both stayed at the same guesthouse, hosted by Saejung-Ang Presbyterian Church through the gracious invitation of Senior Pastor Rev. Deokyoung Hwang.

At the KWMA conference, Ted delivered a plenary address that highlighted the increasing need for more meaningful cooperation regarding missions among the migrants living, working, or studying in the country. He also made a pitch for the need to organize a center that would focus primarily on the equipping of leaders for evangelism and discipleship among the migrants in collaboration with institutions of higher learning.

That same week, the three of us (including Moon) met daily for prayer and brainstorming on how the vision should proceed. Two days before parting ways, we reached an agreement that the hub for offering a campus-based training program would be called the International Center for Diaspora Missions (ICDM). Moon designed the preliminary composition of ICDM, Ted identified the leadership structure, and I developed the curriculum.

Almost six months after our meeting, Ted and I were back in South Korea, this time to join Barnabas Moon in the official launching of ICDM. Members of the board of trustees were invited, comprising some of the nation's respected leaders from various denominations and higher education institutions. Saejung-Ang Presbyterian Church in Anyang City graciously offered ICDM an office to operate on its campus. This allowed ICDM to start its functions immediately, fulfilling networking tasks with selected institutions of higher learning.

Launching the Network Center for Campus-Based Training

On 24 June 2017, ICDM was formally organized and launched publicly. The event was well attended and coordinated. Over three hundred church leaders, educators, and students from various institutions of higher learning, eager to know more about the ICDM, came for potential collaboration. In his plenary address, Ted outlined his vision for mobilizing institutions of higher learning in South Korea to train leaders for diaspora missions:

> For several months, the like-minded among us have been thinking and praying about how to encourage the churches and missionary-training institutions of Korea to become more engaged in the issues related to diaspora mission. Thank you for responding positively to the call we made for the establishment of ICDM as Board members, Advisory Council members, affiliate scholars, collaborative institutions, and well-wishers. Those who share this common cause are many and are found throughout the world. Today's celebratory event is in their thoughts and prayers.[27]

Ted cast a wide net in his presentation of ICDM. He laid out his "second strategy" to train leaders for missions among people on the move, which was specifically a campus-based program.[28] In his two-part address he explained how ICDM came into being and what it was all about:

> The massive population movements of the last century have altered the landscape of missiological reality. During the last few decades, mission specialists have spoken about reaching the unreached by entering restricted-access countries through various creative means. But in recent years, many of those people living in hard-to-reach countries are moving out and often becoming our next-door neighbors. The phenomenon of diaspora is one of the critical issues facing the church today and will be increasingly so in the decades to come. As churches and Great Commission-minded believers, we cannot fail to understand the topic at hand.[29]

In an effort to explain the importance of ICDM, Ted mentioned his role as a former international director of the Lausanne Movement, noting that he remained active as its senior advisor.[30] Commending the wide influence and role of the Lausanne Movement, he explained that the global movement "has been, and is committed fully, to exploring and executing effective ministries

---

27. Tetsunao Yamamori, "The Launching of ICDM," plenary address delivered on 24 June 2017 at Saejung-Ang Presbyterian Church, Anyang City, South Korea, 1.

28. In North America, the closest model to this approach is Tyndale Intercultural Ministries (TIM) Centre on the campus of Tyndale University in Toronto, Canada: https://www.tyndale.ca/tim.

29. Yamamori, "Launching of ICDM," 1–2.

30. Under Ted's initiative as international director, the Lausanne Committee for World Evangelization (LCWE) appointed Sadiri Joy Tira as a catalyst for global diaspora missions. In 2006, Joy and Ted convened the first Global Diaspora Missiology Consultation at Taylor Seminary in Edmonton, Alberta, Canada.

to the diaspora people, the people on the move."³¹ Pointing out that *diaspora* comes from the Greek and refers to the scattering of people, Ted elaborated:

> It refers to the persons or people groups, leaving and settling outside their place of origin, for whatever reasons, voluntarily or by force. These are people who choose to move for business, better economic opportunities, study, family reunions, and travel. On the other hand, there are people who are forced to move because of war, natural disasters, ethnic cleansing, persecution, and religious violence.³²

The world is becoming more diverse and inclusive, a mosaic where cultures meet, worldviews and socioeconomic systems interact, and civilizations intersect because of people's mobility.³³ Ted reminded the audience that the "phenomenon of diaspora is as old as the Bible, but the discussion of diaspora missiology is relatively new among evangelicals."³⁴ He also confided what led him to facilitate conversations on diaspora missions on a global scale:

> Feeling a sense of urgency, I, on behalf of Lausanne, appointed Dr. Sadiri Joy Tira, a Filipino scholar with extensive work with Filipino diasporas in the Middle East, to the position of Senior Associate for Diasporas in 2007. During the 3rd Lausanne Congress held in Cape Town, South Africa, in 2010, Dr. Tira and I initiated the founding of Global Diaspora Network (GDN) to further advance the field of diaspora mission. In a short period of time, GDN has extended its influence far and wide.³⁵

He then struck a high note, describing his respect and hope for Korea as a strategic hub for global missions, including migrants and diaspora communities.³⁶ In precise yet reflective words, he explained,

> Along with Lausanne, I have kept a vigilant eye on the church in Korea. I have always believed that God scattered the Korean people for a purpose as he did with the Jews in biblical times. Earlier,

---

31. Yamamori, "Launching of ICDM," 2.
32. Yamamori, 2.
33. For an extensive treatment, see Doug Sanders, *Arrival City: How the Largest Migration in History Is Reshaping Our World* (New York: Pantheon, 2010).
34. Yamamori, "Launching of ICDM," 2.
35. Yamamori, 2.
36. See Young Woon Lee, "Brief History of Korean Diaspora and Educational Issues of Korean Diaspora Churches," *Torch Trinity Journal* 13, no. 2 (Nov. 2010): 173–90.

the Korean people left their country for such reasons as escaping natural disasters, poverty, and oppression and in more recent years, for the pursuit of higher living standards and educational opportunities. Especially from 1980 with the growth of churches in Korea, Korean Christians began emigrating to various parts for the purpose of evangelizing the world.[37]

Effective collaboration is crucial to the intersection between the *practice* (diaspora missions) and the *theory* (diaspora missiology).[38] Ted had this in mind as he sought out partners for the launching of ICDM. He ensured that both a *practitioner* and an *academic* would be on board during the seminal stage of the ICDM model:

> I shared my ideas and my passion for the church in Korea with Rev. Chang-sun Moon and Dr. Terry Casiño. Rev. Moon is a pioneer in migrant ministry training in Korea and is the founder of Living Hope International Church and Withee Mission International. Dr. Casiño is the head of the Missions Department at Gardner-Webb University in North Carolina, USA. He is a Filipino scholar who taught at Torch Trinity Graduate University for 10 years. Both have been working with me as faithful members of the Global Diaspora Network of the Lausanne Movement. These men became immediate encouragers and ready collaborators.[39]

In hindsight, Ted's desire to see Korean universities and seminaries get involved in training leaders for diaspora missions stemmed from his observations of the realities of migration flow in and outside the country. He stressed that in addition to the fifty million people in Korea, an additional 7.5 million Koreans live in diaspora away from their homeland. In 2016, it was estimated that over twenty-seven thousand Korean missionaries were ministering in 171 countries, most of them in the Asian continent.[40]

While reaching out to their local hosts, many of these missionaries also started and developed churches among the Korean communities overseas.

---

37. Yamamori, "Launching of ICDM," 3.

38. For the intersection between the *practice* of diaspora missions and the *paradigm* of diaspora missiology, see Enoch Wan and Sadiri Joy Tira, "Diaspora Missiology and Missions in the Context of the Twenty-First Century," *Torch Trinity Journal* 13, no. 1 (May 2010): 45–56.

39. Yamamori, "Launching of ICDM," 3.

40. Likewise, Daniel Shinjong notes that "about 43 percent of Korean-American churches sent out short-term mission teams in 2009" ("An Assessment of the Target 2030 for World Mission," *Korea Missions Quarterly* [2012]: 41).

Although many were small in membership, Ted assessed that these could be mobilized as a "powerful force for world evangelization."[41] He recommended further research into this potential so Korean diaspora churches could play their significant role in global missions.[42] On the home front, the number of migrants in South Korea has been growing and is now close to two million. Their work and situations are varied: industrial and factory workers, teachers and highly skilled professionals, students, refugees, and foreigners married to Koreans.

Prospects for Campus-Based Training

Ted was specific in stating the following vision of ICDM:

> To promote diaspora and migrant mission within Korea and to foster an outreach to more than 7.5 million Koreans in diaspora around the world and, through them, to evangelize their non-Korean neighbors cross-culturally. It is a Korean organization boldly venturing out to uncover the God-given maximum potential of the Korean church for global evangelization.[43]

Gleaning from his address, Yamamori envisioned ICDM to offer primarily an "academic component to work closely with partner Christian universities and seminaries in Korea and to help educate current and future pastors, missionaries, and lay leaders in the field of diaspora and migrant mission."[44] Accordingly, the center would also work closely with local churches, denominations, and mission agencies. In encouraging Christian-oriented institutions of higher learning to offer a flexible but relevant curriculum on diaspora missions, Ted put a premium on the integration of *practice* and *theory*, which some schools lacked.[45]

---

41. Yamamori, "Launching of ICDM," 4.

42. Notable challenges exist despite opportunities for diaspora missions among Korean churches. See Chandler H. Im, "The Korean Churches in the USA: Their Concerns and Strengths," in *Global Diasporas and Mission*, eds. Chandler H. Im and Amos Yong (Oxford: Regnum, 2014), 130–47.

43. Yamamori, "Launching of ICDM," 4.

44. Yamamori, 4.

45. Echoing this lack of integration, Tony Cupit notes that "there are institutions whose whole orientation seems to be to send their graduates out to new church planting activities . . . and others who eschew this emphasis and appear to be interested only in training ministers for existing congregations" ("Theological Education Around the World," *Asian Baptist Journal of Theology* 1, no. 1 [April 2007]: 213).

To ensure that the ICDM vision was successfully implemented, the center conducted a three-day conference every two years with a dozen or so invited diaspora specialists (namely, scholars and practitioners) who would present papers that would be published as a textbook a year later. At the heart of this vision was the development of a curriculum that would rotate among six major courses which would constitute a diaspora minor or concentration to be adopted by partner Christian universities and seminaries. Upon Ted's request, I developed the following six core courses for the ICDM curriculum:[46]

- Biblical-Theological Foundations for Diaspora Missions
- Cultural Anthropology for Diaspora Ministries
- Business as Mission for Diaspora Communities
- Case Studies on Diaspora Missions
- Pastoral Care and Counseling for People on the Move
- Contemporary Trends in Diaspora Missiology

Ted wanted to ensure that the ICDM curriculum did not stay on campus for purely academic exercises; he hoped that the program would reach the grassroots level in Christian circles across the nation. To achieve this, ICDM would organize a Speakers' Bureau to promote diaspora topics for churches and mission conferences within Korea and elsewhere in the world where a sizable Korean diaspora population was located. Part of the ICDM strategy is also to pursue other programs:

> (1) To hold discussion sessions among faculty members of the partner institutions on key diaspora topics; (2) To undertake joint faculty research on aspects of diaspora missions; and (3) To create enthusiasm for missions among churches by hosting forums on missions, leading field visits to select countries, and organizing internships with diaspora churches.[47]

Additionally, crucial to Ted's campus-based training strategy is the utilization of resources among diaspora communities for missiological

---

46. Yoon Jong Yoo proposes the following model for the studies on migrant workers based on Old Testament scholarship: "(1) Identifying who are the migrant workers in the Bible by studying terms connected with the migrants, (2) investigating the policy in the Bible for the migrant workers, and (3) providing what kind of policy churches should do for the migrant workers" ("Diaspora Missions in the Old Testament," paper presented at the 1st Symposium on Diaspora Missions, International Center for Diaspora Mission, 14 November 2018, Anyang City, South Korea, 36).

47. Yamamori, "Launching of ICDM," 5.

research.⁴⁸ He made a clarion call to equip leaders for missions among the diasporas with three major reaffirmations:

- Let us reaffirm our commitment to the Great Commission mandate, to reach out to all people within Korea who are yet to know and accept Jesus as Lord and Savior, including migrant neighbors. We pray that these migrants will become followers of Jesus while in Korea and, upon returning to their homelands, serve as soul winners.
- Let us reaffirm our unceasing prayers that the glory of the rapid church expansion of yesterday will repeat itself on Korean soil and the zeal for world evangelization will rise once again.
- Let us reaffirm our missional efforts both to those living in restricted-access countries and to those in diaspora. Out of the world's population of 7.5 billion people, there are 2.1 billion who are yet to hear the gospel proclaimed to them because they have little or no gospel access.⁴⁹ The number of people on the move today is 240 million. Proportionately, those who are living in restricted-access countries outnumber the emerging trend of diaspora people. Therefore, we pray that the Korean Christians will direct their missional efforts to both categories of people in need of salvation.⁵⁰

The first major implementation of ICDM's vision to maximize Korean Christian universities and seminaries in training leaders for diaspora missions took place on 13–16 November 2018 in Anyang City, South Korea. Participants representing various institutions and agencies from six continents attended the first ICDM-WMI-MMTS sponsored international Symposium on Diaspora Missions. The theme of the symposium was relevant and timely: "Biblical Foundations and Case Studies Research on People on the Move." Topics were carefully selected: twelve sessions on biblical reflections and research and six case studies, resulting in meaningful interactions with the participants.

Speakers and delegates from various universities offering theological and missiological educational programs also attended the four-day symposium. The original plan was to publish the proceedings of the symposium as a companion

---

48. For a similar concept, see Fred Farrokh, "Assessing the Value of Diaspora Community Input in Missiological Research," in *Diaspora Missiology: Reflections on Reaching the Scattered Peoples of the World*, eds. Michael Pocock and Enoch Wan (Pasadena: William Carey Library, 2015), 59–75.

49. Kent Parks, "Finishing the Remaining 29% of World Evangelization," *Lausanne Global Analysis* 6, no. 3 (May 2017), https://www.lausanne.org/content/lga/2017-05/finishing-the-remaining-29-of-world-evangelization.

50. Yamamori, "Launching of ICDM," 6.

reader to existing resources that partnering schools would use in their campus-based training program. Throughout the symposium, Ted was fully aware of the changes and challenges that the Korean church faces; yet he understood that these could turn into missional opportunities. Elsewhere, he reflects,

> With the pivotal developments of the last two decades, traditional "host" and "receiving" nations are undergoing dramatic transformations to their immigration and economic policies. The so-called "missions at our doorsteps" model will also require adjustment. While these problems come to pass, the global church must quickly adapt their missional work.[51]

Conclusion

Ted employed a two-pronged strategy to train leaders for diaspora missions because of its efficiency, adaptability, flexibility, longevity (*time tested*), relevance, transferability, and effectiveness. I have personally witnessed his passion for the Korean church as a catalyst for global missionary work, especially diaspora missions.

His missional vision has been compelling, and his pursuit of effective missions among migrants in Korea reassuring. His goal is to see the Korean church and Korean Christian diasporas reaching out to migrants outside their ethnic circles. This has been evident in his unwavering support for training programs offered by WMI, MMTS, and ICDM. Ted can discern the right training mode, offer the most appropriate strategy, and execute a vision that is usually far larger than himself. He knows exactly how to communicate his missional vision to others without imposing his personal ideas.

I have witnessed his patience, diligence, joy, enthusiasm, passion, and humility when serving God alongside others. On many occasions when I had a meal with him, Ted would eat the same food that Koreans eat – a combination of rice, fish, and soup. He is fatherly but not paternalistic, compassionate but discerning. He understands the need of the hour and is very perceptive of the missional and existential realities of the people on the move.

---

51. Tetsunao Yamamori, "Preface to the Revised Edition," in *Scattered and Gathered: A Global Compendium of Diaspora Missiology*, revised and updated, eds. Sadiri Joy Tira and Tetsunao Yamamori (Carlisle: Langham Global Library, 2020), xix.

References

Casiño, Tereso C. "Theological Education of Diaspora Leaders in the Asian Region." *Torch Trinity Journal* 11, no. 1 (Nov. 2008): 45–62.

———. *WITHEE Mission International: A Strategic Model for Diaspora Missions in the Twenty-First Century*. Anyang, South Korea: Withee Mission International, 2015.

Chang, Steven S. H., and Julius J. Kim, eds. *The Global Legacy and Mission of the Korean Church*. Seoul: Torch Center for World Missions/Torch Trinity Graduate School of Theology, 2011.

Cho, David J. "Asian Mission: Historical Perspective." In *Asian Mission: Yesterday, Today and Tomorrow*, edited by Timothy Park, 27–57. Pasadena: Institute for Asian Mission, 2008.

Cupit, Tony. "Theological Education Around the World." *Asian Baptist Journal of Theology* 1, no. 1 (April 2013), 208–219.

Dumapias, Rodolfo Ignacio. *Kingdom beyond Diplomacy: Journey to the End of the Age*. Foreword by Sadiri Joy Tira. Manila: Global Diaspora Network, 2015.

———. "My Journey as a Christian Ambassador." In *Scattered: The Filipino Global Experience*, edited by Luis Pantoja, Jr., Sadiri Joy Tira, and Enoch Wan, 313–26. Manila: LifeChange, 2004.

Farrokh, Fred. "Assessing the Value of Diaspora Community Input in Missiological Research." In *Diaspora Missiology: Reflections on Reaching the Scattered Peoples of the World*, edited by Michael Pocock and Enoch Wan, 59–75. Pasadena: William Carey Library, 2015.

Ha, YongJo. "The Vision and Mission of the Korean Church." In *The Global Legacy and Mission of the Korean Church*, edited by Steven S. H. Chang and Julius J. Kim, 53–58. Seoul: Torch Center for World Missions/Torch Trinity Graduate School of Theology, 2011.

Han, Paul. "The Initial Purpose and Real Intention of Target 2030." *Korea Missions Quarterly* (2012): 13–17.

Im, Chandler H. "The Korean Churches in the USA: Their Concerns and Strengths." In *Global Diasporas and Mission*, edited by Chandler H. Im and Amos Yong, 130–47. Oxford: Regnum, 2014.

Kim, Sang Bok David. "Torch Trinity for Korean Diaspora Students." *Torch Trinity* (Summer 2013): 5–7.

Kim, S. Hun, and Wonsuk Ma, eds. *Korean Diaspora and Christian Mission*. Oxford: Regnum, 2011.

Lausanne Diaspora Leadership Team. *Scattered to Gather: Embracing the Global Trend of Diaspora*. Updated ed. Manila: LifeChange, 2014.

Lee, Young Woon. "Brief History of Korean Diaspora and Educational Issues of Korean Diaspora Churches." *Torch Trinity Journal* 13, no. 2 (Nov. 2010): 173–90.

Moon, Chang-Sun. "From the Editor's Desk." *Vision* 3 (Sep. 1996): 16.

———. "The Reverse Send-off of Non-permanent International Residents." In *21C New Nomad Era and Migrant Mission: The Theory and Practice for Migrant Mission*, edited by Chan-Sik Park and Noah Jung, 293–99. Seoul: Christianity and Industrial Society Research Institute, 2010.

Nam, Jeon Ou. "The Paradigm Shift of the Missionary Concept: From Territory-Centric to Person-Centric." *Korea Missions Quarterly* (2012): 184–200.

Natavid, Sanuel D. "Reach for Victory and for Holiness." *Vision* 3 (Sep. 1996): 2.

Nelson, Marlin L. *Asian Missions Handbook: Practical Policies and Principles*. Seoul: Voice, 1996.

Oh, Doug K. "History of the Korean Diaspora Movement." In Kim and Ma, *Korean Diaspora and Christian Mission*, 181–96.

Parks, Kent. "Finishing the Remaining 29% of World Evangelization." *Lausanne Global Analysis* 6, no. 3 (May 2017). https://www.lausanne.org/content/lga/2017-05/finishing-the-remaining-29-of-world-evangelization.

Sanders, Doug. *Arrival City: How the Largest Migration in History Is Reshaping Our World*. New York: Pantheon, 2010.

"'Seoul Declaration on Diaspora Missiology' at Torch Trinity!" *Torch Trinity* (Winter 2009): 46.

Shinjong, Daniel. "An Assessment of the Target 2030 for World Mission." *Korea Missions Quarterly* (2012): 41.

Wan, Enoch, and Sadiri Joy Tira. "Diaspora Missiology and Missions in the Context of the Twenty-First Century." *Torch Trinity Journal* 13, no. 1 (May 2010): 45–56.

Yamamori, Tetsunao. "Foreword." In Kim and Ma, *Korean Diaspora and Christian Mission*, xi.

———. "The Launching of ICDM." Plenary address delivered on 24 June 2017 at Saejung-Ang Presbyterian Church, Anyang City, South Korea (MS Word format).

———. *Penetrating Missions' Final Frontier: A New Strategy for Unreached Peoples*. Downers Grove: InterVarsity Press, 1993.

———. "Preface to the Revised Edition." In *Scattered and Gathered: A Global Compendium of Diaspora Missiology*, edited by Sadiri Joy Tira and Tetsunao Yamamori, xix-xxix. Revised and updated. Carlisle: Langham Global Library, 2020.

Yoo, Yoon Jong. "Diaspora Missions in the Old Testament." Paper presented at the 1st Symposium on Diaspora Missions, International Center for Diaspora Mission, 14 November 2018, Anyang City, South Korea.

17

Peace in the Land of the Morning Calm

By Barnabas Moon

In February 2017, Ted Yamamori and I were invited to a seminar at the University of the Nations on Kona Island, Hawaii, hosted by a North Korea-related ministry team led by Loren Cunningham, founder of Youth With A Mission (YWAM). We met out of love for North Korea and to promote unification through prayer. Cunningham also commended Dr. Ted, as I fondly call him, for his global work and ministries. Dr. Ted spoke about his involvement in helping North Korea through the ministries of Food for the Hungry International. Likewise, I made a presentation on the assistance that Feed the Children extends to North Korea. At dawn on the third day, Dr. Ted, who was staying in an adjacent room, sent me a text message asking if I could visit his room. When I arrived, he was sitting at a table in a suit, with a Bible open in front of him. He asked me to read the passage where his finger was pointing, which I did: "Therefore confess your sins to each other and pray for each other so that you may be healed. The prayer of a righteous person is powerful and effective" (Jas 5:16). Under these words, a red line was drawn, and small letters were written: "Conflict between Korean and Japanese youth at the Urbana Conference." He was referring to the Urbana Student Missions Conference hosted by InterVarsity Christian Fellowship.

As I considered what the statement meant, Dr. Ted narrated his experience as a speaker at the Urbana Conference. One evening, some young Koreans and Japanese people created a commotion that stemmed from a conflict. This led to a heated argument between two men. Dr. Ted gathered both men in the main hall and shared from James 5:16 to pray and reconcile all night long. While meditating on this biblical text years later, his eyes welled up with gratitude that an aging pastor from Japan and a young pastor from South Korea were bound together by Christ's love with the same passion for North Korea. Then Dr. Ted requested that I bless him, and he prayed for me. I will never forget the feeling I had that morning. I am grateful to Dr. Ted, who continues to have a heart for North Korea, and who prays for the nation despite his age and health issues.

What follows is based on the stories that I heard directly from Dr. Ted while we were traveling to and through numerous countries and various mission fields after 2010. This is a testimony to how much he loves North Korea, how he carries out holistic missionary work, and how committed he is to pray for the North Koreans.

The Guidance of God

Dr. Ted was born in Nagoya, Japan, and grew up in a Buddhist family. He attended a Roman Catholic high school and university and became Christian when a Protestant pastor from Portland, Oregon, shared the gospel with him. Shortly after the Korean War (1950–53), Chaplain Vernon Kullowatz and his family were stationed in Nagoya and Ted connected with him. Ted was interested in learning English, and he did housework for the family. Over time, however, Ted became curious about Chaplain Kullowatz's Christian beliefs, observing how people who believed in God behaved at home. Ted wanted to know if Chaplain Kullowatz's sermons matched his life.

Ted would ask him many questions, and the pastor answered with patience and loving care, but Ted's English was not adequate to fully understand his explanations. So, Ted started attending a Japanese church, and over time he realized that his faith in Jesus Christ was growing stronger every day. It was during this time that he first learned about the Korean War and about the Korean people.

On Christmas Eve 1955, Ted was invited to Chaplain Kullowatz's house for a celebration dinner. After dinner, the pastor's five-year-old son, Scott, brought a package from under the Christmas tree and gave it to Ted. It was a Bible written in Japanese. The following words were written on the first page of the Bible: "May God bless and protect you with eternal love, I pray." Ted recalled the evening he had spent at Chaplain Kullowatz's house. His heart began to fill with what he had learned from the American pastor about the teachings from the Bible. He realized that night that it was a *Kairos* moment for him, so before heading back home, he accepted Jesus as his Savior and Lord. Just a few days later, Ted was baptized by Chaplain Kullowatz.

Since he became a disciple of Jesus Christ in 1955, Bible verses have played a significant role in Dr. Ted's life. One day, he came across a couple of verses in Romans that proved to be a turning point in his young life: "It has always been my ambition to preach the gospel where Christ was not known, so that I would not be building on someone else's foundation. Rather, as it is written: 'Those who were not told about him will see, and those who have not heard will understand'" (Rom 15:20–21).

The apostle Paul aimed to preach the gospel to those who had not yet heard it, and Dr. Ted became passionate about this commitment as well. It is no wonder that Dr. Ted would later write numerous articles on strategies for evangelizing the lost and bringing to faith and repentance those who did not yet believe in Jesus Christ. In 1993, he was asked to write a book for the Urbana Conference that year. He chose a captivating title: *Penetrating Missions' Final Frontier: A New Strategy for Unreached People.* In his mind, he considered North Korea. For him, this nation was at the last frontier of missionary work. By 1998, North Korea had suffered a series of natural disasters, including earthquakes, floods, and drought.

At that time, Dr. Ted was chairman of Food for the Hungry International (FHI). Because of his interest in North Korea, he oversaw relief activities that included providing $7 million in milk powder to feed North Korean children for three years. He made seven trips to North Korea during the same period. Dr. Ted heard about North Korea's atrocities through the stories of North Korean defectors and reports from human rights organizations. He learned of the nation's spiritual and moral condition – murder, enslavement, torture, long-term detention, rape, forced abortion, religious persecution, the trafficking of women, forced marriage, prostitution, and women who murdered children with sticks for stealing rice. One might wonder why Dr. Ted became interested in North Korea and loved the people of this isolated country. In the following pages I share what I heard directly from Dr. Ted about why this was the case.

In 1945, when Ted was just seven years old, he almost starved to death due to famine. During World War II elementary school students fled to the countryside of Japan. There they had little to eat. At first, Ted felt the pain of hunger, but the pain gradually became numb. As he told this story, Dr. Ted also described Mother Teresa as an example of how to care for those in these types of situations. He recounted how he and his wife visited Mother Teresa's "House for Poverty Death" in Calcutta. It was there she told them, "No one should die alone. The children of God must be able to die with dignity." The home was a place for those who entered to depart from the world surrounded by the love of the caregivers.

In October 1979, Dr. Larry Ward, Founder of Food for the Hungry International, visited Biola University in Los Angeles, where Dr. Ted taught. He told the story of Pol Pot's atrocities in Cambodia. Pol Pot's soldiers killed one million of his people. Ward spoke of the desperate needs of Cambodian refugees and pleaded with Biola University to send a nurse to work with FHI in Thailand. Dr. Ted took fifty-seven nursing students and faculty members to Thailand in the summer of 1980. They worked among refugees from Laos, Cambodia, and Vietnam. Many of the nurses were assigned to a refugee camp called Khao-I-Dang on the border between Cambodia and Thailand, accommodating 130,000 Cambodians.

Cambodian men remained in the country to fight Pol Pot's army. Women, children, and the elderly reached the Thai border through a province called Batambang. Survivors reached the refugee camps through the region, but the camps were in a terrible condition. The nurses worked hard day and night and some people said they could not understand why God allowed such a terrible thing to happen. Dr. Ted had to serve the nurses, and in doing so he also began to see his own face in the faces of dying children. At that moment, his childhood memories came back, and when he returned to Biola in the fall of 1980 he could no longer concentrate on teaching. He joined FHI as an employee a year later, leaving behind eighteen years of teaching experience. He went on to serve FHI for twenty years, for seventeen of which he was president.

How Can We Know God's Heart toward North Korea?

"God's heart toward North Korea is nothing more than a heart toward the world, a lost world without Christ. With North Korea at the final destination of missionary work, we must accept the basis for global evangelism and pay maximum attention to North Korea and its people." This is what Dr. Ted says as he considers God's heart for the people of North Korea. He outlines eight primary reasons for global missions and intentional outreach in North Korea:

1. Christ commanded a worldwide missionary work. Acts 1:8 says, "But you will receive power when the Holy Spirit comes on you; and you will be my witnesses in Jerusalem, and in all Judea and Samaria, and to the ends of the earth."

2. Our Lord seems to have established worldwide missionary work as a precondition for his return. Matthew 24:14 says, "And this gospel of the kingdom will be preached in the whole world as a testimony to all nations, and then the end will come."

3. As Christians, we have received precious gifts to be shared as widely as possible. Therefore, we should share our biggest gift as widely as possible. Faith in Jesus Christ is the root of eternal life. Romans 10:17 says, "Faith comes from hearing the message, and the message is heard through the word about Christ."

4. Every individual is important. Every individual's spiritual hunger must be satisfied. Obviously, John 3:16 emphasizes this divine purpose of universal access to salvation: "For God so loved the world that he gave his one and only Son, that whoever believes in him shall not perish but have eternal life."

5. If we can't love our neighbors in the global community who yearn for change, they will be easily influenced by evil forces. To find out the truth, we should pay more attention to North Korea.

6. Christian enemies are becoming increasingly ruthless. It is necessary to grasp the evil that instills a heart that isn't dedicated to others.

7. Only a changed life can change society, and only a changed global society can truly live in peace. This is Dr. Ted's favorite maxim. Since surrendering his life to Christ nearly sixty years ago, he has been increasingly confident that he can achieve "horizontal" peace in the world only when he achieves "vertical" peace with God.

8. Various forms of Christian missionary work are very attractive. We should hope to value the pure passion of working abroad to help others find salvation.

We should keep in mind these eight reasons when cooperating to reach out to North Koreans.

To Follow God's Heartbeat for North Korea

In his 1993 publication, Dr. Ted introduced the nomenclature or descriptor of "God's Envoy." "Envoy" is a diplomatic term for an ambassador. Therefore, God's envoys are God's ambassadors. In 2 Corinthians 5:20, Paul uses the description "Christ's ambassadors." Today, God's ambassadors are fully aware of the global missionary situation, which is the basis for their motivation to participate in global outreach. The current world missionary situation calls for a large mobilization of God's people – that is, God's special envoys, God's ambassadors, and the ambassadors of Christ who are prepared to address both the physical and the spiritual needs of the poor in the world.

Today, South Korea is known as a country with a high percentage of Christian believers. The country is host to the world's largest church, which has nearly eight hundred thousand members. However, God's involvement in the Korean peninsula dates back to the past. The first Protestant missionary to Korea was a Welshman named Robert Jermain Thomas, who was martyred in September 1866. He was stabbed, beaten, and beheaded in Pyongyang.

Revivals

There have been two major revivals in Korea. The first was known as the Wonsan Revival Movement. Wonsan is a port city, and to get there it takes about six hours by car from Pyongyang in the direction of the East Sea. A revival took place in 1903. In 1904, there were ten thousand believers, and in 1906, more than thirty thousand new Christians joined the movement. But for some reason, the flames of revival were put out.

Another revival took place in Pyongyang, which was called the Great Revival Movement of Pyongyang (1907–10). On 14 January 1907, Korean Christians and Western missionaries gathered at a church outside Pyongyang to study the Bible. God stirred their hearts as they did so. People gathered to study the Bible began to repent of racism, hatred, anger, and envy. They asked God for forgiveness, and when God responded to their cries, revival took place. Thousands of people repented publicly; churches began everywhere, and the movement grew and spread quickly. By 1907, fifty thousand people had given their lives to Christ. The rapid growth of the church led to persecution by the Japanese military, who tried to force Koreans to bow to the Japanese emperor. Once called "Oriental Jerusalem," Pyongyang was oppressed.

Dr. Ted's Continued Engagement in North Korea

After twenty years of serving with FHI, Dr. Ted retired in 2001. In 2004, he was invited to serve as the international director of the Lausanne Committee on World Evangelization, now simply referred to as the Lausanne Movement. North Korea was the least evangelized country in the world, and Dr. Ted's burden for North Korea remained. By 2008, God called Dr. Ted to be an interim CEO of World Serve Ministries in Canada and the United States, focusing on the Chinese Family Church Movement, Cuban churches, and ethnic groups in other creative access and closed countries.

But North Korea never left his mind. After two and a half years of serving with World Serve Ministries, Dr. Ted spent time in northeastern China, where he would secretly assist North Korean defectors. He wanted to learn more about this compassionate service for personal growth. Apparently, God was not finished with Dr. Ted yet, so God granted him another ministry opportunity. On 1 February 2011, Dr. Ted met Dr. Kim Jin-kyung, who established two international universities, namely, Yanbian University of Science and Technology in China (1992) and Pyongyang University of Science and Technology in North Korea (2010). Dr. Kim asked Dr. Ted to serve as senior vice president of the two universities. He also requested him to be an advisor to help him on governance and succession issues. This was known territory for Dr. Ted, having served as a professor, dean, and vice president at several universities for eighteen years before he joined FHI.

Dr. Ted then became chairman of the Seoul-based NAFEC (Northwest Asia Foundation for Education and Culture) board of directors, which governs both universities. Dr. Kim and Dr. Ted came to trust each other, a beautiful testimony to how God can use leaders from historically conflicting nations for his glory. Although the animosity between Koreans and Japanese remains deep in some sectors of society, Dr. Ted (a Japanese) and Dr. Kim (a Korean) can work together because of their common cause for and bond in Jesus Christ.

A Ray of Hope for North Korea

Although I offer an account of Dr. Ted's involvement in North Korea, it is equally important to share a miraculous story about Dr. Kim Jin-kyung's life and achievements. This is a story of a man whom God used in developing Pyongyang University of Science and Technology, which provides a ray of hope for North Korea.

After living in the United States for many years, Dr. Kim, who was educated as an entrepreneur and had established several successful businesses, established Yanbian University of Science and Technology in 1992, the first Chinese-foreign joint university. In the aftermath of the North Korean famine in 1988, Dr. Kim and his colleagues were fully aware of North Koreans' desperation for aid and relief. They brought food, medicine, and blankets to North Korea. However, in September 1998, Dr. Kim was arrested on charges of being a CIA agent; he was imprisoned and handed a death sentence.

Ahead of the scheduled death penalty, Dr. Kim wrote four letters – one for his wife, a second for faculty and students at the Yanbian University of Science and Technology (YUST), one for the top authority in the North

Korean government, and one for the US State Department. In his letter to the North Korean government, Dr. Kim wrote, "Use part of my body for medical development for the benefit of North Koreans." In his letter to the US State Department, he wrote, "Do not retaliate." Although he suffered torture and tremendous hardships there, Dr. Kim's response was remarkable: his imprisonment was a simple misunderstanding.

On 24 October 1998, Chairman Kim Jong-il, father of the current North Korean Supreme Leader Kim Jong-un, ordered Dr. Kim's release after monitoring the situation. Dr. Kim's letters to the North Korean government and the US government impressed Chairman Kim. Two years later, in January 2000, Dr. Kim received a phone call from Kim Jong-il in Pyongyang and decided to meet him. At the meeting Chairman Kim apologized to Dr. Kim for his imprisonment. Kim Jong-il then asked Dr. Kim to establish a similar educational institution in Pyongyang. At that point, YUST had achieved the highest status in Chinese higher education. It had become one of the top one hundred universities in China, with more than 2,500 students and 388 faculty members. Dr. Kim's response to Kim Jong-il's request was positive. Chairman Kim allocated 248 acres of land in southern Pyongyang for the establishment of Pyongyang University of Science and Technology (PUST).

The building was completed, and education began in 2010. All education was conducted in English and was conducted by prominent overseas faculty. Currently, there are five hundred undergraduate students representing seventeen countries; one hundred graduate students; and ninety-five faculty members. The PUST campus can accommodate two thousand students. These students are selected from the top graduates of prestigious schools in the Democratic People's Republic of Korea; they are also trained according to the educational philosophy of "globality, practicality, and creativity" and are considered to be the best talents to contribute to their compatriots. But beyond that, there is also a hope for world peace.

Dr. Ted's PUST: Peace, Unity, Service, and Trust

The first core value of PUST is *peace*. In Dr. Kim Jin-kyung's language, "love-ism" is the foundation for peace. PUST students are expected to learn what this "love-ism" is. He proposes seven principles that love-ism should practice:

1. Understand others
2. Seek reconciliation
3. Practice forgiveness

4. Respect others and their desires
5. Be willing to sacrifice to maintain peace
6. Apologize or say "I'm sorry"
7. Say "thank you" to those who helped you

PUST's educational philosophy is to create a peaceful world by producing graduates who can function most efficiently and productively as contributors rather than wasting resources in modern society. The seven principles proposed by Dr. Kim are guidelines to help create a peaceful and harmonious society. PUST's faculty are peace-loving scholars from all over the world who voluntarily decided to participate in this educational experiment because of their love for North Koreans. They do not get paid.

The second core value of PUST is *unity*. Dr. Kim describes the diverse members of the PUST community as a family. PUST's faculty come from various backgrounds and cultures around the world. The students come from various parts of their country. However, while at PUST, all students are treated like members of the same family. They eat together, study together, and play together. They all want to be productive members of society. Dr. Ted used to tell students that he would continue to help them by introducing Dr. Kim and PUST's unique stories to more audiences around the world through his networks. Dr. Ted stresses that to succeed in this effort, PUST graduates must be able to prove their qualifications. The reputation of a university depends on the quality of its graduates. He reminds the students that they are responsible for doing their best for PUST, assuring them that one day they will be proud that their university is one of the best in the world.

The third core value of PUST is *service*. Dr. Ted desires to see students learn about the meaning of volunteer work at school. Acts of service are defined as helpful activities. All faculty members voluntarily participate in PUST and decide to come to help by providing their educational expertise. In the 1990s, when North Korea suffered a severe natural disaster and needed outside help, Dr. Ted wanted to help, saying that Dr. Kim's sacrifice for the North Korean people was unquestionable and that he was deeply moved by Dr. Kim's love for North Koreans and his commitment to educating tomorrow's leaders who would serve North Koreans and deal with international issues across borders. By providing education in English, PUST aims to produce graduates who can function globally and work at international universities. Dr. Ted advises students as follows: "Show us what you can do for your country to improve the quality of your life, and if you are given the opportunity, show us on the international stage the spirit of service you have learned, and make your country proud."

The fourth core value of PUST is *trust*. If North Korean leaders had not trusted Dr. Kim, there would be no PUST today. PUST's faculty operates according to the principle of trust. Trust is an intrinsic characteristic necessary to operate PUST, and Dr. Ted hopes that every graduate of PUST will become a person of integrity recognized and respected by the world as a contributor to society and peace.

Is PUST Looking to the Future of North Korea Going in the Right Direction?

In his 2015 book *The Real North Korea: Life and Politics in the Failed Stalinist Utopia*, Russian North Korea expert Andrei Lankov writes, "Only North Korea itself can change North Korea.... Therefore, the solution is to increase internal pressure to change the system. As such, the main way to achieve this is to raise North Korea's awareness of the outside world."[1] Lankov commends all efforts to expose North Koreans to the outside world. He urges others to utilize the officially approved academic, cultural, and other human exchanges approved by the North Korean authorities.

Over the past few years, PUST has sent students to visit the best universities in China. Also, European universities have begun offering full scholarships to PUST students for further research. The UK's University of Westminster and University of Cambridge have each offered scholarships to several students. Sweden's Uppsala University has offered eight scholarships. More universities in Europe are considering a similar system.

As a full-fledged university, the PUST academic system is rigorous. There are currently three departments in the university with multiple foci for students:

- *Division of the Arts and Sciences*
    - IFM: International Finance and Management
    - ALS: Agriculture and Life Sciences
    - ECE: Electrical and Computer Engineering
- *Division of Medical Sciences*: in 2014, PUST opened five new programs:
    - School of Dentistry
    - School of Public Health

---

1. Andrei Lankov, *The Real North Korea: Life and Politics in the Failed Stalinist Utopia* (Oxford: Oxford University Press, 2013), 215.

- School of Medicine
- School of Nursing
- School of Pharmacy
- *Division of Research and Development*

Dr. Ted has emphasized that a highly trained and motivated ambassador of Christ is needed to fill a strategic place of service at PUST. Three months prior to Chairman Kim Jong-il's death (17 December 2011, at the age of seventy), the North Korean leader asked Dr. Ted to arrange a meeting with Dr. Kim. High-ranking officials attended the meeting, and North Korean leader Kim Jong-il lavished warm praise on Dr. Kim. Then, Kim Jong-il recommended that Dr. Kim be awarded an honorary doctorate in education, signed by the Chairman himself; he would also be granted honorary North Korean citizenship to allow him to freely enter the country. The honorary citizenship was signed by Kim Jong-il himself, which meant that Dr. Kim could go in and out of North Korea without restrictions. This had never happened before, and perhaps will never happen again.

When Kim Jong-il died, PUST's foreign faculty members were invited to see the deceased leader's remains. New leader Kim Jong-un greeted the faculty members one by one. Kim Jong-un knew that his father had great respect for Dr. Kim and PUST. Dr. Ted whispered prayerfully as he recalled this: "In the past few years, 50–70 percent of Chinese YUST graduates have become believers. I pray that what is happening in China's YUST during the time of God will be repeated in North Korea's PUST."

Feed the Children, Korean Ministry

In 2013, during a diaspora missions meeting in Manila, Dr. Ted shared with me a compelling childhood story: "When I was a child, I grew up in Nagoya, and there was one thing I couldn't forget. One morning, many Koreans came up to the front of our house and cried around my father, singing 'Arirang,' and leaving. My father was also crying while sending them. Later, when I grew up, I realized how much Japan had harmed Korea. I was so sorry and heartbroken. So, I decided to do my best to help the Korean peninsula in the areas I could. God entrusted me, who was lacking, to serve the FHI, to work for the Lausanne Committee, and to engage in YUST and PUST. Now, I would like to suggest that you set up a South Korean committee for Feed the Children. Cooperate with the FTC headquarters in Oklahoma, USA, to carry out relief activities and nutrition projects for North Korean children."

As a result, the Feed the Children Korea Committee was established in May 2015. Dr. Ted's love for North Korea will continue through this committee. North Korean children need help. According to a recent report by the World Food Programme (WFP) and the United Nations Children's Fund, the nutrition status of North Korean children has improved slightly, but it is still serious. The report is heartbreaking. There is severe malnutrition (affecting 7 percent of children); chronic malnutrition (affecting 37 percent); many are underweight (affecting 23 percent); and 1 in 3 pregnant women suffers from malnutrition and anemia.[2] The nutrition status of children in the mountainous areas of Hamgyeong-do and Ryanggang-do is equally serious.

Dr. Ted says that whenever he remembers a situation in which he almost died of malnutrition during World War II, he sees himself through North Korean children who suffer. He is a Japanese American, but his blood is purely Japanese. But he has been loved and appreciated in the Korean peninsula as he continues to love the Korean people. I am confident that Dr. Ted will not cease praying for the Korean peninsula until God calls him to eternal glory. I join Dr. Ted in the conviction that God will lift up and use the Korean peninsula, a country of "Morning Calm," as Dr. Ted constantly wishes for peace and unification with great enthusiasm. I am also convinced that God will use the Korean peninsula for world missionary work according to the divine plan.

My numerous travels with Dr. Ted – learning from him and soaking in his wisdom – have made my heart and mind more open to North Korea. As I walked around the mission field with Dr. Ted and listened to his stories, my mission became clearer and more certain. I thank God for allowing me to meet this exemplary leader, and for giving us many opportunities to minister together with one shared vision. I hope that my ministry to North Korea and Dr. Ted's love for North Korea will continue to create a synergy in line with God's will for the Korean peninsula.

References

Lankov, Andrei. *The Real North Korea: Life and Politics in the Failed Stalinist Utopia.* Oxford: Oxford University Press, 2013.

---

2. United Nations Children's Fund (UNICEF), "Analysis of the Situation of Children and Women in the Democratic People's Republic of Korea", 2019, 54.

Afterword

By Sadiri Joy Tira

Publishers and authors are always asking at least two questions: "Who will read this book?" and "How can we make money out of it?"

Certainly, this Festschrift is not about making money. It is about honoring Dr. Ted Yamamori for his contributions, passion, commitment, and exemplary leadership in global missions. These, we believe, need to be shared with others, particularly with the younger generations. This book calls them to preach the "whole gospel, to the whole world, by the whole church" – this being the goal of the Lausanne Movement, in which Ted is held dear.

At the time of writing, Russia has invaded Ukraine, leading to extreme human suffering, dislocation, separation of families, the scattering of refugees, massive property destruction, global economic upheaval, and the deaths of both soldiers and civilians. And the war isn't just regional: the global community is impacted as well, with rumblings of cyber insecurity and the possibility of a nuclear war on the table.

When the atomic bomb was dropped by the Americans on Hiroshima, Ted Yamamori saw the human tragedy that resulted in the thousands of deaths and extreme suffering among his Japanese people. He experienced hunger from the scarcity of food and clean water.

In addition to the current Eurasian crisis, we are still struggling physically, economically, psychologically, sociologically, and emotionally to survive the global impact of COVID-19. This pandemic has been pervasive, sparing no country. The death toll is heartbreaking, economic growth has slowed, and educational advancement has been hindered. We have not fully assessed the negative and positive impacts of the pandemic. That will take years of study and multidisciplinary research to understand.

Since he was a boy, Ted Yamamori was chosen to serve God with his mind, his heart, and his hard work. His reach goes far – into communities of poverty, urban centers, local churches, higher education institutions, and among the political elite and the corporate world. Now in his golden years, Ted Yamamori has left us a road map and guidebook to continue the work.

The Lausanne Movement will celebrate its fiftieth anniversary in 2024 in Seoul, Korea. Our hope is that this publication will inspire the participants – younger leaders of the global church – to stand on the shoulders of missionary giants such as William Carey, Hudson Taylor, A. B. Simpson, C. T. Studd, Mother Teresa, Billy Graham, Bill Bright, Donald McGavran, Ralph Winter, John Stott, Francis Schaeffer, Leighton Ford, Tom Wang, George Verwer, Ray Bakke, Luis Bush, Douglas Birdsall, Chris Wright, and, of course, Tetsunao Yamamori.

Bibliography of Tetsunao Yamamori's Books

The following list was provided by our friends at the library at the International Graduate School of Leadership in Quezon City, Philippines. The list is in chronological order.

Yamamori, Tetsunao. *Church Growth in Japan.* Pasadena: William Carey Library, 1974.

Yamamori, Tetsunao. *Church Growth in "Brathiosia": A Study in the Development and Prospect of CMF work in Brazil, Ethiopia, and Indonesia.* [n.p.], 1974.

Yamamori, Tetsunao, and E. LeRoy Lawson. *Introducing Church Growth: A Textbook in Missions.* Cincinnati: New Life Books, 1975.

Yamamori, Tetsunao, and Charles Taber, eds. *Christopaganism or Indigenous Christianity?* Pasadena: William Carey Library, 1975.

Yamamori, Tetsunao. *The Church Growth Handbook.* Edited by Win Arn. Pasadena, CA: Church Growth Press, 1979.

Yamamori, Tetsunao. *God's New Envoys.* Portland: Multnomah, 1987.

Smith, Katie, and Tetsunao Yamamori. *Growing Our Future: Food Security and the Environment.* Boulder: Kumarian, 1992.

Yamamori, Tetsunao. *Penetrating Missions' Final Frontier: A New Strategy for Unreached Peoples.* Downers Grove: InterVarsity Press, 1993.

Yamamori, Tetsunao. *Unerreichte Völker: Neue Strategien für einen grossen Auftrag.* Translated by T. Doreen. Neuhausen/Stuttgart: Hañssler-Verlag, 1994. (Original work published 1993.)

Yamamori, Tetsunao. *Mijŏndo Chongjok Irŏk'e Chŏpkŭn Hara* 미전도종족이렇게접근하라 [Approach the Unreached People Like This]. Translated by Lee Hyunmo. Sŏul T'ŭkpyŏlsi: Jyoi Sŏn'gyohoe, 1994. (Original work published 1993.)

Yamamori, Tetsunao, Bryant Myers, and David Conner, eds. *Serving with the Poor in Asia.* Monrovia: MARC, 1995.

Yamamori, Tetsunao. *Kirisutosha no kyōseiteki hataraki: Nijūisseiki no sekai senkyō* キリスト者の共生的働き:二十一世紀の世界宣教 [Symbiotic Ministry a Strategy for Christian Relief and Development]. Tokyo: Inochi no Kotobasha, 1996.

Yamamori, Tetsunao, Bryant Myers, Kwame Bediako, and Larry Reed, eds. *Serving with the Poor in Africa.* Monrovia: MARC, 1996.

Yamamori, Tetsunao, Bryant Myers, René Padilla, and Greg Rake, eds. *Serving with the Poor in Latin America.* Monrovia: MARC, 1997.

Yamamori, Tetsunao, Bryant Myers, René Padilla, and Greg Rake, eds. *Servir con los Pobres en America Latina: Modelos de Ministerio Integral*. Translated by S. Escobar. Buenos Aires: Kairos, 1997. (Original work published 1997.)

Yamamori, Tetsunao, Bryant Myers, and Kenneth Luscombe, eds. *Serving with the Urban Poor*. Monrovia: MARC, 1998.

Padilla, René, and Tetsunao Yamamori, eds. *El Proyecto de Dios y las Necesidades Humanas: Mas Modelos de Ministerio Integral en America Latina*. Buenos Aires: Kairos, 2000.

Yamamori, Tetsunao, and Kim-kwong Chan. *Witnesses to Power: Stories of God's Quiet Work in a Changing China*. Carlisle: Paternoster, 2000.

Padilla, René, and Tetsunao Yamamori, eds. *Mision Integral y Pobreza: CLADE IV – Congreso Latinoamericano de Evangelizacion*. Buenos Aires: Kairos, 2001.

Chan, Kim-Kwong, and Tetsunao Yamamori. *Holistic Entrepreneurs in China: A Handbook on the World Trade Organization and New Opportunities for Christians*. Pasadena: William Carey International University Press, 2002.

Monk, Robert, Walter Hofheinz, Kenneth Lawrence, Joseph Stamey, Bert Affleck, and Tetsunao Yamamori. *Exploring Religious Meaning*. 6th ed. Upper Saddle River : Prentice Hall, 2003.

Yamamori, Tetsunao, and Kenneth Eldred, eds. *On Kingdom Business: Transforming Missions through Entrepreneurial Strategies*. Wheaton: Crossway, 2003.

Yamamori, Tetsunao, David Dageforde, and Tina Bruner, eds. *The Hope Factor: Engaging the Church in the HIV/AIDS Crisis*. Waynesboro: Authentic Media, 2003.

Padilla, René, and Tetsunao Yamamori, eds. *La Iglesia Local como Agente de Transformación: Una Eclesiología para la Misión Integral*. Buenos Aires: Kairos, 2003.

Padilla, René, and Tetsunao Yamamori, eds. *The Local Church, Agent of Transformation: An Ecclesiology for Integral Mission*. Translated by B. Cordingly. Buenos Aires: Kairos, 2004. (Original work published 2003.)

Miller, Donald E., and Tetsunao Yamamori. *Global Pentecostalism: The New Face of Christian Social Engagement*. Berkeley: University of California Press, 2007.

Miller, Donald E., and Tetsunao Yamamori. *Wae sŏmginŭn kyohoe e segye ka yŏlgwang hanŭn'ga : Kidokkyojŏk sahoe ch'amyŏ ŭi saeroun model, Sŏngnyŏng undong* 왜 섬기는 교회에 세계가 열광하는가 : 기독교적 사회참여의 새로운 모델, 성령운동 [Why the World Is Enthusiastic about the Church We Serve: A New Model of Christian Social Participation, the Holy Spirit Movement]. Translated by Kim Seong-geon and Jeon Jong-hyun. Seoul: Gyohoeseongjang-Yeonguso, 2008. (Original work published 2007.)

Yamamori, Tetsunao, and Kenneth Eldred, eds. *Kingdŏm Bijŭnisŭ* 킹덤 비즈니스 [Kingdom Business]. Translated by Choe Hyŏng-gŭn. Seoul: Joy Sŏn'kyohoe, 2008. (Original work published 2003.)

Monk, Robert, Walter Hofheinz, Kenneth Lawrence, Joseph Stamey, Bert Affleck, and Tetsunao Yamamori. *Zong jiao yi yi tan suo* 宗教意义探索 [Exploring Religious

Meaning]. Translated by Z. Daiqiang, Z. Yalin, and S. Shanling. Chengdou: Sìchuān rénmín chūbǎn shè, 2011. (Original work published 2003.)

Yamamori, Tetsunao. *The People of God and Global Workplace Mission*. Wilmore: Asbury Theological Seminary, 2014.

Tira, Sadiri Joy, and Tetsunao Yamamori, eds. *Scattered and Gathered: A Global Compendium of Diaspora Missiology*. Eugene: Wipf & Stock, 2016.

Tira, Sadiri Joy, and Tetsunao Yamamori, eds. *Diasŭp'ora sŏn'gyohak* 디아스포라 선교학 [Diaspora Missiology]. Tŏ Meik'ŏ. 2018. (Original work published 2016.)

Tira, Sadiri Joy, and Tetsunao Yamamori, eds. *Scattered and Gathered: A Global Compendium of Diaspora Missiology*. Rev. and updated ed. Carlisle: Langham Global Library, 2020.

Yamamori, Tetsunao. *Ai no shisetsu: "Tozasareta-koku 々" Ni fukuin o tsutaeru tame no yūki aru senryaku* 愛の使節 : "閉ざされた国々"に福音を伝えるための勇気ある戦略 [Envoy of Love: A Courageous Strategy to Preach the Gospel to "Closed Countries"]. Translated by Kyoritsu Christian Institute. Kyoritsu Christian Institute, n.d. (Original work published 1987.)

Yamamori, Tetsunao. *Nihon no kyōkai seichō* 日本の教会成長 [Church Growth in Japan]. Translated by K. Ariga. Tokyo: Inochinokotobasha, n.d. (Original work published 1974.)

Editors and Contributors

Editors

Sadiri Joy Tira, DMiss, DMin, is convener of the Jaffray Diaspora Net Research of the Jaffray Centre for Global Initiatives at Ambrose University. He is also a Diaspora Missiology Specialist and sessional Professor of Intercultural Studies at Ambrose. Tira served as the Lausanne Movement senior associate/catalyst for Diasporas from 2007 to 2019. He is currently serving with PALM Ministries Association as a staff worker.

Laurie Nichols is Founder of Common Goods Communications, which provides strategic communications and content development for some of the largest faith-based and nonprofit organizations in the world. She has over twenty years of experience in communications and marketing, having worked for fifteen of those years heading up editorial and communications at the Wheaton College Billy Graham Center and serving in leadership roles for a number of publications, including *Evangelical Missions Quarterly*. She is the Founder of the Heromakers Movement. Nichols holds degrees in journalism and communications (BA, Valparaiso University) and interdisciplinary studies (MA, Wheaton College).

Contributors

Douglas Birdsall, PhD, is honorary Chairman of the Lausanne Movement. He has served as a pastor, as a missionary in Japan, as President of Asian Access, and as Vice President of Advancement of the Alliance Theological Seminary/Nyack College in New York.

Tereso C. Casiño, ThD, PhD, is Professor of Missiology and Intercultural Studies at Gardner-Webb University School of Divinity, North Carolina, USA. He is the Founding Director of Asia-Pacific Institute of Missions in the Philippines and Vice President of International Center for Diaspora Missions in South Korea.

Leiton Chinn is Former Senior Associate/Catalyst for International Ministries for the Lausanne Movement. He has been mobilizing the church for ministry among international students for forty-five years, including serving as President of the Association of Christians Ministering among Internationals (ACMI). He served as the International Coordinator for the World Consultation on Frontier Missions: Edinburgh 80. He is a member of the WEA Mission Commission.

Joseph W Handley, Jr., PhD, is president of A3 and author of *Polycentric Mission Leadership*. Previously, he was the founding director of the Office of World Mission, Azusa Pacific University, California, USA, and lead mission pastor at Rolling Hills Covenant Church, California, USA. Joe also serves as co-catalyst for the Lausanne Movement in Leadership Development and as faculty member/tutor for doctoral studies in World Christianity and Global Leadership.

Stanley John, PhD, is Associate Dean for Global Initiatives at Alliance Theological Seminary, New York, USA. He is also a member of the Board of Directors for Langham Partnership (USA).

S. Hun Kim is Director of the Korean Diaspora Institute, ARILAC, in Korea, and a reflective practitioner and Bible translator with Wycliffe College, Canada. He completed the translation of the Bible for Southern Azerbaijani in Iran and published in 2013. He was also engaged in the Lausanne Global Diaspora Network. Kim operates a program for training refugees in Germany and Europe with Equip7: Learning Community.

Masanori Kurusawa, DMiss, is Former President and currently Professor Emeritus of Tokyo Christian University, Japan. He is also Chairman of the Japan Lausanne Movement.

LeRoy Lawson, PhD, served as President of Hope International University in California, USA, and as Pastor to Central Christian Church in Arizona, USA.

David S. Lim, PhD, is Chairman of the Philippines Lausanne Movement, President of the Asia School for Development and Cross-Cultural Studies (ASDECS), and a member of the steering group of SEANET.

Cody Lorance is an author and a lecturer with expertise in business, community development, migration, diaspora studies, and religion. He is co-CEO of Endiro Coffee, a tree-to-cup company with operations in Uganda and the USA. He is an anthropologist, missiologist, and theologian by training with degrees from Wheaton College Graduate School, Illinois, USA, and the University of Science and Arts of Oklahoma, USA.

Wonsuk Ma, PhD, is Dean of Theology and Ministry and Distinguished Professor of Global Christianity at Oral Roberts University, Oklahoma, USA. He is a writer and educator at the Korean Pentecostal School and served as Executive Director of Oxford Centre for Mission Studies, UK. Ma is editor of the Regnum Edinburgh Centennial 2010 Series.

Barnabas Moon is a mission mobilizer and pastor in Seoul, Korea, and Director of WITHEE International and Feed the Children (Korea). Moon is also Vice President of the Global Diaspora Network.

Nigel Paul is the Founder and International Director of MoveIn, a movement "to see thousands of regular Christians prayerfully moving in among the unreached, urban poor globally." Nigel grew up in Zambia, Pakistan, and Kenya and studied Internet Business at the University of Waterloo, Canada. Paul also leads an on-the-ground MoveIn team, which is planting a church.

Lorajoy Tira-Dimangondayao is a Master of Theological Studies student at St. Stephen's College at the University of Alberta, Canada. She has a BTh from Ambrose University (formerly Canadian Bible College), has served as administrative assistant to Dr. Sadiri Joy Tira since 2001, and is particularly interested in diaspora missiology in the Canadian context.

Sadiri Tonyvic Tira Jr. is a church planter with the North American Mission Board and SEND Network. He is Pastor of Edmonton Supper Club and served as Senior Manager of Hope Mission in a downtown Edmonton shelter home for the homeless and marginalized community.

Mats Tunehag is Chairman of BAM Global and has been developing the Business as Mission (BAM) concept as well as national, regional, and global strategic alliances of people and BAM initiatives for more than thirty years. He initiated the first global think tank on BAM and serves with a global investment fund based on Christian values that helps small and mid-size enterprises to grow in size and holistic impact. Tunehag served for many years as a senior leader on Business as Mission in both the Lausanne Movement and the World Evangelical Alliance.

Juliet Lee Uytanlet, PhD, teaches mission courses and Cultural Anthropology at the Biblical Seminary of the Philippines. She is the Program Coordinator for the PhD program at Asia Graduate School of Theology, Philippines, and served as a Lausanne Movement Catalyst from 2016 to 2018. Uytanlet is author of

The Hybrid Tsinoys: Challenges of Hybridity and Homogeneity as Socio-Cultural Constructs among the Chinese in the Philippines (Wipf and Stock, 2016).

Philip Yan is Founder and Director of the Centre for Redemptive Entrepreneurship (CRE) at Tyndale University, Canada, whose vision is to equip Christian entrepreneurs as culture-shaping catalysts in advancing their redemptive ventures. Yan runs Genesis XD and is co-Founder of KLINCK Coffee and Red Propeller, which sells services and products to employ people with barriers to employment.

Steven Ybarrola, PhD, is Dean of the E. Stanley James School of World Mission and Evangelism, and Professor of Cultural Anthropology at Asbury Theological Seminary, Kentucky, USA. He served with Operation Mobilization (OM) in Europe and Latin America. Ybarrola's areas of specialty are anthropology, migration, ethnicity, race, intergroup relationships, and identity.

International Graduate School of Leadership (IGSL) Librarians

Princess Mae Bucton is Library Assistant and holds a BSc in Hotel and Restaurant Management from Palompon Institute of Technology, Philippines.

Redentor Bhien Luz is a Library Assistant and holds a Bachelor of Library and Information Science from the University of the Philippines.

Alexis B. Obiena holds a Bachelor of Secondary Education from Metro Manila College, Philippines, and is currently taking master's studies in Library and Information Science from the University of the Philippines.

Tributes

For more than five decades, Dr. Ted Yamamori has been a pioneer and bridge-builder – from his foundational studies on the dynamics of growing churches, to his leadership in the understanding and practice of holistic ministry, his engagement with universities in Asia as well as North America, and his championing of the new field of diaspora missiology. He has been a mentor and an inspiration to Christian leaders in dozens of countries, and one of the key figures in the revitalization of the Lausanne Movement and its networks in the twenty-first century.

His gracious manner, his attention to the individual, and his encouraging notes testify to his Christlike servant spirit. Hebrews 13:7 says, "Remember your leaders, who spoke the word of God to you. Consider the outcome of their way of life and imitate their faith." Dr. Ted Yamamori is a leader deserving of imitation.

Dr. David Bennett
Global Associate Director for Collaboration and Content,
Lausanne Movement

I came to know Ted during the 2010 Lausanne gathering in Cape Town, South Africa. He and Joy Tira approached me regarding the Oxford Centre for Mission Study joining in their work to engage in diaspora mission scholarship. As was usual for Ted, he had his finger on the heartbeat of mission, the soul of scholarship, and the good news of Jesus Christ in world mission. We were given a good-sized room to meet with other delegates about diaspora mission, but demand for the group far exceeded the space provided, and thus a large hall was opened, which filled to capacity as well.

I mention this because this incident captures for me the essence, insight, and prophetic scholarly wisdom of Ted. He knew what was happening and why it was important well before most in the mission world. Further, he knew better than most that scholarship matters in mission. Missionaries are by nature people of action. This is good, but at times they grow impatient with those who think, analyze, and (in a good sense) critique those actions. Ted realized that the secret to mission is considered action that weds enthusiasm and thoughtful reflection.

Because of this, Ted's work and contribution continues to reverberate globally. Our words of honor will call attention to his life and legacy, but the most important are these not issued by us: "Well done, good and faithful servant."

Dr. Tom Harvey
Academic Dean, Oxford Centre for Mission, UK
Researcher on Church and State in China

It is both an honor and a delight for me to write this tribute from Japan, the country of Ted's birth. To me, Dr. Tetsunao "Ted" Yamamori was, is, and will be "Ted Sensei." In Japanese society, not every professional is called *sensei* (先生). *Sensei* is a title of honor, generally translated into English as "teacher" or "master," although its literal meaning is "a person born before (you)." The title of honor is conventionally used in Japan to refer to and address certain professionals: teachers/educators, ordained ministers/pastors, and medical doctors (i.e. specialists who can teach, nurture, heal, and/or cure others). The honor is given to them for their wisdom, expert knowledge, and/or specialized skill they possess regardless of their age.

Ted Sensei was born and raised in Nagoya, the fourth-largest city in Japan. Since earning a PhD in Sociology of Religion from Duke University in 1968, over half a century ago, he has worn many hats: author, scholar, professor, theologian, mission catalyst, international director of a global mission movement (Lausanne), CEO of an NGO (Food for the Hungry International), and so on. He has not been an armchair Christian scholar, but a man of action to change the world for the better. He is a man for all seasons, like the four distinct and beautiful seasons of Japan.

Over the past fifteen years, I have met and interacted with Ted Sensei about a dozen times on four different continents: Africa (South Africa), Asia (Philippines and South Korea), Europe (France), and North America (Canada and USA). When I first met him, he showed a keen interest in my PhD topic – Interreligious Dialogue between Korean Christians and Buddhists on Suffering. In retrospect, I surmise it was because he was born into a Buddhist family and was an expert in East Asian religions, Buddhism in particular.

His full name consists of four Chinese (kanji) characters: *yama* (山); *mori* (森); *tetsu* (鉄); *nao* (直). Globe-trotting and constantly on the move, his life has embodied diverse attributes of a mountain (山), a large forest (森), steel (鉄), and straightforwardness (直). I believe he has lived up to his name's full meanings. His family, friends, and numerous colleagues would be extremely proud of his towering accomplishments in and for the kingdom of God. He has been running his race well, similar to what the apostle Paul claims: "I have fought the good fight, I have finished the race, I have kept the faith" (2 Tim 4:7). Ted Sensei, *otsukaresama deshita* (You have done a fabulous job)!

Dr. Chandler Im
Secondary School Principal and Chaplain,
Wadeda International Christian School, Tokyo, Japan

I remember being introduced to Dr. Ted Yamamori by Dr. Sadiri Joy Tira during the 2010 Lausanne gathering in Cape Town, South Africa. What I noticed about him was how he vigorously championed the urgency and significance of diaspora missions and the emerging field of diaspora missiology under the overarching framework of holistic mission. I distinctly experienced and felt his influence and encouragement upon us who were preparing our written contributions and presentations in the lead-up to the Global Diaspora Forum held in Manila in 2015. His vast and diverse range of academic, personal, and professional experience proved invaluable in investing in the published output of the Forum the requisite intellectual, practical, and spiritual gravitas to further cement diaspora missiology as a legitimate sphere of global missiology.

But even before his formal involvement with the Lausanne Movement, Dr. Yamamori had already undertaken an integral and pivotal role in global evangelism and missions through being a prolific scholar and global mission strategist who had authored over twenty books on evangelism and missiology. After retiring as president emeritus of Food for the Hungry International in 2001, he was soon asked to serve as the international director for the Lausanne Committee for World Evangelization. What resonated with me most was his remarkable statement:

> There is no retirement for a Great Commission Christian. The Lord has given us marching orders. Until he calls off that command, the order remains in effect. The truth of the matter is that when Jesus calls you into ministry, you must respond. I have reached seventy years of age, but I am healthy, and my mind is still somewhat intact. I want to serve the Lord wherever I am needed for as long as the Lord provides me with good health. I suspect that until I draw my last breath, my conscious thought will be ministry, ministry, ministry.

In 2008, he felt led into his fourth ministry opportunity – to serve as president/CEO of WorldServe Ministries. Dr. Yamamori's unforgettable legacy as a Christian statesman has been the unique way in which he has creatively harnessed his God-given gifts to produce eternal fruit for the kingdom arising from his creative synthesis of Christian theory with praxis in the crucible of reality.

Dr. Amador A. Remigio
Consultant and Mentor,
Pastor of Spiritual Formation

The collaborative partnership of several friends, contributing writers, and the following agencies, organizations, and institutions made this book project a reality:

Centre for Redemptive Entrepreneurship

Edmonton Supper Club

International Graduate School for Leadership

Heromakers Movement

Jaffray Centre for Global Initiatives

Langham Partnership

Lausanne Movement

PALM Ministry Association

WiThee Mission International

Their enthusiastic endorsements, encouragement, generous practical support, and fervent prayers even at the height of global pandemic are acknowledged and appreciated.

Ingram Content Group UK Ltd.
Milton Keynes UK
UKHW020925050523
421284UK00015B/267